RISK MANAGEMENT FOR
COMP

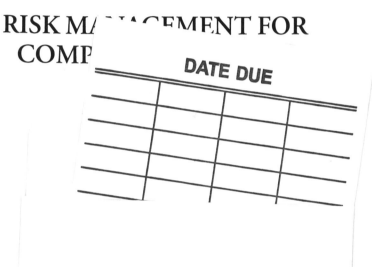

DATE DUE

RISK MANAGEMENT FOR COMPUTER SECURITY

Protecting Your Network and Information Assets

By Andy Jones & Debi Ashenden

ELSEVIER
BUTTERWORTH
HEINEMANN

AMSTERDAM • BOSTON • HEIDELBERG • LONDON
NEW YORK • OXFORD • PARIS • SAN DIEGO
SAN FRANCISCO • SINGAPORE • SYDNEY • TOKYO

Elsevier Butterworth–Heinemann
30 Corporate Drive, Suite 400, Burlington, MA 01803, USA
Linacre House, Jordan Hill, Oxford OX2 8DP, UK

♾ Recognizing the importance of preserving what has been written, Elsevier-Science prints its books on acid-free paper whenever possible.

Library of Congress Cataloging-in-Publication Data
Jones, Andy.
    Risk management for computer security: protecting your network and information assets/Andy Jones and Debi Ashenden. —1st ed.
        p. cm.
    Includes bibliographical references and index.
    ISBN 0-7506-7795-3 (alk. paper)
        1. Industrial safety—Management.   2. Computer security.   I. Ashenden, Debi.   II. Title.
    T55. J655 2005
    658. 4'78—dc22   20040755

British Library Cataloguing-in-Publication Data
A catalogue record for this book is available from the British Library.
ISBN: 0-7506-7795-3

For information on all Elsevier Butterworth-Heinemann publications
visit our Web site at http://books.elsevier.com/security

Printed in the United States of America
05 06 07 08 09 10   10 9 8 7 6 5 4 3 2 1

T
55
.J655
2005

Working together to grow
libraries in developing countries

www.elsevier.com | www.bookaid.org | www.sabre.org

ELSEVIER   BOOK AID
              International   Sabre Foundation

To my wife, Kath, who has always given support and shown tolerance and patience and without whose support I would not have been able to complete this book.

Dr. Andrew Jones, MBE MSc. MBCS
University of Glamorgan
United Kingdom

Contents

Foreword by Dr. Jerry Kovacich   ix

Preface   xiii

Acknowledgments   xix

About the Authors   xxi

SECTION I: AN INTRODUCTION TO RISK MANAGEMENT   1

1   Introduction to the Theories of Risk Management   3

2   The Changing Environment   11

3   The Art of Managing Risks   25

SECTION II: THE THREAT ASSESSMENT PROCESS   35

4   Threat Assessment and Its Input to Risk Assessment   37

5   Threat Assessment Method   55

6   Example Threat Assessment   89

SECTION III: VULNERABILITY ISSUES   131

7   Operating System Vulnerabilities   133

8   Application Vulnerabilities   143

9   Public Domain or Commercial Off-the-Shelf Software?   149

10   Connectivity and Dependence   165

SECTION IV: THE RISK PROCESS   183

11   What Is Risk Assessment?   185

12   Risk Analysis   195

13   Who Is Responsible?   207

SECTION V: TOOLS AND TYPES OF RISK ASSESSMENT   213

14   Qualitative and Quantitative Risk Assessment   215

15   Policies, Procedures, Plans, and Processes
of Risk Management   219

16   Tools and Techniques   231

17   Integrated Risk Management   243

SECTION VI: FUTURE DIRECTIONS   253

18   The Future of Risk Management   255

Index   261

Foreword

This book, *Risk Management for Computer Security: Protecting Your Network and Information Assets*, as the name obviously implies, is a book about managing risks. But not just any type of risks—risks to information systems and computers. Computers may be networked or stand alone, although very few these days are not somehow connected to one another through local area networks, wide area networks, and the "mother of all networks," the Internet, as well as the information they display, store, process, and transmit. It is about cost-effectively managing those risks.

You are probably saying "so what?" There are thousands of such books on the market, so why this one? I anticipated that question because I also was a potential reader of this book and did not want to waste time reading a book that was not practical and only provided "scholarly" information but was of little practical application for me in establishing and managing a risk management program.

I asked myself the same question. After all, why should I endorse this book? To find the answer to "our question," I decided to do some research. I went on-line to one of the world's most well-known on-line booksellers (who shall remain nameless) and found 90,316 "hits" on risk management books and magazines. The books and magazines listed ran the gamut from risk management topics related to finance, product development, insurance, investing, computing, security, personal credit, healthcare, and the like. I narrowed the search to "computer security risk management" and found "only" 53,872 hits. That helped but still didn't work very well. Therefore, I decided to see what these 53,872 books were about.

I found that many were very narrow in focus, dealing with risk issues pertaining to U.S. Government matters, a new health law, vulnerabilities of some networks, risk stuff related to the Internet, and the like. Some were somewhat dated, actually out of date based on the rapidly changing world of our information environment. To narrow my book choices down even more, I looked at the information provided about many of the books' authors. Some were written by individuals who may be nice people, good writers, and researchers but obviously either have little or no experience in the "real-world" of doing risk management processes, projects, establishing risk management programs, and the like—or if so, their experiences seemed to be limited (based on the information provided). This became apparent by looking at their degrees as well as their jobs as presented on the on-line books' web pages. In addition, they, for the most part, seemed to be focused on risks without actually putting the emphasis where it belongs—applying it to businesses, thinking like a business person, and looking at it from a business perspective. In other words, how can I do it at the least cost to my business while balancing those costs with some acceptable level of risks? After all, even governments have limited budgets for information assets protection and have developed a "business approach" to dealing with this issue.

Some books' web pages I looked at indicated that the books were basically information systems security—computer security—books with some risk management things thrown in. Some had "cutesy" titles to get your attention, but when looking at the reviews by those who had purchased their books, the number of pages, table of contents, and authors' backgrounds, well, many just didn't seem to be worth reading.

So, there we have it. I found many books published that at least alluded to risk management, but very few really seemed to be written by those whose duties involve managing risks to automated information and the information systems. Many seemed to be outdated, whereas others seemed to lack the approach used in this book.

Now, there is this book you are reading—or at least reading this Foreword. What I found enjoyable about this book is that it really is a "handbook" that is easy to read and covers "everything you always wanted to know but were afraid to ask" on the topic of managing risks of information assets, with emphasis on costs versus risks. Let me say it this way: It is a business-oriented approach where costs are an important issue that must be considered. In other words, how much protection is enough? How much does it cost? Is it worth the costs? Are we getting our money's worth? How do we know? How much risk am I accepting? Is it too much? Not enough based on costs?

As the authors point out: ... *if the risk assessment is not carried out effectively, then the organization will either waste money or be exposed to an unacceptable risk.* This says it all. This is what risk management is all about, and this is the authors' driving thought behind this book. Now, how does one establish a program to include processes and such to address the risk management issues associated with information assets protection at least cost? In other words, using management terminology, effectively and efficiently (good and cheap).

Speaking of the authors, look at who they are—look at their educational background and experience as noted in the "About the Authors" part of this book. Their experience is not just in information systems security, even though that background is needed. More importantly, look at their experience in actually establishing and managing risk management projects and programs. Andy Jones and Debi Ashenden indeed have "been there and done that." They are writing based on their actual experiences in the business of managing the risks to information systems and the information that our modern systems display, process, store, and transmit. Indeed, if you could only have one book on risk management to guide you to successfully managing systems and information risks in the business world as well as in a government's information environment, this would be the one to choose.

What is also nice about this book is that it is not some statistically driven look at managing risks written by someone with a PhD in statistics and one that requires the reader a similar degree to understand what the author is talking about. No, this is an easy-to-read common business sense approach to the topic. It has information that can be easily applied by both the novice and experienced information systems security practitioners. Furthermore, it is a book that can easily be read and understood by the businesses management professionals so they, maybe most importantly, understand what risk management is all about when it pertains to information and system. This is a book that provides managers the necessary background to make informed decisions on managing risks. After all, when it comes down to it, it is they, not the security practitioner, who are responsible for making the major risk management decisions and it is they who bear full responsibility for those decisions.

So, read this book, apply what you have learned from this book, and make your systems and information assets cost-effectively safer. You may also want to buy a copy of this book for your nonsecurity boss so that he or she too can make better informed decisions on managing risks to today's most valuable information assets.

Dr. Gerald L. Kovacich
ShockwavWriters.Com
Whidbey Island, Washington
United States of America

Preface

In an increasingly interconnected environment, we are consistently required to develop better and more cost-effective defenses for our information systems. In the past when information security was the realm of governments and the military and when security was only concernd with the confidentiality of the information, then the concept of "absolute" security was adopted and millions (billions?) of dollars spent in chasing this holy grail. In more recent years, the requirements of the commercial sector, a growing level of experience, and a touch of reality have changed this, and it is now the norm to seek "cost-effective security." There is also a growing realization, in trying to achieve this aim, that some degree of "risk" must be accepted and managed. In cold hard terms, if the risk assessment is not carried out effectively, then the organization will either waste money or be exposed to an unacceptable risk.

A global environment in which there is dependence on available technologies presents a very different problem from that which pertained just a few years ago. In the past, when risk was assessed, it was normally in terms of the natural and physical disasters or possibly the loss of research and development knowledge to a competitor. Now, as shown by recent experience, the problem has shifted considerably. Unfortunately, so far, the way in which we address the problem has not.

Operating within a global business environment with elements of a virtual workforce can create problems not experienced in the past. How do you assess the risk to the organization when information can be accessed remotely by employees in the field or traveling internationally? How do you assess the risk to employees who are not working on company premises and are often thousands of miles from the office? How do you assess the risk to your organization and its assets when you have offices or facilities in a nation whose government may be supporting the theft of the corporate "crown jewels" to assist their own nationally owned or supported corporations? If your risk assessment and management program is to be effective, then these issues must be assessed.

As we have just indicated, personnel involved in the risk assessment and management process face a much more complex environment today than they have ever encountered before. Unlike other attempts to provide information and guidance on risk assessment and management, this book covers more than just the fundamental elements that make up a good risk program. We provide an integrated "how to" approach to implementing a corporate program. It is completed with tested methods and processes and checklists that can be used by the reader and immediately implemented.

Yes, the world is an increasingly dangerous place and maybe more so today than ever before. Thus, the role for risk assessors has never been more challenging. They are faced with a dynamic business environment they must understand and support. They are faced with a greater number of threats than ever before and the potential for more sophisticated attacks against corporate assets. They are faced with management and employees who no longer are loyal to the organization, and they are faced with a range of threat agents, including hostile nations, terrorists, criminals, hackers, and competitors who seek to steal information or assets, prevent the organization from making best use of them, or generally gain advantage against us.

The challenges are many and this book has been written to help the reader in meeting their challenges as we progress through the twenty-first century.

COVERAGE

This book is intended to provide an up-to-date holistic approach to risk assessment that can be used by both individuals who are new to the subject and experienced professionals. There are a range of factors that need to be considered and a number of methods, processes, and procedures provided to the reader. They should then be able to make immediate use of this information. The text consists of six sections and 18 chapters. Section I (Chapters 1–3) provides an overview of the global business environment and an introduction to the theory behind risk management. It describes the purpose and processes of a risk assessment and risk analysis. Section II (Chapters 4–6) describes and demonstrates a threat assessment for a fictional organization and shows how this contributes to the risk assessment. Section III (Chapters 7–10) looks at the types of vulnerability that must be taken into account when carrying out a risk assessment and ways in which they can be mitigated. Section IV (Chapters 11–13) addresses the risk process and covers risk assessment, risk analysis, and the position of the risk process within an organization. Section V (Chapters 14–17) covers the different types of risk assessment that can be carried out and the types of tools, both manual and automated, that can be used to support the process. Finally, in Section VI (Chapter 18) we look at the future of risk management, from the development of professionalism to the training and awareness of staff.

Section I: An Introduction to Risk Management

This section looks at the general issues and explains what the term "risk management" means.

Chapter 1: Introduction to the Theories of Risk Management
This chapter gives a brief history of risk management from the pencil to the software application. It also includes definitions for risk management, risk assessment, and risk analysis.

Chapter 2: The Changing Environment
This chapter introduces the reader to the interconnected and global environment in which organizations must now operate. It looks at the aspects that have changed and the impact this has had, particularly in the areas of corporate governance, regulatory requirements, and operational risk. It describes a changing environment that requires a change in the way we think of risk.

Chapter 3: The Art of Managing Risks
This chapter looks at the skills and thinking that are necessary in the management of risk.

Section II: The Threat Assessment Process

This section describes a process for the assessment of threat, giving a taxonomy of threat agents and a method for determining the potency of a potential threat.

Chapter 4: Threat Assessment and Its Input to Risk Assessment
This chapter examines the role of threat assessment and its importance in the accurate and effective assessment of risk.

Chapter 5: Threat Assessment Method
This chapter shows a method for the assessment of threat. It looks at the different types of threat agent and outlines a method for determining the level of threat that is posed by a specific threat agent to the organization.

Chapter 6: Example Threat Assessment
This chapter shows a worked example of the threat assessment method for a fictitious organization. It looks at the threat posed by a number of threat agents and shows the areas where countermeasures can be implemented. It also shows the potential for modeling different scenarios to allow for effective decisions to be made.

Section III: Vulnerability Issues

This section of the book looks at the vulnerabilities that will have an impact on the level of risk that the information systems are exposed to. It looks at vulnerabilities in the operating systems and the applications and also looks at the effect of increased reliance on and connectivity to the Internet. This section also looks at the differences between commercial off-the-shelf and public domain software.

Chapter 7: Operating System Vulnerabilities
This chapter gives examples and details of the types of vulnerabilities that exist in operating systems and the problems they cause.

Chapter 8: Application Vulnerabilities
This chapter gives examples and details of the types of vulnerabilities that exist in applications and the problems they cause.

Chapter 9: Public Domain or Commercial Off-the-Shelf Software?
This chapter compares and contrasts public domain and COTS software and the merits and disadvantages of each.

Chapter 10: Connectivity and Dependence
This chapter looks at the effects of the use of the Internet and the increasing reliance of most organizations on an infrastructure over which they have no influence.

Section IV: The Risk Process

This section of the book looks at the range of processes that form the risk management process. It looks at what is involved, how to analyze risk, and the responsibilities of the individuals involved.

Chapter 11: What Is Risk Assessment?
This chapter describes the risk assessment process and the issues that must be addressed from a corporate perspective if risk is to be addressed holistically. It also discusses why the risks are greater now than ever before. It provides a rationale, with examples, to show the value of properly conducted risk assessment.

Chapter 12: Risk Analysis
This chapter provides details of the process and the issues that have to be considered when carrying out a risk analysis.

Chapter 13: Who Is Responsible?
This chapter introduces the role of the risk manager and identifies the level within the organization at which they must operate to be effective and the characteristics needed to be successful. It also explores the various stakeholders in the organization who need to be taken into account when developing the risk assessment process.

Section V: Tools and Types of Risk Assessment

This section looks at the types of risk assessment that can be carried out and the range of tools and techniques available. These tools and techniques are compared against each other to determine their feature richness and their effectiveness. It also looks at the structure of the risk assessment organization and the role of the risk manager.

Chapter 14: Qualitative and Quantitative Risk Assessment

This chapter describes different types of risk assessment that can be carried out and examines why one may be more effective in some circumstances than another.

Chapter 15: Policies, Procedures, Plans, and Processes of Risk Management

This chapter explains and provides examples of how to identify and describe risk management duties, responsibilities, processes, plans, policies, procedures, and projects.

Chapter 16: Tools and Techniques

This chapter describes a number of the more common tools and techniques that can be used when carrying out a risk assessment. It describes the features of the tools, the advantages and shortcomings of various techniques, and compares them with each other. It also explains why one approach may be better for some organizations than another.

Chapter 17: Integrated Risk Management

This chapter addresses the management and administrative aspects of risk management to include dealing with executive management, peers, and employees; the budget process; and how to use a proven metrics management system.

Section VI: Future Directions

This section addresses the function of corporate risk management in the twenty-first century and looks into the future challenges of the task.

Chapter 18: The Future of Risk Management

As the global marketplace continues to change and become more dependent on technology, the need for corporate risk management will become greater and more complex. Risk aware organizations must be staffed with professionals who are technologically aware. The stereotypical view of the type of individual tasked with risk management as being an ex-policeman is totally unrealistic both now and in the future. This chapter addresses some of the current trends in both business and technology and how they relate to the need to provide protection to a company and how these changes affect the risk management professional.

CLOSING COMMENTS

We hope you find this book useful and that it provides information that you can easily apply to the risk management process in your organization. We appreciate hearing from you and gladly accept your comments, constructive criticism, and advice as to what we should add, delete, or expand upon in a second edition. We can be contacted through our publisher, Elsevier Butterworth-Heinemann. See their website at http://books.elsevier.com/security.

Acknowledgments

This project, from an initial idea to the successful publication of this book, has taken the time and effort of a number of people in addition to its authors. It has taken the support and understanding of our families; professional input of our business, law enforcement, and security colleagues, friends, and those involved in the management of risk; as well as the publisher's team assigned to this project.

We are grateful to all of them for their support on this project. We send a special thanks to

Dr. Jerry Kovacich

Phil Swinburne

Arnold Drenth

To the staff and project team of Butterworth-Heinemann, Mark Listewnik, Pam Chester, George Morrison, and Linda Hah thanks for all your efforts and for your support and guidance, which has made this book possible. We look forward to your continued professional support and expertise.

About the Authors

Andy Jones has over 30 years of military intelligence, information warfare, business security, criminal and civil investigations, and information systems security experience in the British military and in the international business sector. He has spent a considerable period in defense research into information warfare and information systems security management and computer forensics. He has experience in both government and commercial investigations and security audit and as an international lecturer and consultant on these topics. Andy is currently working as a principal lecturer at a university in information security and computer crime and as a consultant and continues to conduct research in these topics. He holds a PhD in The Measurement of Threats to Information Systems.

Debi Ashenden has a background in risk assessment in government and the finance, insurance, and media sectors. She has a well-developed set of specialist skills in information assurance and corporate intelligence analysis. She has carried out a broad range of roles, addressing business needs and process analysis for information assurance, business security risk analysis, intelligence assessment, and project management. Debi was previously the Head of Professional Services in the Trusted Information Management department at QinetiQ, the privatized element of what was previously the Defence Evaluation and Research Agency and is currently a Senior Research Fellow in Information Assurance at the Royal Military College of Science, Cranfield University.

Section I

An Introduction to Risk Management

1

Introduction to the Theories of Risk Management

Here we introduce a brief history of risk management through the changing scope of information security risk, the evolving methods for carrying out a risk assessment, and the changing configurations of drivers for undertaking risk assessment. We also consider the definitions of risk assessment and risk management in the information security environment.

In this chapter we outline the different approaches to risk and how the demands of these approaches vary. These include technical risk, information security risk, and business risk and how these three are interrelated with respect to the field of information security. We review some of the complications involved in risk assessment, such as where risk is measured in organizations, how it is measured, and, perhaps most importantly, to whom it is communicated.

Information security risk assessments first focused on individual Information Technology (IT) systems and their implementation. This was at a time when software was often custom-made, and systems were usually stand-alone rather than interconnected. Risk assessments tended to focus on technical vulnerabilities, only paying scant attention to the risk associated with the people using the systems or the processes that underpinned the operation. As systems became interconnected, it was recognized that attention needed to be paid to the points of connection—to what happened in the virtual space between systems. Now risk assessment focused on the risks exposed by connecting systems together, information leakages, and unexpected ways of being able to access systems and the information they held. The next step in the evolutionary process was to consider information security risks at the project level. In some respects this was a significant move forward because information security risk assessments within a project setting tend to take into account not just the system itself, but also the people and processes that surround the system. Considering information security risks also means that the risk assessment process is exposed to a greater number and variety of people and becomes a more rounded consideration in the process.

The final stage of evolution for risk assessment is for it to be seen as an enterprise-wide issue, and this is what we are seeing at the moment. Information security risk assessments become one part in the enterprise-wide risk assessment process. This often covers all aspects of operational risk and is usually undertaken to comply with corporate governance requirements, which means the Board running an organization needs to understand all the risks associated with that particular business. There is still much work to be done in this area if information security risk is to become a respected and valued part of this process; information security risk is still in danger of being seen primarily as a technical issue, and it must mature to become a management issue. Assisting this maturation process should be one of the main aspirations for today's information security risk manager.

So what of the future for information security risk assessment? It needs to take its place in the wider enterprise-wide risk process, but it also has to broaden out so that risk dependencies are better understood across the enterprise. This is particularly relevant in an international organization or a national body. As our IT infrastructures become increasingly intertwined, we need ways of carrying out IT security risk assessments that are lightweight and flexible yet allow us to understand interdependencies of risk in a complex and dynamic environment.

As the scope of information security risk assessments has changed over the years, this has had a number of important implications for the risk assessment process. The consumers of information security risk assessments have changed significantly from a small group of technically literate individuals who would read the risk assessment report and implement the findings as part of a functional process. A risk assessment today is more likely to have a variety of readerships, ranging from the technically literate to the less technically focused project team through to the business focused senior management team and finally the Board. These different stakeholder groups have to be taken into account if the risk assessment process is going to continue to deliver benefit. As we discussed, information security risk assessments are now often part of a wider process, and they need to be undertaken with this awareness in mind. They are often one part of a much bigger picture; for example, today's information security risk assessment in a financial sector organization is likely to form part of the overall operational risk assessment that will be used to meet the Bank of International Settlements requirements for Basle II. The other part of the Basle II risk report will be the credit risk assessment that the organization undertakes. Information security risk has to fit in with other forms of risk assessment.

From this last example it is apparent that the drivers for undertaking risk assessments have changed significantly over recent years. At the micro level, information security risk assessments were carried out in the past purely to ensure that security was maintained, usually using the principles of confidentiality, integrity, and availability to guide the assessment process. In recent years this has expanded to become more of an assurance issue, now incorporating issues of the quality of information and the dependability of systems. At a macro level, the most overwhelming drive for information security risk assessments in recent years has been regulatory requirements and corporate governance. Originally risk assessments were carried out to manage IT security risks and to provide evidence that this had been done to ensure systems achieved accreditation (either internally or from a third party). This was particularly the case for military and public sector IT systems. In recent years we have seen the development of the British Standard BS 7799 for information security (part one of which has now become ISO 17799). Organizations can be accredited to this international standard through BS 7799:2, which outlines the requirements for compliance with the standard. The first step to implementing the standard and the first documentary evidence that an auditor will expect to see are a risk assessment process and a completed risk assessment. This standard has provided a baseline measurement for a number of organizations and is seeing an increasingly enthusiastic take-up in South East Asia. As we explore in later chapters, we are now witnessing organizations undertaking information security risk assessments to comply with corporate governance requirements such as the Turnbull Report in the United Kingdom; for the finance sector there is the Sarbanes Oxley Act and Basle II, both demanding that adequate account is taken of information security risks. These changing drivers have an impact on the type of risk assessment that is carried out and, more importantly, the skills required to do so successfully.

As you might expect, the tools for carrying out information security risk assessments have changed dramatically over recent years. In basic terms the methodology has remained fairly static, but the ways in which it is implemented reflect not only the different sectors in which it has matured but also the changing drivers and scope. When risk assessments focused on a single IT system, it was relatively easy to carry out a risk assessment with a pen and paper using a simple matrix framework. As the requirements for risk assessments broadened, these frameworks become more complex. The step change came about when we had to consider the risks in connecting systems and the risks at the project level. It was at this point, as has already been noted, that people and processes began to be considered in greater detail. This made the process more complicated, and the solution from an IT perspective was to build a software tool to support the process.

(In the United Kingdom, this led to the software solution called CRAMM, which is tellingly still the preferred method for addressing information security risk in the public sector.) Over the next few years we saw a proliferation of such software tools, all following the same basic methodology but with variations to suit different types of organizations. As we moved toward enterprise-wide risk assessments, we started to see attempts to site information security risk assessment within the wider business environment. This led to balanced scorecard type approaches to looking at information security risk assessment (e.g., FIRM from the Information Security Forum). There have also been attempts, largely unsuccessful, in recent years to use corporate finance risk assessment techniques in the information security environment. These were primarily driven by a downturn in the IT market that led to a push to provide return on investment figures for IT spending, particularly in the security field. The search for an ideal risk assessment method continues, but many organizations are now beginning to realize that a custom-made, or at least customized, approach is the best way forward.

So what for the future of information security risk assessment? A central part of understanding risk and making sure that it works for the business rather than against it is in aligning it with the business strategy. This involves looking outside as well as inside the organization, making the most of business opportunities but in a controlled evaluated way in the fast-moving business environment. It is also important to remember that risk can be a positive attribute in the business environment and that organizations are increasingly becoming proactive rather than reactive in their activities.

Presenting information security risk to the Board is an area where there is a great deal more work to be done. In recent research undertaken by Henley Management College in the United Kingdom, the point was strongly made that information security needs to move from a functional concern to a core part of business strategy. In many cases, however, this simply is not happening. The research discussed how Boards could start to make this move and offered a roadmap to help with this transition. The reality is that few Boards will read a specialist piece of research on information security. How then will the gap between the functional and strategic threads of information security be closed? What roles are there within companies that will understand the benefits offered by this approach? How, in real terms, will information security become aligned with business strategy when it is still the case that IT strategy is not always aligned with business strategy?

It seems that risk could be the linchpin that connects the two threads of function and strategy in the security arena. This was brought out in a document by the Information Assurance Advisory Council named "Engaging the Board."

Risk can be broken down into a number of areas to be addressed and all apply to information security: technology, business processes, the environment, and people.

In organizations with a mature approach to information security, technology risk is probably well understood. It is a way of protecting assets within the business and should bring together an understanding of business processes with the technology that supports them. Organizations have focused a great deal of attention in this area already, although undoubtedly there is still work to be done, particularly in the area of metrics and dependency risks.

If we look at the environment in which organizations operate, we can see the impact that corporate scandals have had and how this has led to vigorous moves to tighten up corporate governance. Regulation is one way to ensure that Boards address information security issues. We have seen legal regulations such as the Data Protection Act (in Europe) and Money Laundering requirements for those in the finance sector, along with the operational risk requirements such as those proposed by the Basle II and standards such as ISO 17799.

Ideally, however, our aim should be to make information security a core competence within organizations at all levels, and risk assessment could be the starting point for embedding this understanding. In the long run it is the integrity and ethical stance of individuals that poses the highest risk; if this is skewed, then regulations can always be subverted. This is the area that is undoubtedly the most difficult to address: people and the organizational culture. We need IT governance and information security risk to become part of an organization's corporate social responsibility, and it is obvious that this is not an area where information security is struggling on its own. If we assess company business strategies, the strongest areas are likely to be the matching of company strengths and weaknesses against the opportunities and threats offered by the industry sector. The areas most likely to be out of alignment are the values of the senior managers in an organization and the expectations of society as a whole. This area encompasses the whole problem of building trust between individuals within an organization and between the organization and the society in which it exists. All these areas need to be aligned for a business strategy to be successful, and information security and risk assessment has to be accorded its proper place if there is to be a mapping between the culture of the organization, its reason for being, and the environment in which it operates.

Future chapters outline the demands and complications of any risk management approach, and consideration is given to the various tools and techniques used to manage risk. We also address whether qualitative or quantitative approaches should be used; this is especially relevant in view of the general lack of actuarial data that exist in the field of information security. We look at future developments for risk assessment, particularly in the field of corporate intelligence and threat assessment.

First, however, we need to understand the basics. A generally accepted definition of risk in the information security environment is that risk is a function of the level of threat, vulnerability, and the value of the information asset. (The terms "risk", "threat", "vulnerability", and "impact" are defined in Chapter 4.) Without either a threat agent, a vulnerability, or an impact there will not be a risk. There must be a threat agent to exploit a vulnerability, and this exploitation must cause an impact for there to be a risk to the organization. It is easy to see how the key terms are interconnected, and organizations are becoming more mature in their approach to risk and more skillful at understanding their vulnerabilities and the impact these could cause. They are becoming better at looking inward at their organizational processes and practices, but unfortunately they are not so good at looking outward at their environment, an important aspect if they are to get a true measure of risk. We return to this subject in Section II. We use the term "threat agent" in our definition of threat. Many people use the terms "threat" and "vulnerability" synonymously, but here we are specifically talking about the agent that exploits the threat (addressed in Chapter 5).

We have a theoretical definition of risk, but in reality what constitutes a risk for an organization? It will vary from one organization to another. Some companies are risk averse, whereas others are not, and this will depend on their organizational culture, their strategy, the success of the business, and the industry sector in which they operate. The way that organizations prioritize confidentiality, integrity, availability, and nonrepudiation will depend on these factors. The outcome of a risk that is realized, whether the purpose is to degrade information, destroy it, or deny access to it, will depend on the type of information affected.

Given the many different forms of risk assessment that take place, we have to consider what we mean when we aim to minimize risk and ensure a successful recovery for information assets. Are we aiming to reassure stakeholders in the business, to achieve a financial advantage, or to gain a tick in the box from a regulatory authority? From an information security perspective, we may mean that we would like to preempt an attack. This seems an unlikely achievement on the face of it but one that perhaps we should aspire to achieve. If this is our aim, how will we know when we have achieved it? This is the perennial security problem: If our information security is working and protecting our networks, then there won't be any security breaches. Therefore, is lack of attack proof that it is working? We may have intrusion detection sensors on the IT networks that enable us to track and monitor attacks, but these will only prove that security is working on the infrastructure—it does not address the wider issues of protecting information in the environments through which it flows across the information network. It may be the case that trapping attacks, monitoring activities, and prosecuting where unlawful intrusions have taken place is accepted as successful recovery for some organizations; this may be the case for commercial business, but would it be sufficient for the government or the military? For some organizations, successfully defeating an attack against an information network could just mean a successful physical recovery, and this will have implications for business continuity. When is the recovery deemed successful? This too can have different meanings in different circumstances. It may mean recovering the physical information and the infrastructure, but as many organizations discovered in the wake of September 11, psychological recovery is also a vital element. The importance of understanding the risks to information networks, in the broadest sense, rather than just IT networks is apparent. These questions all need to be considered when risk mitigation strategies are planned.

What we are attempting to demonstrate is that there are many definitions of risk even within the information security environment. There are also many different motivations at play across both public and private sector organizations, and all organizations will have a fluidity according to circumstances and scenarios. We can see there is no simple answer to defining risk in an information environment. Various factors have to be considered, and as with all strategic decisions, there needs to be sufficient flexibility within an organization to anticipate and respond appropriately as the situation demands. However, just as we can see many different approaches to understanding risk within individual organizations, the difficulties of aligning processes for risk management in the organization is further complicated by the usual concerns. These encompass issues of lack of time and money and the need for business cases for security spending. There will also be company issues to consider. These can be important when a large part of a company's assets are tied up in its reputation. There may also be political considerations surrounding third party connectivity, whether it's taking place upstream or downstream in the value chain. It may be easier to impose risk management techniques downstream in the value chain but harder to achieve upstream. Organizations may not put confidentiality as a business priority, but they still have to comply with legal and regulatory issues that demand attention to confidentiality. Finally, there is a need to align business strategy with IT, to ascertain what will work best for the organization and to balance the two.

To expand on this last point further, we need to think more carefully about the value of strategic agility in attempting to manage risk. The best way to develop a strategic approach to an issue is to think about situations from different perspectives—or through different lenses—combining an appreciation of past experience, an understanding of planning and control, with an ability to think innovatively. This is a tall order and depends on having access to timely well-developed information and to act upon it within a time scale that ensures an advantage and on anticipating future scenarios. It can also depend on collaboration between organizations in the form of strategic alliances. In the face of increasingly turbulent, fast-changing, and uncertain business environments (often termed hypercompetitive environments), organizations need to acknowledge that any advantages gained through risk management may be temporary and that success may depend more on the ability to adapt to situations in the short term, building up the speed of reactions, acting flexibly, and encouraging innovation. This is just as applicable to the success of managing information security risks as it is to the general business environment. We need good flow across all information networks to facilitate an understanding of risk and to ensure that we can reap the benefits of indirect action, be creative in our responses, and perhaps ensure that the unexpected is not totally unplanned.

In conclusion then, if we are to address risk holistically at a basic level, we need to define a methodology that is suitable for the organization and can be incorporated into an enterprise-wide approach to managing risk. Most importantly, there is a need to understand the usefulness of a strategic approach to risk both in terms of the business and in terms of IT and to think about risk beyond the boundaries of the organization. When we can do this, we will have a holistic approach to risk that can be communicated at all levels of the business. The following sections cover in more detail the issues outlined in this chapter. By the end of the book you will have a toolbox of techniques and approaches to put together your own risk assessment methodology and to tailor it to your specific organization. The tools and techniques described will give you the sufficient breadth to address information security risk holistically.

2

The Changing Environment

In this chapter we introduce the reader to the interconnected and global environment in which organizations must now operate. We look at the aspects that have changed and the impact of those changes, particularly in the areas of corporate governance, regulatory requirements, and operational risk. We describe a changing environment that requires a shift in the way we think of risk.

Since the start of the 1990s, there has been a significant change in the level and type of risk that all sectors of government and industry have been exposed to. At the level of nation states, we have seen the collapse of the soviet block and communism, which the West has hailed as a victory. In reality, although capitalism seems largely to have triumphed over communism, the global stability that we enjoyed as a result of two superpowers in tension has also disappeared and we live in a much more volatile environment. Not only has there been a shift in the balance of power between governments, but regional pressures and multinational corporations now must also be taken into consideration, with the power and influence of individual nation states on the decline. The significant issue here is that whereas in a Western democratically based system we can influence the actions of governments (we periodically have the opportunity to vote the government out of office if we do not like the way they operate), the actions of multinational corporations are very much more difficult to affect. Also, in very much the same time frame, we have seen the globalization of communications accessibility and the wide scale availability of information technology that have led to a massive take-up of access to information, brought about as a result of these developing technologies. Concurrent with and partially as a result of the drive for faster and more reliable communications and information technology, we have also seen a convergence in the disparate technologies. Communication systems are now almost exclusively managed by computer systems and computer systems rely extensively on a wide range of communications technologies. As the processing power of the computer systems has increased, so has the development of the applications and facilities that were previously not possible.

From the rather pedestrian start in the 1990s of computers connecting to bulletin boards to the concept of the World Wide Web at 14.4 kilobits per second (Kbps) (improved to a nominal 56 Kbps), today it is not unusual for home users to be connected via one of a number of methods. Such methods are the asynchronous digital subscriber line (ADSL) with a potential 500 Kbps downstream and 256 Kbps upstream and, more recently, systems such as asynchronous broadband connections that give a downstream speed of up to 2 megabits per second (Mbps) and an upstream speed of 56 Kbps. Homes that are connected to cable service providers can also connect at potential high speeds of up to 2 Mbps, although more realistically the actual access speeds are probably nearer to 512 Kbps and the use of satellite broadcast technology as an alternative delivery means. Other options include connection via radio/microwave at speeds of 2 Mbps or via satellite with a potential downstream speed of 3 Mbps or wireless optical connections with a potential speed of 10 Mbps in each direction.

In the same sort of time frame we have seen the processing speed of home and off desktop computers increase from the 486–33 MHz system to the 3 gigabit system. Storage capacity has increased from an average of 10 or 20 megabits to a staggering 250 gigabits over the same period. With these increased processing and communications speeds have come applications that make use of them. It is now quite standard to use streaming video, music on demand, video conferencing, and a range of other facilities.

These advances in technology have coincided with and underpinned the infrastructure for social changes and have provided the opportunity for people to change their lifestyles by adopting options such as home working, where they can remove the drudgery of commuting on increasingly congested roads and rail systems. In Western societies, as a result of the changes in business practices, the workforce has become more mobile, and the concept of a "job for life" with a loyal and long-standing workforce has largely disappeared. Overcrowded roads and rail transport systems are part of the social change that has taken place, resulting in an increasing demand for people to work from home and avoid the frustration of commuting. This also works to the advantage of business, because a workforce that does not occupy office space comes at a lower cost and increases competitiveness. As the pace of business increases, so do the demands on the infrastructure to cope with a workforce that needs to be highly mobile and that requires the same level of access to facilities and information they would have if they were working in the office.

Figures 2.1 and 2.2 give an indication of the huge expansion that has occurred in access to and use of the Internet in just over a decade. Although this enormous increase in the use of the Internet has had huge potential benefit for industry and commerce in that it has provided access to the global markets, it has also created problems due to a common infrastructure to which all users have equal access. Another significant issue to remember is that not all populations of the world are English speaking and that well over half of the users of the Internet do not use English as their first language.

Another significant change occurred because of the attacks on the U.S. infrastructure on September 11, 2001, by a terrorist organization. Although this attack in itself did not change the world economy, it was a new departure, in its scale, from anything that had previously been experienced and has added a new and very real dimension to the risks that organizations face. Issues such as business continuity were tested on a scale that had rarely been seen before and in some cases were found to be inadequate. The asset that was found to be most poorly accounted for was not the equipment or the data but the skilled personnel to use them.

In the public sector, there are a range of reported incidents that illustrate the types of events that can affect an organization. These events, given next, were accidental, so just think what the impact might have been if they had been intentional.

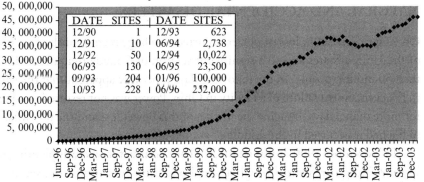

Figure 2.1. *Hobbes' Internet timeline. (Courtesy of http://www.zakon.org/robert/internet/timeline)*

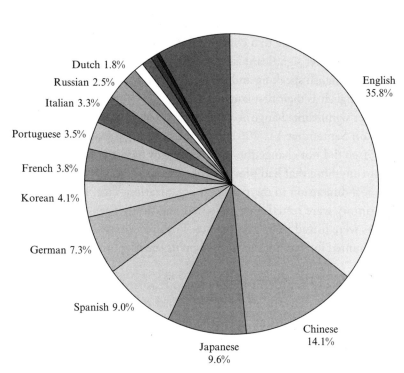

Online Language Populations
Total: 729 Million
(March 2004)

Dutch 1.8%
Russian 2.5%
Italian 3.3%
Portuguese 3.5%
French 3.8%
Korean 4.1%
German 7.3%
Spanish 9.0%
Japanese 9.6%
Chinese 14.1%
English 35.8%

Figure 2.2. *Internet language populations. (Courtesy of http://global-reach.biz/globstats)*

NATURAL AND ACCIDENTAL DISASTERS

On August 14, 2003, loss of power occurred to a large section of the East Coast of the United States and to a significant section of Canada that affected more than 50 million people. In the following days it became apparent that the trigger to the events was a failure of a facility in Ohio. Power was not restored to all users for more than 3 days. Imagine the impact of this power loss and the potential loss of life had it occurred in the middle of winter.

In November 1990, it was reported[1] that a contractor who was planting trees in the Chicago area cut through a telephone cable, disconnecting services to 150,000 telephones. The following year, according to the same source, an AT&T

---

1. Computer Related Risks, Peter G Neumann, ACM Press, 1995

crew, while removing an old cable, cut through a fiber optic cable carrying more than 100,000 calls. Among the organizations affected were the New York Mercantile Exchange and the Federal Aviation Authority Air Traffic Control, which led to lengthy flight delays. In another incident that affected Air Traffic Control in 1991, a contractor cut through a 1500 circuit cable in the San Diego area, causing an outage of approximately 16 hours.

MALICIOUS DISASTERS

In a separate attack, Bob Brewin reported that Art Money, the U.S. Assistant Secretary for Defence for C^3I, had stated that "Cyberterrorists have hacked into and altered the Defense Department's medical World Wide Web pages that contain information on troops' blood types." According to the report, the intruders had apparently gained access to and then altered databases that contained medical information at Department of Defense hospitals in the southeastern United States. The report stated that this incident had caused the Department of Defense to review its policy with regard to the types of information it made available on its web pages.

COMMERCIAL SECTOR

In the commercial sector we have seen a range of disasters, some foreseeable and avoidable and some not, but the result has been the introduction of a range of legislation to control the greater excesses of commercial organizations and to make them more accountable. Legislation has been introduced to compel legal accountability by individuals and organizations, from corporate manslaughter to environmental issues and privacy and good governance of the business.

Enron

Few business failures to date have gained as much attention or have started as many lawsuits and investigations as the collapse and bankruptcy filing of Enron. Investigations into the collapse included separate investigations by the U.S. Departments of Justice and Labor, the Securities and Exchange Commission, the Financial Accounting Standards Board, relevant U.S. Senate and House committees, a number of other government regulators, the National Association of Securities Dealers, and groups of investors.

Before its Chapter 11 bankruptcy filing, the Enron Corporation was one of the world's largest energy, commodities, and services companies. It had marketed electricity and natural gas, delivered energy and other commodities, and provided services in the financial and risk management areas to customers worldwide. The company, which was based in Houston, Texas, was formed in July 1985 by the merger of Houston Natural Gas and InterNorth of Omaha, Nebraska. From this base as a natural gas pipeline company, it rapidly evolved from just delivering energy to brokering energy futures as the energy markets were deregulated. In 1994, it started to market electricity and then entered the European energy market in 1995. In 1999, the company initiated a plan to trade in high speed Internet access bandwidth. In the year 2000, the company had interests in nearly 30,000 miles of gas pipeline, a 15,000-mile fiber optic network, and electricity generating operations around the world. In that year it reported revenues of $101 billion.

Although what actually took place at the company before its collapse is still under investigation and will, in due course, be decided by the courts, the underlying issues include corporate power abuse, conflicts of interest, and inadequate auditing. What the collapse did reveal was that there was no entirely satisfactory way in which to account for complex deals that extend over a number of years.

The failure of Enron also caused the collapse of the accountancy firm that had audited its accounts, Arthur Andersen. The culpability of that accountancy firm in the eventual collapse has not yet been determined, but its very involvement resulted in the company itself becoming nonviable.

WorldCom

The next major company to collapse was WorldCom Inc., the nation's second-largest long-distance company, in July 2002 with an alleged accounting irregularity of US$3.9 billion. It was alleged that a fraud had taken place to show the earnings of the company were in line with the expectations of Wall Street and to support the stock price for WorldCom. This allegation was contained in a fraud suit filed in the federal court in Manhattan, arguing that WorldCom had falsely portrayed itself as a profitable business when it should have reported losses of a total of US$1.2 billion for its last full year of trading and the first 3 months of the year in which it collapsed.

According to the *New York Times*, the fraud was first identified when an internal WorldCom auditor found that expenses incurred in the last full year of trading had not appeared where they should have in the company's books. Instead, the were spread across a series of capital expenditure accounts. The internal auditor's report stated that the shift in expenses was significant and potentially fraudulent. At WorldCom, the normal costs of connecting a customer to its fiber optic network were transferred (incorrectly) from the profit-

and-loss statement to the balance sheet as capitalized expenditures. These improper transfers involved costs at both the WorldCom group, which primarily catered for large commercial customers, and the MCI group, which serviced small-business and residential customers.

Whenever a company spends money to acquire a new asset, whether it is miles of fiber optic cable or a modem, it must ask itself how long the asset will continue to have value. If the answer is less than a year, then according to experts the expenditure probably should be treated as an ordinary business expense and deducted from earnings in the same quarter. However, if the asset will continue to have value into the next year or longer, there may be a good argument for capitalizing it, that is, turning it into an asset that can be depreciated over a number of years instead of deducted from earnings right away. This highlighted a set of issues as to when costs are part of ordinary day-to-day business and when they can be considered capital expenditures. In business, the ordinary costs are immediately deducted from revenue with the result of a reduction in earnings. On the other hand, capital expenditure, the outlay of money for longer term assets such as buildings, infrastructure, routers, and other hardware and software, can be depreciated over time.

Within the business opinion was clear: The actions had been taken in an effort to maintain the company's stock price. Despite problems that had been mounting throughout 2001, its stock traded within a range of $10 to $20 a share in the period, and this stock value was supported by the company's public reports of continuing profits of a net $1.4 billion during its last full year and $130 million in the first quarter before the collapse. It eventually became clear these earnings did not exist and had been engineered to satisfy the fixation of the stock market on near-term results. In the volatile labor market, where short contracts are the norm, the pressure is on corporate executives to match or exceed investors' expectations of performance to maintain their positions. The problem is exacerbated by the often generous stock options that are provided for both executives and other employees who can profit only if the company's earnings and stock price climb ever higher.

THE GOOD OLD DAYS

In the past, the environment in which we lived and worked was very different. Organizations tended to be based in the same area as their customers and, as a result, were locally accountable. For example, the power company was an independent organization that served the local community. If for some reason the supply failed, then the community that it served was probably without power until the service could be restored. Over a period of time, as a result of pressures from the users and for good business economic reasons, the industry started to organize and the companies began to connect to each other to trade surplus production and to provide some degree of resilience so that a failure in one generation plant could be compensated for by increased production elsewhere. In general, this was a successful step forward, although in the United States it has from time to time led to "brown outs" over wide areas, where the pain of insufficient supply has been shared by many instead of a few. For those who live in areas with a good supply who suffer the effects, the benefits might be argued.

This effective isolation and lack of interconnection and interdependence meant that any effect of failure was normally only local, which might be catastrophic for those involved, but was contained to one area or group of users. It also meant that the organization had a clear relationship with its suppliers and that the consumer would probably have a direct relationship with the supplier and that organizations were locally accountable (if the consumers were unhappy, they would either complain directly or turn to another supplier). In the current environment, with huge multinational corporations operating all aspects of the infrastructure on which we rely, the structure of the organizations is far more complex, and in many cases the organizations themselves do not appreciate the level of interdependency of the structure on which they rely. For the consumer, it is now significantly more difficult to know who we are really dealing with and, if there are problems, to be heard.

REGULATION

Partially as the result of the increased importance and significance of the globalization of trade and partially as the result of a number of high profile corporate excesses, we have seen increasing levels of legislation introduced to protect the shareholder and the consumer. As a result of the increased legislation and also the changed environment, the need to assess the risks to the business, the operation, and the information systems on which both of these rely has become increasingly important.

One significant aspect that has emerged with the widespread use of information systems is the issue of individual privacy. Data on individuals are increasingly collected and stored on information systems by corporations and governments for a wide range of purposes. These range from your bank and credit rating agency to your local superstore, where they want to know your shopping habits to better target you for future promotions. Unless these organizations are conscientious and there is strong legislation, the individual may have little protection from the storage and use of incorrect information or inappropriate use of correct information.

Also, given that not all organizations (including government departments) deal with the protection of privacy with the same rigor, how does the citizen ensure that information about them is not collected, stored, or used inappropriately?

As people use information systems to communicate through e-mail and in chat rooms, there is an increasing reliance on these systems. With increasingly strong legislation in place to protect the rights of the individual, how do organizations protect themselves from liability that results from the misuse of these facilities by their staff while at the same time protecting the rights of the individual?

When companies had a single function—the power company produced electricity and the water company delivered water—the structures of the companies could be very simple. However, in efforts to spread the risk of doing business, returning a good value to the investors and gaining economies of scale, companies have merged and grown into multidiscipline multinational conglomerates that are now hugely complex with convoluted chains for decision making and a presence in a number of legal jurisdictions. It is now difficult, with some companies making more profit than the gross national product of small countries, to determine which jurisdiction applies and where (and even if) the company should pay tax. As a result of the increasing globalization of trade and banking and in recognition of a changing trading environment, the Basel Accord was introduced to strengthen the confidence in the banking systems and to create a more even playing field for all participants.

The Basel Accord

The Basel Capital Accord, first published in 1988 with full implementation completed by the signatories by the end of 1992, was developed with two fundamental objectives, which were the core of the Committee's work on regulatory convergence. The first objective was that the framework should serve to strengthen the stability of the international banking system, and the second objective was that it should be fair and have a high degree of consistency in its application to banks in different countries. In the subsequent years, increased volatility in the market as well as a number of incidents such as the Asian and Russian monetary crises, the collapse of Barings Bank, and the problems with Sumitomo Capital prompted a review at the Capital Accord to produce a detailed update to attempt to address some of the underlying issues identified as a result of these incidents.

In June 1999, the Basel Committee released a proposal to replace the 1988 Capital Accord with a more comprehensive and risk-sensitive framework that covers the market, credit, and operational risk areas. The initial consultation for the new document was held in January 2001, and a draft directive was issued. After a second consultation period through the spring and summer of 2001, the Committee released a complete and fully specified proposal for a further round of consultation in the early part of 2002. The Committee produced the final version of the New Accord during 2003, and an implementation date of January 1, 2007 is projected.

In the region of 110 countries have become signatories to the new Basel Accord, and in a number of jurisdictions, including the United Kingdom, the United States, the European Union, Canada, Singapore, and Australia, there are plans to accelerate the implementation of this new accord. The New Accord is based on three mutually reinforcing pillars, which together should contribute to safety and soundness in the financial system. The first pillar is the minimum capital requirements that, for the first time, include all areas of banking business and operations, including retail banking, small and medium enterprise lending, information technology, and operations risk. The second pillar deals with the supervisory review process, which sets out some basic standards for bank supervision to minimize regulatory arbitrage. The third pillar deals with market discipline, which requires much more disclosure and transparency by both the banks and their regulators.

As stated earlier, in recent decades we have seen a massive move forward in the globalization of trade and commerce, and with it has come the requirement for commensurate regulation in the form of industry accords and self-regulation and national, regional, and international laws. A large number of companies are now "global" in their operations, with interests in from a few to many countries. Companies like Microsoft™ truly span the globe and have an annual turnover that dwarfs that of some countries. One of the major problems with international or multinational companies is who regulates them—which country has primacy in imposing its laws on the organization? Do the companies pay tax in the country where profits were earned? Where do they write off losses? This issue is one that plagues countries as well as the companies. Countries want to attract investment and industry to their region and so will make concessions to companies to encourage them to invest, so how can a fair and level playing field be ensured? In reality, international law is so slow in coming into being that it is almost irrelevant. I once heard it said that it took nearly 40 years for the law of the sea to come into being and that even now not all nations have signed on. What chance is there of getting any effective international law in place in a realistic time frame?

Other options, which include laws within single nations or common law across groups of nations, for example, the European Union or the G8 countries, all have a place and can be effective in some regions. However, there are other ways in which effective regulation can be achieved. One example of this is the U.S. Sarbanes-Oxley Act of 2002, introduced by the Securities and Exchange Commission to restore investor confidence after the spectacular collapse of Enron.

Some indication of the progress that has been made and the attitudes that now exist with regard to risk can be seen from a speech made at a conference in the United Kingdom in March 2002 on managing information risk in a changed world, where a member of the British Parliament, who had previously held the post of Minister of State for E-Commerce and Competitiveness, Mr. Douglas Alexander, said the following: "It has always been clear to me that the problems we face are, at heart, management ones rather than technical ones. The right behavioral model for any organisation is to understand the nature of the risk it faces and take appropriate, and auditable, actions to address that risk." He then went on to speak of what needed to be done to manage that risk in a changed and constantly changing world. He recognized that in order to prosper, there is a need for organizations in government and the private sector to work together. He spoke on the U.K. government's role in ensuring the security of the nation and the importance of its policy in protecting the critical national infrastructure and the approach to regulation in the area of e-business, describing it as "a light touch" that would be based, probably, on the issuing of guidance of "E-policy principles," which obliges everyone preparing new legislation to prove that, first and foremost, it is friendly to the on-line environment. His view was that one role of regulation in the information security field was to ensure that it was possible to capture and punish offenders. In the United Kingdom, the main instruments of legislation, the Regulation of Investigatory Powers Act and the Anti-Terrorism Crime and Security Act, have addressed the requirements of the law enforcers in the information age, but there may be a need for further updating of the laws in this area. He also referred to current initiatives in the area, including the SAINT initiative, which has similarities with the Information Sharing concept developed in the United States.

In the European Union, the Council passed a resolution at the end of 2001 that called on Member States to carry out a basic agenda of activities to improve network and information security. This resolution included improving awareness raising efforts and increasing the importance of information security in education and the intention to create a cyber-security task force to enhance the ability of Member States to prevent, detect, and respond to incidents. At the same time, the Organisation for Economic Co-operation and Development was in the process of reviewing the 1992 Guidelines on Information Security.

CORPORATE GOVERNANCE

In the current highly connected environment, the careless or inadvertent actions of the owners of one system have the potential for enormous ramifications for other systems and the networks themselves. As a result, information security is now a core aspect of good corporate governance. It will probably require a cultural change in the way we look at business to bring this issue out of the operations room and into the boardroom. One of the key challenges that we face is how to properly value the protection of our information assets. The current widely held basis of investment analysis simply treats enhanced protection for information systems as an overhead. If the situation is to be properly addressed, we will have to find ways of addressing this problem so that investment decisions can be taken quickly and effectively.

Turnbull

Another initiative from 1999 from the United Kingdom was the Turnbull Report. This report was the product of a working party led by Nigel Turnbull to provide guidance to companies, specifically those listed or intending to be listed on the London stock exchange, on the adoption of a risk based approach to establishing a system for internal control and review. The potential benefits of effective risk management were listed at length, but examples of the perceived benefits included higher share price over the longer term, a reduction in management time spent "fire fighting," a lower cost of capital, and the achievement of competitive advantage. The guidance requires directors of companies to exercise judgment in reviewing how the company has implemented the requirements of the code relating to internal control and the subsequent reporting to shareholders.

RISK

Risk is present in organizations at all levels of operation from the strategic level to the operational level to the tactical level but is normally described as business or operational risk.

Strategic Risk

Strategic risk is best described as the enterprise or organizational risk issues that are addressed at the highest level of management within the organization. Decisions that affect the goals, objectives, key risks, and stakeholders are all made within the strategic context of achieving a mission and a vision for the organization. It is the normal business practice to adopt a risk assessment approach to examine any threats and opportunities to the organization.

Tactical Risk

Tactical risk is a term that describes the level of risk between the strategic and the operational level. It is the area where the broad implementation of decisions and the achievement of goals takes place. Tactical risk refers to the medium term choices and decisions that occur within the framework set at a strategic level. The term describes the *tactics* by which the strategy is achieved and will normally be owned by the middle tier of management.

Operational Risk

Operational risk really describes the day-to-day risks that an organization will encounter in carrying out its operations. Operational risk occurs within the framework of the tactical decision-maker's focus. Although this level focuses on implementing tactical and operational decisions, it is important to understand all the risks faced by the organization as they carry out their business. Within the financial sector, the Basel Committee on Banking Supervision has defined operational risks as "the risk of direct or indirect loss resulting from inadequate or failed internal processes, people and systems or from external events."

Approach to Risk Management

The insurance industry has a long experience of managing risks. They have been operating for centuries and have gained a wealth of experience in establishing the level of risk that exists in a range of environments. So why do they still get it wrong? In reality, largely they do not. When they set a premium to insure against an event, it is based on a long background of historic information and is calculated to allow them to make a profit, given that, in a percentage of cases, the event will occur and they will have to pay compensation. However, the insurance companies have no more experience of the implications of globalization and the convergence of technologies than anyone else. Also, insurance knowledge and some of the input to the assessment of risk is based on historical knowledge, but when the situation changes at an ever increasing rate, this type of knowledge is not available.

This attitude is significant, because it shows the realization that the management of risk does not mean the elimination of risk. It means reducing the risk to a level that can be tolerated. Many organizations still view it as the former, with the expectation that risk management will make the problem go away. They cannot accept that, in reality, risk management just means reducing the probability of an event happening to a much lower level.

Governments have been particularly notable in this regard. If you look at the security of information, a breach of national security was considered to be improbable, and as a result there was an attitude of risk avoidance rather than risk management. It was only in the early 1990s that this approach became unacceptable, starting a significant change in policy. Although it is possible, in a relatively short period of time, to change policy, reeducating career civil servants who implement these policy changes is much more difficult. In many cases, even though the public sector organizations talk of risk management, they actually still think of risk avoidance.

There is an increasing requirement for a more dynamic way to deal with risk that can make allowance for and deal with the fast changing environment and allow cost-effective action to be taken to reduce the risk to a manageable and acceptable level. Whatever method is used, it must be transparent and understandable—if you want to persuade the board of your organization to invest significant funds in a course of action designed at the reduction of risk, it is essential that you can demonstrate to them what the costs and benefits are. The old days when "experts" gave their assessment and assured the organization they understand the problem and were trusted to be correct are no longer sustainable, because whatever method is used, it must be able to be replicated.

JUST IN TIME OR JUST TOO LATE?

Another development that has had a significant impact in recent years is the adoption of the "just in time" principle to reduce the capital investment required to carry out business. In the past we had vast warehouses full of stock and raw materials that cost money to buy, store, and insure. As communications have improved and confidence has grown, it has been possible to avoid these costs by ensuring that materials and stock arrive at the appropriate place within a very narrow time frame. The adoption of this principle has, potentially, huge benefits, but the downside is that any disruption to the delicate and often complex supply chain, even for a relatively short period of time, will result in a disruption to the business. When just in time turns into just too late, disaster looms.

COMPETITIVENESS

The underlying factor that drives all the changes in the way commercial organizations operate is competitiveness. The more competitive an organization is, the greater it will prosper and the longer it will survive. If we can reduce operating costs by the more effective management of our information security risks, this will help in the reduction of operating costs.

3

The Art of Managing Risks

In this chapter we consider the skills and thinking necessary in the management of information security risk. The risk manager needs a very broad set of skills and thought processes to be successful. Although many risk managers only possess a subset of the skills and thought processes outlined in this chapter, this should not deter them. Although many of these skills can be learned, the strength of many of them will depend on individual personalities. The successful risk manager is one who recognizes his or her limitations and takes steps to improve skills in areas where he or she identifies weakness. The unsuccessful risk manager is one who works in a very narrow field, refusing to appreciate that risk is primarily dependent on context and not looking beyond his or her own area of specialist expertise. This is the risk manager who will miss important changes in the environment both at a macro and micro level and will not be able to ensure that the information security risk profile of his or her organization remains aligned with corporate strategy. As a result, it is likely that either unnecessary risks will remain unexamined or the approach to information security risk will be too inflexible to allow the business to achieve its maximum potential.

In this chapter we refer back to the importance of the context that surrounds risk management decisions. Information security risks cannot successfully be managed in isolation but have to be clearly located within the whole organization's business strategy and the industry sector in which the organization does business. Context is key when it comes to understanding the art of managing risks. Another way of looking at this is through appreciating the risk manager's need to understand risk dependencies between information assets, different technology implementations, different stakeholder groups within the organization, and the different environments in which the organization operates. In this chapter we introduce a heavy weight of expectations on the successful risk manager.

A useful concept to help introduce the art of managing risk is that of "bridging"—that is, using thinking and skills that cross disciplines and boundaries. In recent years this has become an increasingly useful attribute for an information security risk manager. It means understanding the technology in business terms (understanding the context), knowing the implications that should guide the selection of countermeasures when mitigating risk, and how this will affect the business (usually in terms of profitability, take-up by customers, usability, etc.). Information security risk managers need a certain amount of business knowledge, coupled with technical understanding and good communication skills. Because they need to be able to communicate across a wide range of individuals in the organization, they need to be able to appreciate the interests of other stakeholders, other roles, responsibilities, and drivers, and this is where bridging skills are invaluable.

There is always a need for organizations to work toward ensuring that people, processes, technology, structure, and strategy are aligned; in this way the organization will achieve its full potential and true competitive advantage. This is probably best demonstrated by the Scott Morton model (Figure 3.1). The model comprises the elements of structure, processes, procedures and people, technology, and strategy and locates these elements both within the micro-environment, which is internal to the organization, and the wider external macro-environment. Morton

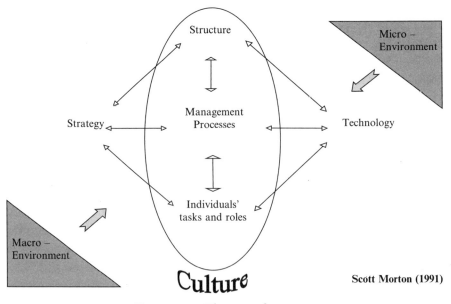

Figure 3.1. *Elements of structure.*

suggests that each element in the model needs to remain aligned if the organization is to succeed.

From the perspective of a successful information security risk manager, this means he or she needs to understand the organizational strategy and how technology will be used to support this strategy. She or he also needs an understanding of the structure, processes, and roles and responsibilities that underpin the business. Furthermore, he or she needs to understand the environment in which the organization operates (both at a national or international level as appropriate) and, perhaps most importantly, the organizational culture. This latter attribute is key in determining whether risk mitigation strategies will succeed or fail.

Whatever area we are focusing on to understand the risk to information security (people, process, or technology), we are usually assessing the risk because some type of change has occurred. This often causes a knock-on effect (consequential effect) in the organization to the extent that the elements outlined in the Scott Morton model become distorted and need to be realigned. For example, in many cases it is the introduction of new technology that causes this distortion. In this case it is not sufficient just to understand the security risks involved in implementing this new technology, but our appreciation of risks and the possible countermeasures has to extend to include the people and the processes that surround the technology. Without this, the elements in the model cannot be realigned, and little real progress will be made in ensuring that effective countermeasures are in place. For this reason we return to the concept of bridging when we consider the art of managing risk. Without having at least a basic understanding of all the elements in the model, it will be difficult for the information security manager to understand how to assist with realigning them.

Therefore, the successful information security risk manager will understand the risks at a number of different levels; also, these risks need to be defined, analyzed, and mitigation strategies selected and communicated across these same levels. This is a tall order and one that many risk managers fail to achieve. As our appreciation of security risk management has matured, so the demands on its practitioners have expanded. Risk management once focused solely on technology risk—examining the specific vulnerabilities in a system. As systems were connected together, a new appreciation arose that the risk environment would change; however, risk silos still existed. Project risk was addressed as a separate issue and even now does not always include security risk. As a result of this focus on technical risk and vulnerabilities, security risk management was perceived as difficult to understand—a point of view that was probably underpinned by risk reports that were impenetrable to anyone from a nontechnical background. With today's focus on corporate governance, the issue of risk pervades the organization, and information security risk assessment plays a relatively small but vital role in helping to manage risk across the enterprise. For this to happen, the information security risk manager needs to understand the broad context of risk across every facet of the organization and has to interface successfully with other risk managers who specialize in different areas.

This is most apparent in recent times with the introduction of Basel II by the Bank of International Settlements into the finance sector and the accompanying requirement to bring together an understanding of credit risk with an analysis of operational risk. The aftermath of the Enron bankruptcy raised issues of corporate governance. This was reflected in an address given by the Chairman of the Basle Committee's Accounting Task Force (May 8, 2002) when he talked about the impact on issues of trust, confidence, accounting, and, in particular, the ethics that underlie the financial reporting systems. This also tied in with U.S. recommendations from the National Association of Corporate Directors to the House Committee on Energy and Finance (March 1, 2002). In this document the National Association of Corporate Directors called for the Securities and Exchange Commission to urge the adoption of a system similar to the U.K. Combined Code (as implemented in the Turnbull Report in the United Kingdom). Furthermore, the recommendations pointed to other countries that have followed the U.K. example, such as Canada with the Dey Report. The core recommendations include that audit committee duties should encompass "not only assurance of financial reporting quality, but also oversight of risk." We can see from this brief outline of recent events how risk and corporate governance are being forced on the Board's agenda.

In 1988 the Basel Committee originally ruled that a bank's total capital should never fall to a level of less than 8% of risk weighted assets, and it set out rules for calculating the risk weighted figure. It has since been recognized that a single risk measure for all banks is inappropriate, and as a result, the Committee developed a new system that will be more risk sensitive and flexible. Furthermore, the Committee sought to widen the range of risks that form the basis of the capital adequacy process and to attune this calculation to the bank's own internal methodologies for measuring and controlling risk. The Committee sought to reward those banks that manage risk effectively by allowing them to reduce the levels of capital maintained to support their business. This means that those banks demonstrating good risk management processes will reduce levels of capital maintained, whereas banks failing to convince that their systems are robust will be penalized with a higher capital charge. Risk weighted assets now encompass market and operational risk (including security risk). In this instance information security risk sits within the overall concept of operational risk. The successful information security risk manager in a finance organization will be able to communicate an understanding of security in the wider concept of operational risk and appreciate the broad implications of the situation with regard to credit risk. Although we focused on the finance sector in this example, it is likely this approach to risk will soon pervade other sectors.

With this in mind, we can start to appreciate the different levels at which information security risk assessments take place. In some circumstances they are still technical risk assessments, but the risk manager also needs to provide both analysis and support for project risk assessments (usually into project teams) and needs to understand the role of the security risk assessment in enterprise-wide risk assessments, particularly those produced and reported to the Management Board to meet corporate governance requirements. The different levels at which the risk manager has to produce risk assessments are further complicated by the purpose of the risk assessment: to meet audit requirements, to satisfy regulators, to be used internally, or to demonstrate risk mitigation for customers (particularly in the case of e-business initiatives). It is necessary to distinguish carefully between those risk assessments produced to protect the business and those that have business promotion as their aim.

If this sounds as if the risk manager has to be all things to all people, then it is probably not far from the truth. If the risk manager sees his role as purely a risk reporting job, then many of the issues outlined above may be ignored, but as the discipline of information security becomes more established and the business environment remains reliant on technology to achieve competitive advantage, then the information security risk manager needs to demonstrate an increased return on investment for his role. In this latter case, the thinking and skills that underpin the work of the risk manager are varied and increasingly complex.

The ability to think broadly characterizes the successful information security risk manager. He or she needs to understand the culture within the organization and to use it to guide the way that risk assessment is carried out. Both a technical understanding and an ability to deal with "soft" issues are necessary. Undoubtedly, the successful information security risk manager needs to recognize his or her own limitations and call in specialist assistance when necessary. He or she needs to maintain a sense of balance and proportion when assessing security risks and to understand the implications of countermeasures in terms of the business. Furthermore, the information security risk manager needs to understand dependencies that may exist, in terms of technology, processes, and people. Finally, a risk manager needs an element of creativity in his or her thinking. This will be invaluable in developing risk mitigation strategies that assist rather than hinder what the business is trying to achieve. Creative thinking is also often necessary to deal with the organizational politics that a risk assessment process can exacerbate as individuals try to defend their own positions or push forward their pet projects.

Breadth of thinking is important because the risk manager needs to encompass the whole context of the organization and the business it operates. This understanding should be at a level that will enable the risk manager to gather information across a broad section of the workforce. It is of little use for the risk manager to only gather information from technical staff or from the project team; it is vital for the risk manager to move beyond specific interested parties to ordinary users. It is only with the ordinary user (that is, the people who have the day-to-day responsibility for using a process or operating technology) that the risk manager will get a true picture of the security risks. It is well recognized that although formal processes may exist to govern the use of technology, these are often disregarded or reinterpreted at the practical hands-on level. This is the information the risk manager needs if he is to manage risk effectively and for risk mitigation strategies to be anything more than superficial. For this reason the risk manager needs to have good soft skills to encourage individuals to share information. He needs to create a participative and non-threatening environment and yet be able to construct a thorough data gathering process. Information security risk managers will often be treated with suspicion, and it is important that the risk manager mediates the messages that are heard. For example, it is often the case that people become defensive in an attempt to protect themselves or a project, and this will distort the information that they give. The risk manager needs to be able to spot such distortions and manage them constructively, giving reassurance that the primary aim is to understand all the risks to develop risk mitigation strategies that will not hinder the way that business is done.

On the other hand, the risk manager also needs to have sufficient understanding of technical issues to establish a certain level of credibility. Without this credibility, it will be difficult to get a sound understanding of the technical issues that are being tackled and technical staff could become an obstacle, often deciding to develop their own working practices. An important part of the risk manager's role is to understand his or her own limitations, and this is particularly relevant as far as the technology is concerned. Where necessary, the risk manager must recognize when a specialist should be called in and should ask that specialist to prepare a brief on the subject area. It is often easy for technical staff to only give a fraction of the information they have at their disposal simply because they either do not or cannot explain the technological implications adequately. Risk managers should be sufficiently robust in their thinking to pursue lines of inquiry with rigor and not be dissuaded from their endeavors.

To elicit the right information, the risk manager should be able to articulate, to himself or herself at least, the style of the organizational culture. Culture is a term that is often used in a very vague way to describe the intangible facets of how an organization works; for example, there is said to be a public sector culture that is different from a private sector culture and, in some cases, this is often true. To reach a definition of a "culture," we have to consider the complexity that exists in understanding organizational culture. Organizational culture is embodied in the attitudes and beliefs of the individuals within the organization. The culture of an organization is often taken for granted, but the risk manager needs to use the organization's culture to help determine how a risk assessment should be carried out. In organizations that have a strong "need to know" culture, it can be very difficult to gather information, and careful thought needs to be given to what medium should be used to get the best results.

Finally, the risk manager needs to be able to think creatively. For risk mitigation strategies to work within a specific organizational culture, some compromise is undoubtedly necessary, and it may be necessary to think of countermeasures from a range of viewpoints—not forgetting the spread of people, process, and technology. It may even be the case that long-term risk mitigation strategies rely on external relationships. This could take the form of agreements with partners and suppliers or even political lobbying in some cases.

Even within the organization it is likely that creativity is needed to present the findings of the risk assessment in a way that ensures constructive action is taken. The findings should not provoke a "witch hunt" or place undue pressure on specific individuals but should steer a path toward a set of risk mitigation strategies that are broadly acceptable at all levels of the organization. These can then lead to detailed countermeasures being implemented that are workable and are accepted by all stakeholders.

Ultimately, there needs to be a sense of balance in the way a risk manager thinks. He needs to understand the implications of any risk mitigation strategies and to convey clearly this understanding. Furthermore, he needs to understand the dependencies in the risk mitigation strategies. It may be the case, as outlined at the beginning of this chapter, that by changing the technology and the processes to minimize risk, it is also necessary to retrain individuals. In this case the information security risk manager needs to develop countermeasures that will assist the business and not hinder its progress. By achieving this only once, the risk manager will learn that others will be happy to cooperate with risk assessments in the future as they begin to understand that it can be a constructive undertaking.

We discussed the thinking required to become a successful risk manager: understanding context and organizational culture; bridging disciplines, boundaries, and environments; thinking creatively; and maintaining a sense of balance. Now we need to translate this understanding into practical skills. Unsurprisingly, the information security risk manager requires a broad range of skills that encompass both the general domain of information security and its specific application in the technical environment. In addition, the risk manager needs analytical skills to decide how to carry out risk assessment in his or her own organization. As we shall see in later chapters, as risk assessment matures in the information security environment, it is increasingly important that the risk assessment manager accepts that there is no one single off-the-shelf method that can be applied in all organizations and will achieve the same results for all instances of risk assessment. Frequently, methods need to be adapted to organizations and the specific requirements that the risk assessment manager has identified. Other skills include data analysis (both qualitative and quantitative), which is not only useful when it comes to drawing conclusions from the information gathered but also helps to inform the method used during the initial stages of the risk assessment. Skills in this area include designing the format for interviews, running successful workshops, and putting together questionnaires. This is particularly important because, in general, the success of the risk assessment depends on the information gathered during the early stages.

The information security risk manager also needs good negotiating skills to ensure that his or her risk mitigation strategies are implemented. A combination of communication and compromise is needed to ensure the technology supports the business in the best possible way. To this end, report writing skills are essential because a risk assessment is of little use if the results cannot be communicated successfully—both to a technical and nontechnical audience as appropriate and in an acceptable medium. The medium used could vary between formal report, presentation, or web page. The risk manager needs to decide which style of delivery best suits the risk assessment, and this depends on the requirements for carrying out the risk assessment and the roles and responsibilities of other stakeholders who have played a part in the exercise.

Verbal communication skills are also vital. These will come into play during interviews or when running workshops—two of the most common methods used for gathering initial risk data and understanding the risk appetite in a particular context. The risk manager needs to be able to hear and interpret the subtext of the different discourses that come to light on these occasions.

Finally, in the modern organization it would be surprising if the risk manager did not also have a supervisory role. This may encompass both a formal element, as the risk manager may have a small team to manage, and a less formal element, as a virtual team may exist where individuals are pulled in to assist the risk manager on an ad hoc basis as the requirement for their skills dictates. As the risk assessment process matures in an organization, the risk manager may also delegate aspects of the job to other parts of the organization (for example, into project teams). This often leads to the development of a baseline approach to risk where projects with relatively low level, or well understood, risks develop their own risk mitigation strategies, only reporting upward to the risk manager when they need assistance or the risk profile of a particular project is exceptional. In this way the risk manager should not be focusing on mundane risk assessments but should only be required to take a hands-on approach with more complex risk assessments.

The art behind a successful risk assessment process is the ability to set information security and the technology which it often underpins in the context of the business as a whole. This holistic approach is vital if all the elements in the organization are to be aligned in the manner recommended by Scott Morton. The risk manager needs to be able to understand the similarities and differences between the various levels of risk assessment. This understanding must span the technical risk assessment to the enterprise-wide approach to risk as well as the information security risks from specific projects through to ensuring compliance with regulatory and corporate governance requirements. Allied to this understanding must be an appreciation of the different purposes for which a risk assessment may be undertaken. This could be for routine audit purposes, to prove regulatory compliance, to communicate business risk internally, or to promote the business externally. Each purpose may require a different approach to the risk assessment process and needs to be handled appropriately. The method used for the risk assessment will often depend on how the output will be used.

The thinking behind a successful risk assessment needs to encompass the culture of the organization and the breadth of the business itself. It needs to be able to address both hard and soft issues and to keep a sense of proportion and balance in the development of risk mitigation strategies. Ultimately, the risk assessment manager needs to be able to recognize his or her own limitations and to bring a sense of creativity to the process. This thinking translates into skills that encompass technology, people, and processes. The skills needed include analytical capabilities, some technical capability, report writing and communication skills, quantitative and qualitative data gathering techniques, and supervisory and negotiating skills. It is unlikely that a risk manager will naturally possess all these attributes. Some successful risk managers have come from a technical background and built their business skills to enable them to fulfill the evolving role in which they have found themselves. Many still do not appreciate the need for communication and people skills in their role. It is likely that this will change over the next few years, just as it is probably that we will see more information security risk managers who have started out in a business role. In the main, however, information security risk managers will be successful if they do not neglect the intangible attributes that contribute to the delivery of the risk assessment process.

Section II
The Threat Assessment Process

4

Threat Assessment and Its Input to Risk Assessment

In this chapter we examine the role of threat assessment and its importance in the accurate and effective assessment of risk.

THREAT

It seems appropriate to start this chapter by explaining what is meant by a threat assessment. In information security, this is probably one of the most abused and misunderstood terms and is often used interchangeably with the term "vulnerability." In this book, the word "threat" is used to describe those "things" that may pose a danger to the information systems, and for clarity, the term "threat agents" is used. What we are actually referring to is those agents, either intentional or accidental, that have the opportunity and that may exploit a vulnerability in the security of information systems.

The Internet Request For Comments (RFC) Glossary of terms describes threat in the following ways to cover differing environments:

[Internet usage] A potential for violation of security, which exists when there is a circumstance, capability, action, or event that could breach security and cause harm. That is, a threat is a possible danger that might exploit a vulnerability. A threat can be either "intentional" (i.e., intelligent; e.g., an individual cracker or a criminal) or "accidental" (e.g., the possibility of a computer malfunctioning, or the possibility of an "act of God" such as an earthquake, a fire, or a tornado).

In some contexts, such as the following, the term is used narrowly to refer only to intelligent threats:

[U.S. Government usage] The technical and operational capability of a hostile entity to detect, exploit, or subvert friendly information systems and the demonstrated, presumed, or inferred intent of that entity to conduct such activity.

British Standard (BS) 7799, which has been developed into International Standard (ISO/IEC) 17799:2000–Code of Practice for Information Security Management, is one of the most relevant documents and standards in this area and defines threats, risks, vulnerabilities, and assets as follows:

Threats are anything that could cause harm to your assets, and vulnerabilities are weaknesses in your security arrangements that make it easy for these threats to occur. For example: if you have no backup of your data you are vulnerable and make the threat "loss of data" likely to occur.

Risks describe the probability that a damaging incident is happening (when a threat occurs because of a vulnerability), as well as the possible damage if this incident takes place.

Assets. Something that has value to your company and how it is carrying out its business operations.

The BS 7799 definition of information security also defines those aspects that it is safeguarding, as follows:

Confidentiality of information—ensuring that it is accessible only to those authorized to have access;

Integrity of information—safeguarding its accuracy and completeness;

Availability of information—ensuring that authorized users have access to it when required.

In developing a common vocabulary of terms, it is important that we recognize other standard definitions such as the ISO/IEC Guide 73 Vocabulary for Risk Management–Guidelines for Use in Standards. In this document, risk is defined as "the combination of the probability of an event and its consequence." Risk assessment is defined as "overall process of risk analysis and risk evaluation."

THREAT ASSESSMENT

A threat assessment is an integral and essential element of the risk assessment and risk management processes. If an organization wants to undertake an effective risk assessment for its information systems to enable rational and considered decisions to be taken, then it is essential that an accurate picture of the threats to the organization are understood. It must be clearly understood that risk assessment is a business process. The need to carry out these assessments of the risks to information assets or to other assets of an organization has been brought about as a result of the proliferation in the use of information and communications technologies and the convergence of these technologies over the last three decades. This massive increase in the use of these systems and the subsequent dependence on them has resulted in significant changes in the level and type of threat to the information environment that we have, whether knowingly or in ignorance, come to rely on.

The way in which we assess the threat that is posed to an information environment has not developed at a pace that has matched the rate of change and adoption of the technologies, with the result that we are still using tools and techniques from a previous environment. It is also a reality that the way in which we assess threat has not yet transitioned from art to science. As a result of using tools and techniques that were developed for nontechnology based systems, there is currently no way in which the threats, as opposed to the vulnerabilities, to information systems can be either modeled or quantified in any meaningful or repeatable manner that will allow the decision makers to take informed decisions.

In this heavily dependent and rapidly changing environment, where technology is offering new opportunities and the matching problems, all types of organizations, from governments to commerce to academia, are increasingly needing to produce meaningful risk assessments on which they can make decisions on the appropriate level of investment required to establish and ensure that they maintain the appropriate levels of confidentiality, integrity, and availability to their information. This is not possible without assessing threats as well as vulnerabilities.

Security standards such as BS 7799 and the related ISO 17799 start from the assumption that organizations and governments understand the threats they face to their information systems. For them to achieve a better quantification of the risk to an information environment, it is increasingly important that the information on which decisions are based is as up-to-date and accurate as possible and is expressed in terms that have a common meaning and basis. If a term is used in the assessment of threats to one information system, it should be understandable to those involved in the preparation of a threat assessment for another system, not least because interdependence between systems is a fact of life in the networked world. Unfortunately, in the high technology environment reality is far from this. Even common terms such as "threat" and "vulnerability" are used almost interchangeably. If the input on the level of threat that is used in the risk assessment process is to be improved, then an accurate representation of the threat to information systems must be achieved.

The threat agent is not the only factor that must be considered when determining the level of threat to an information system. Other issues that must be addressed include the probability of an attacker carrying out a successful attack and the impact that a successful attack would have on the business. After all, no matter how capable and motivated a potential threat agent might be, if the countermeasures in place at the target are already at a level higher than the attacker can overcome, then there is no prospect of a successful attack. Also, if the information asset that is being targeted is of little or no significance to the business, then the potential impact to the business is low or nonexistent. (It may be appropriate in the last case to question why the system is being used if it has no value or impact to the business; the very existence of a system is a cost to the organization in terms of hardware, software, management, and maintenance.)

For the owners, the custodians, or the insurers of information systems to understand the risks that come into effect as a result of using a particular high technology device in a particular set of circumstances, it is necessary to carry out a risk assessment of the relevant information environment. The assessment of the risk is essential in the modern environment because it will provide guidance on the system with regard to the likelihood of an event occurring after all the identified threats and vulnerabilities have been taken into account and the selected countermeasures have been implemented. From this, the relevant parties will have a better understanding of the residual risk they will be accepting if they choose to operate the system in the manner that has been defined. They can explore the relative benefits of options that are available to them as well as the relative costs and benefits of those options in order to reduce this residual risk even further. The following factors must be considered when conducting such a risk assessment:

- The Agent that is causing a Threat to the system;

- The exploitable Vulnerability within the system (Note: The significant word here is *exploitable;* if it cannot be exploited, then it does not require investment to protect it.);

- The Impact of a successful attack;

- Mitigating factors (countermeasures).

SOME HISTORY

The assessment of threats in the political and physical environments has been undertaken since time immemorial at the national and international governmental level. More recently, large organizations in the commercial sector have also started to undertake threat assessments to meet legal and regulatory requirements and to ensure that the protection they implement is cost effective. At the government level, assessments have been undertaken by experienced and skilled analysts who have carried them out over an extended period of time. The assessments produced by these analysts have then been applied to potential threats to the nation states' physical assets. The analysts who have, historically, carried out the analysis of the threat have worked in an environment where the time scales were relatively long and the assets they were analyzing had a physical basis.

Even in this environment, we have seen how difficult it is to produce an effective analysis of something like the threat from a nation state. A recent example is Iraq, where despite U.N. weapons inspection teams trying to detect weapons of mass destruction over a number of years, there was still considerable disagreement between a number of nation states on the capabilities of the country. With the benefit of good old 20/20 hindsight and a unique scrutiny from the United States, the United Kingdom, and other countries of the strength and accuracy of the intelligence that was used by the coalition governments to justify their actions, the picture became even more confused. Given that this is an assessment of the threat in which physical assets were being analyzed, you may begin to understand the problems that exist when we move into the new and more complex arena of information and information technologies.

Typically, threat analysts have looked at the threat that is posed by other nation states and terrorist groups. Every country will look at the threat that is posed to its interests, both at home and abroad, and will have skilled analysts who spend their careers specializing in, in all probability, a small section of the threat spectrum. They may concentrate on the threat from one geographical area or country and, over time, gain an in-depth knowledge of the threat capability of that entity. They will isolate key indicators of intent and capability, such as the movement of ships or aircraft, the movement of troops, or perhaps even the movement of key individuals. They will look for indicators of intent in the diplomatic arena (remember that countries normally use the military as a last resort). The point is that where physical action is contemplated, the time scales are normally protracted, with a period of diplomatic activity that is then followed by a period of preparation, where the logistics and armaments are moved to locations that will enable the country to undertake operations. In this period, there is time for the analysis of likely actions and outcomes. If the group of interest is a terrorist group, although there may be no diplomatic phase, the group will still need to acquire the knowledge and equipment necessary for them to carry out the attack and to deploy its resources to the location where they are going to carry out the attack. Although the same is fundamentally true of an attack on an information system, the level of resources required, the preparation time, and the number of observable indicators are all significantly different. In an attack on an information system, the attacker is likely to have available the resources to carry out the attack, and they are not detectable as other types of weapons would be. The preparation time is shortened because there is no requirement to move resources to a location from where they can reach the target, and the threshold for initiating the attack may be at a far lower level.

The threat posed to such an intangible and volatile environment as an information system has never, to date, been successfully assessed. That is, it has not been carried out in a provable and replicable manner. In the past, the threat agents considered have been, primarily, either other nation states or terrorist organizations. An example of how difficult the problem is was highlighted in February 1998, when the U.S. Department of Defense computer systems came under what was, at the time, described as a systematic attack. The attack pattern was highly indicative of preparations for a coordinated attack on U.S. Defense Information Infrastructure at a time when the U.S. Air Force was being readied for a deployment against the Iraqi Regime. The attacks all appeared to be targeted against Department of Defense network domain name servers and were exploiting a well-known vulnerability in the Solaris Operating System. (Incidentally, the patch for the vulnerability had been available for quite some time.) The attack profile consisted of a probe to determine whether the vulnerability existed in the server, which was then followed by the exploitation of the vulnerability to enter the computer. Once into the system, the attacker would insert a program that gathered data and, at a later date, return to retrieve the data collected.

The attacks were widespread and appeared to be well coordinated, and a large number of the attacks followed the same profile. The attacks seemed to target key elements of the defense networks, and over the period the attackers collected a large number of network passwords. The attacks could not be characterized or attributed to a specific source, but there was an obvious potential connection with the deployment for impending operations in the Persion Gulf.

After a considerable period of investigation (reported as up to 17 days), involving a wide range of the resources available to the U.S. Government, it was discovered that the attackers were what became known as the Cloverdale Kids, two youths aged 15 and 16 from Cloverdale, California, who operated under the nicknames of Too Short and Makaveli. They had also been given assistance and "mentoring" by a third person, identified as an 18-year-old Israeli youth, Ehud Tenenbaum, who used the nickname of Analyzer.

The reason for giving this example is that an attack, which was considered to have been initiated by a foreign nation and which involved a wide range of the resources available to the United States, was eventually attributed to three youths with the resources and equipment that can be found in the average home. This gives some insight into the level of difficulty we currently face. It is also worth pointing out that if this incident had occurred in almost any other country in the world, the time taken to isolate the perpetrator would probably have been considerably greater. If the attacker had indeed been a foreign power, how much damage could they have caused?

The threat posed both by, and to, commercial organizations or non-terrorist non-government organizations has not, in the past, been considered. In the current environment, however, it has been demonstrated that the potential impact from, and to, these other groups could be much more significant than was previously thought. The threats posed to non-government organizations and the elements of the Critical National Infrastructure have not been considered until recently, because in the past there was no single individual or group that was concerned with or had a sufficient understanding of the problem.

WHAT IS A THREAT AGENT?

To understand what a threat is, it is necessary to identify the separate elements that make up a threat. The elements identified below are not an exhaustive set but have been selected to demonstrate a good cross-section. The characteristics of these elements are as follows:

1. Natural threats and accidents: This group consists of non-intentional threat agents and includes those natural incidents such as earthquakes, typhoons, naturally occurring fires and floods, and the unintentional actions of humans. They are described separately as natural and accidental.

2. Malicious threats: This group consists of those threat agents that result from the intentional actions of individuals and groups and have the following characteristics that affect them:

   • Capability
   • Motivation

- Catalysts
- Access
- Inhibitors
- Amplifiers

Natural and Accidental Threats

These are two relatively well-known and understood groups of threats, and some knowledge of them can be gained from the insurance industry and the actuarial history they retain regarding the effects of earthquakes, fires, wind, water, and lightning. For the second group, accidental damage, there is, again, a wealth of information available within the insurance industry with regard to the likelihood of an accident occurring in the physical domain (i.e., someone dropping a piece of equipment). What cannot be avoided is our inability to accurately predict the incidence of such incidents. Unfortunately, in the electronic environment, with the exception of the cases recorded by Peter G. Neumann in his book, *Computer Related Risks*,[1] there is little or no documented information that is publicly available for incidents that have occurred in the electronic environment; as a result, there is little that can be gained from any past experiences in this domain.

For this group of natural and accidental threat agents, each type is reviewed in isolation because they have only tenuous links to each other, and the main area of commonality is that they are not planned or directed.

- Earthquake: The possibility of damage as a result of an earthquake is largely geographically dependent, but again there is considerable experience and documented case histories in the insurance industry of underwriting this type of event.

- Fire: The likelihood of a direct effect on an information system from fire can easily be calculated, and there is considerable experience and a large number of documented case histories in the insurance industry of underwriting this type of event.

- Wind: The possibility of damage from wind, normally most often thought of as a result of tornados or hurricanes (typhoons), is largely geographically dependent, because some locations are far more prone to wind damage than others. Again, there is considerable experience and

---

1. Neumann, P. G. 1995. *Computer Related Risks*. Addison Wesley, ISBN 0-201-55805-X

documented case histories in the insurance industry of underwriting this type of event.

- Water: The likelihood of a direct effect on a system from water, either from tidal wave, flood, rain, or damaged pipes, is again easily calculable, and there is considerable experience and documented case histories in the insurance industry of underwriting this type of event.

- Lightning: Again, the likelihood of a direct effect on a system from the effects of lightning is easily calculable, and there is considerable experience and documented case histories in the insurance industry of underwriting this type of event.

- Accidents: The threat to an information system from accidental misuse or damage is very different from the categories in the other groups above, because it can and will be affected over time by the attitude, disposition, and training of the staff, in addition to the environment. What separates this group from the malicious threats discussed later is the absence of malice or motivation. Again, this type of threat is generically well understood, and the probability of an event occurring as the result of an accident can be reasonably predicted from the actuarial data held by the insurance industry.

It is possible that more than one of these natural threats will affect an information system at the same time or shortly after each other. An example of this might be an earthquake that is followed by a fire as a result of the disruption to the gas or electrical services that the initial event caused. It may then, in turn, be affected by water used by the emergency services to douse the fire.

Malicious Threat Agents

For a malicious threat to exist, there must be an "agent" (an individual or a group of individuals) that will implement the threat. That agent must have sufficient motivation to carry it out, the capability and the opportunity to do so, and something to cause them to carry it out at that specific time (a catalyst). The threat agent will also be affected by other factors that will either enhance or reduce the likelihood of it being initiated by an attacker or an attack being successful (amplifiers and inhibitors).

- Motivation: The motivation of an attacker to carry out a malicious attack on a system could arise from any number of drivers, which may affect the attacker either individually or in combination. There are a number of commonly accepted motivational drivers:

Political
Terrorism
Secular
Personal gain (including recognition)
Religious
Revenge
Power
Curiosity

- Capability: The capability of an individual or a group formed into some type of organization to mount an attack and to sustain it at an effective level will vary with the complexity, resources, and sophistication of both the attacking force and the target. It may be sufficient for an attacker (threat agent) to mount an attack at any level to achieve their objective, but it may also require a high level of resources over a long period to have the desired effect on the target.

- Opportunity: For an attacker to initiate an attack on a system, the attacker must have the opportunity to carry out the attack. This may be the result of a number of circumstances coming together, but for the purposes of this book, we constrain opportunity to mean either physical access or direct or indirect electronic access to the target. For a threat agent to carry out an attack on an information system, it must gain either physical access to the system (the threat agent gaining direct access to the place where elements of the system are located) or through either direct electronic access (through a connection from other networks) or indirect electronic access (eavesdropping). Without this, there is no opportunity for an attack to be initiated.

- Catalyst: A catalyst is required to cause a threat agent to select the target and the time at which the attack will be initiated. The catalyst may be something that has an effect on either the target or the threat agent. An example of a catalyst might be the one that was considered earlier, when the U.S. Air Force was deploying to the Persion Gulf. This could have been the catalyst for Iraq or its sympathizers to carry out an attack on the U.S. military in an attempt to prevent or delay the deployment.

- Inhibitors: A number of factors (affectors) inhibit a threat agent from mounting an attack either on a specific target or at a specific time. As mentioned before, these may affect either the target or the threat agent. An example of this may be the perception by the attacker that the target system is well protected and that any attempt to attack it will be quickly detected. Another inhibitor might be the fear by the attacker of being caught as a result of publicity of successes by relevant law enforcement agencies.

- Amplifiers: A number of factors (affectors) may encourage a threat agent to carry out an attack at a particular time against a particular target or group of targets. Again, these may affect either the target or the threat agent. Examples of this may be the perception that the target system is not well protected during a certain time period and that an attempt to attack it will not be detected or, even if detected, that no follow-up action will be taken.

- System: For a threat agent to carry out a successful attack on a system, there are at least two system related factors that must be present. The first is that there must be an exploitable vulnerability in the system the threat agent can use. For a vulnerability to be exploitable, it must be known, or there must be an expectation that it will be known, to the attacker and they must have sufficient access to the system to carry out the attack. The vulnerability may exist in the hardware, the operating system software, the applications software, or the physical environment in which the system is contained. The second factor is that the target system must be important enough to the organization that the loss of it or a degradation in its confidentiality, integrity, or availability would have a large enough impact on the business process of the organization to be considered a success by the attacker and/or the organization. Alternatively, it may be the only target available to the threat agent that will satisfy their requirements.

SEQUENCE OF FACTORS INVOLVED IN A THREAT

As described above, for a threat agent to pose an actual threat to an information system, a number of factors have an influence. In reality, for it to pose a real threat to an information system, the threat agent must possess a capability and be able to gain either physical or electronic access. The level of access and its capability will influence the potential impact that such a threat agent will have. The likelihood of the threat agent being able to mount a successful attack will be reduced by factors that inhibit its ability but will be enhanced by other factors. In addition, some type of catalyst will cause the threat agent to act when it does, depending on the motivation of the threat agent. The components of a malicious threat and their interrelationships are detailed in Figure 4.1.

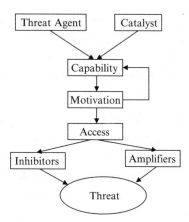

Figure 4.1. *Sequence of threat agent relationships.*

Malicious Threat Agent

Malicious threat agents can be categorized into one of a number of groups. The groups detailed below are neither exclusive (the threat agent may belong to one or more of them) nor exhaustive. The main groups are shown in Figure 4.2. A malicious threat agent can be generated from any one of the groups or group combinations identified in Figure 4.2. This is not an exhaustive list of potential sources or groupings of malicious threat agents, because these change over time as high technology, education, national and international politics, culture, and a host of other factors have an effect.

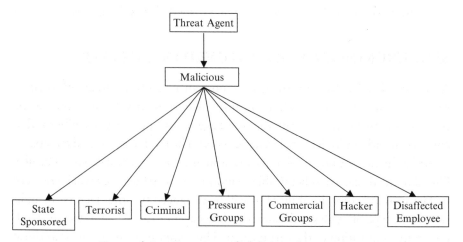

Figure 4.2. *Groupings of malicious threat agents.*

Capability

For a malicious threat agent to be effective, it must have the perceived or actual capability to carry out and, if necessary, to sustain an attack and perhaps totally destroy the target and any subsequent replacement. The main constituent elements of the capability of a threat are detailed in Figure 4.3. For malicious threat agents to be able to carry out an attack, they must have the means in terms of personnel and equipment and the necessary skills and methods to be successful. They must also, in some cases, have a sustainable depth of capability to achieve their aims.

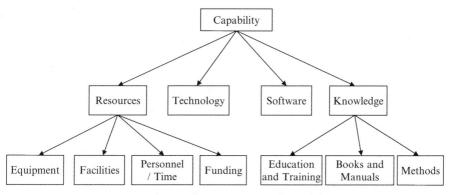

Figure 4.3. *The components of capability.*

Inhibitors

A range of influences and factors may either inhibit or assist a malicious threat agent in carrying out a successful attack. These have been labeled as inhibitors and amplifiers. It is possible that the same influence, with a different value or in different circumstances, may act to inhibit or amplify either the likelihood of an attack or the potential for success of an attack. An example of this might be the security measures in place to defend a system. If they are weak, this will encourage an attacker to mount the attack; if they are strong, it may deter an attacker or prevent them from succeeding.

The influences that might act as inhibitors are detailed in Figure 4.4. An inhibitor may work in a number of ways. First, it may reduce the inclination of a threat agent to initiate an attack. Second, it may prevent a threat agent from initiating or carrying out a successful attack. Third, it may minimize the impact a successful attack will have. The fear of being captured as a result of conducting an attack may well act as a sufficient deterrent to the threat agent and cause it to decide not to carry out the attack. If the threat agent perceives their peers or indeed the public will hold him or her in contempt for attempting the attack (for example, if the target was a hospital or a charity), this may be sufficient to inhibit the attack. Also, if the level of technical difficulty that the threat agent encounters is sufficiently high, the threat agent may decide it is not worth the investment of effort required to attempt or continue the attack either on the initial target or at the current time. The factors that come together to inhibit an attack are, or may be, used as part of the protection and defense of the system and may assist in the reduction of the risk to the system.

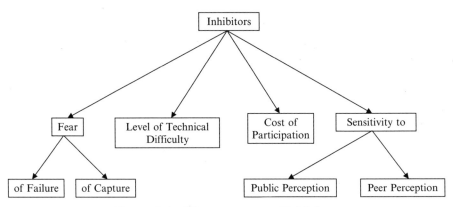

Figure 4.4. *The components of inhibitors.*

Amplifiers

As mentioned above, the influences that may be an inhibitor in one environment may be an amplifier in another. The influences that might act as amplifiers to an attack taking place or being successful are detailed in Figure 4.5. The types of influences that amplify or increase the possibility of an attack occurring or being successful are varied and are dependent on the type of threat agent but include factors such as peer pressure or the level of skill or education. In the first of these amplifiers, there is the desire of the threat agent to be well regarded by his or her peers. His or her desire is to gain the recognition and respect of peers through the

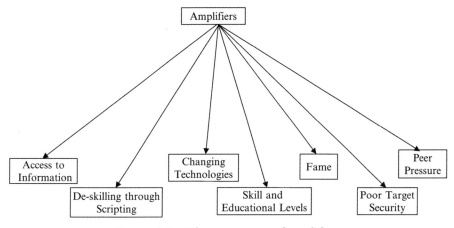

Figure 4.5. *The components of amplifiers.*

demonstration of skills, and this will strengthen his or her resolve to carry out the attack. The level of education and skill an agent possesses, or can gain access to, improves the confidence of the threat agent and also increases the likelihood of a successful attack. Another factor may be the ability to gain access to the information the agent needs to mount an attack, in terms of information on the target, other relevant information systems, organizations, or in terms of programing scripts and tools that can be run to conduct an attack; these may also increase the possibility of a successful attack.

Catalysts

The causal factor in a threat agent deciding whether to and when to carry out an attack on an information system may be the result of an event, such as a publicity event for an organization with which the threat agent has a dispute or a dislike, or perhaps the start of an armed conflict between the threat agent's country, or one for which they have sympathy, and an opponent. Another factor may be the circumstances of the threat agent, and any change (perhaps in location, social grouping, or employment status) may affect their ability or desire to carry out an attack or to be successful.

An attack may also be triggered by the advent of a new technology that makes what was previously not achievable a possibility. Finally, the commercial imperative to gain advantage against a competitor may cause a threat agent to conduct an attack. Figure 4.6 details some of the main groups of factors that may act as catalysts for an attack being initiated.

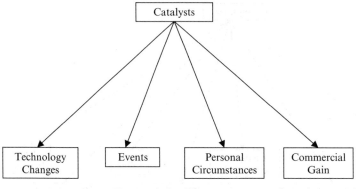

Figure 4.6. *The components of catalysts.*

Motivation

The motivation of the threat agent is, by definition, a subjective area, and the threat agent may be influenced by a wide range of factors. Influential factors depend on the grouping or combination of groupings from which the threat agent originates. In some cases a number of these will act together to influence the threat agent. Figure 4.7 lists some components of motivation; this is not

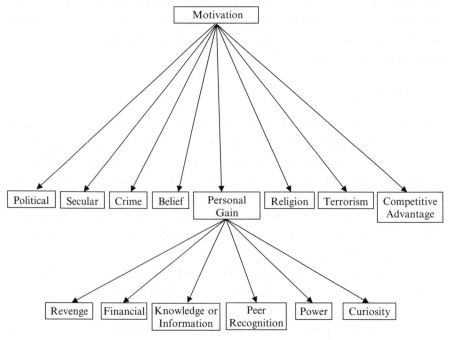

Figure 4.7. *The components of motivation.*

intended to be a comprehensive list but rather gives an indication of the range and diversity that may have an influence.

In this chapter the term "threat", as it is used in this book, has been defined and explained, and the elements that need to be present for a threat agent to cause a problem have been examined. In summary, for a malicious threat agent to be effective, it must have the capability to carry out its attack and also the motivation and the opportunity.

5

Threat Assessment Method

In this chapter we show a method to assess threats to information systems. We look at the different types of threat agent and outline a method for determining the level of threat that is posed by a specific threat agent to the organization.

In 2002, the authors developed a method that could be used to place common and understandable value on the potency of a threat that was posed by a threat agent to a system or an organization. It must be made clear from the outset that this method is not, and never was intended, to be used in isolation. The measurement of the threat only has any meaning when used as an input to a risk assessment. An understanding of the threat informs the risk assessment process and allows for the modeling of actions that can be taken to mitigate the threat to the system or the organization. This method was exposed to considerable testing across a wide range of scenarios, during the course of which it was refined to the state that is shown in this chapter. It is almost certain that as the model is used on a wider range of scenarios, further development will take place.

As discussed in Chapter 4, threat agents can be split into a number of groups. These groups are not exclusive, and a threat agent may belong to a number of the groups at the same time. An example of this may be a person who is a hacker but who also has strong beliefs in a subject and would be classified as part of a pressure group. In developing the method, each of the identified threat groupings was looked at in isolation and evaluated separately, due to the huge range of capabilities that exist in the different groups and the range of factors that influence them.

It was also believed that better results could be obtained if the effects of each of the other elements—the amplifiers, the inhibitors, the catalysts, and the motivation—were evaluated separately to understand the relationships between them. Subsequent testing of the method produced consistent results that were within the bounds of expected outcomes. It is always worth remembering that if the inputs to a method are subjective, the outcome can only be subjective.

Given the lack of "facts" available in the areas we are discussing, one should be clear that the outcome of the method is subjective but that it provides one with at least two different benefits. First, it provides a framework of areas to consider when conducting the threat assessment. It was not designed to be a box ticking method, but if it helps the person to carry out a consistent and repeatable threat assessment, then why not. Second, having followed the logic of the processes, you will have been forced to identify the inputs that provided the values that you ascribed; therefore this method provides you with an evidence trail to allow you to justify your decisions at a later date. (Don't the U.S. and British Governments wish they had been able to do that with regard to the intelligence on weapons of mass destruction in Iraq—or perhaps not.) In the commercial world where the return on investment has to be demonstrated, this is a potentially very powerful tool for a security/risk manager who is trying to convince the Board to spend money on improving the countermeasures. It will also provide some level of confidence the organization can demonstrate that it has taken account of the threat and that good corporate governance is in place.

THREAT AGENTS

When the individual groups were examined, it became apparent that a common set of metrics could be developed for each of the groups but that the values derived were not comparable between the different groups. For example, it would not be rational to expect that the values derived from a hacker group or a disaffected employee would have the same meaning as those that might be derived for a nation state. What must be understood from the method is that it gives an indication of the potential severity of the threat from a number of sources, but some consideration should be given to how these individual threat agents compared with each other.

There is also a potential relationship between the types of threat agent and the potential targets. For example, if the threat agent is a nation state, then it is probable that the target will be another nation state or, within another nation state, a significant industry or institution (perhaps elements of the critical national infrastructure?). On the other hand, the target of a commercially sponsored threat agent is likely to be another commercial company. The level of resources that are available to a commercial threat agent is not likely to be proportionally less than that which is available to one sponsored by a nation state; the target is likely to have a similar scaling in its resources. As a result of this, although the metrics for each of the groups have been based on a potential out 100% for a total threat agent capability, they should not be compared with each other. Each of the values is relative.

NATION STATE SPONSORED THREAT AGENTS

To calculate and express the potential threat from a threat agent that is sponsored by a nation state, it is necessary to draw on a wide range of indicators. The sources of information that are available will depend on the level and type of organization for which the threat assessment is being carried. If the threat assessment is being carried out on behalf of a government, then the normal sources of openly available information may be used, but it is far more likely the traditional sources of "secret intelligence" will be used. To use anything other than the best sources available would be negligent. However, it is worth remembering that in the environment of information security, the expertise and knowledge from traditional sources may not be available. If the organization conducting the threat assessment is a commercial or non-government organization, then it has to rely on intelligence collected by its own sources (or perhaps shared resources; there is no reason why a group of organizations from a geographical area or industry sector cannot cooperate) or is available from "open sources."

Table 5.1 shows a set of open source factors that can be used to provide an indication of the potential threat from a nation state sponsored threat agent. These factors could be modified or added to, depending on the sources available. The selected indicators take into account those factors that affect the capability of a nation state to sponsor a threat agent. There is no attempt here to give the impression of a precise prediction—there is neither the information available nor any great history of attacks to learn from. What this does provide is an indicator with regard to the potential threat, while at the same time acting as an aide memoir to the user to consider a range of indicators. The factors included were selected because of their relevance to potential threat capability generation. The level of adult population is the raw resource pool from which a capability might be generated. The level of literacy will modify the level of potential threat—if the literacy level is low, then a lower proportion of the population will be able to contribute to the capability pool. The gross domestic product (per capita) provides a crude indicator of the relative prosperity of the country and the likelihood of high technical equipment being available to the population. The inputs for power consumption, level of access to the telecommunications infrastructure, and the availability of Internet access all give an indication of the access that a potential threat agent living in the country would have. They also act as indicators of the level of knowledge and experience that is likely to be available on Internet and telecommunications technologies. The known or inferred levels of technological development and technical expertise, together with the indigenous information warfare capability, give another indication of the capability that may be available within the country. The known or inferred capability of other countries with which the threat state has alliances or agreements cannot be ignored, because there may be a transfer of technology or knowledge or a "loan" of capability.

Table 5.1   Nation State Sponsored Threat Agents

Factors	Country
Adult population (in millions) (P)	
Level of literacy (L)	
Gross domestic product per capita (G)	
Power consumption per capita (PC)	
Level of telecommunications infrastructure (TI)	
Internet access (IA)	
Technological development level (TL)	
Technical expertise (T)	
Known indigenous information warfare capability (I)	
Allied nations capability (N)	
Cultural factors (CF)	
History of relevant activity (H)	
Other factors (AB)	
Government (Go)	

The cultural influences and the type of government both have an effect on the capability. For example, a country that has a tight control over the population and does not have to rely on popularity to remain in power is far less affected by the influences of the opinions of the population than a liberal democracy. Cultural factors within a country may also have an influence on the capability of the threat agent. These may be religious or secular but cannot be ignored because they may affect capability. If the population is averse to technology, it will reduce the capability; on the other hand, a strong influence to preserve religion, local culture, or any number of other factors may cause the threat agent to have a higher motivation. Finally, other influencing factors such as a conflict or hostility with another nation state may again influence the motivation of the threat agent.

To convert these individual and varied factors into a form that is of use and in which the different elements provide a suitably weighted input and to enable it to be replicated for all countries, it is necessary to add a weighting that can adjust the importance of the values that are applied to each part. Table 5.1 lists the inputs to the model that can be extracted. For this information to be used as metrics for this type of threat agent, it is necessary to assign values to each of these elements, as shown in Table 5.2. As a result, it is now possible to derive a metric value for the nation state threat agent that can be modeled with different values for each of the attributes.

To provide an appropriate and effective value to these diverse inputs, it is necessary to apply a range of weightings to them. The potential threat capability can be derived by applying the weightings, as follows. The threat capability can be broken down into three groups of influences. The first group relates to the population and provides an input to the overall assessment of approximately one-third:

[Adult Population (P) × Literacy (L)] + Power Consumption per capita (PC) will give a maximum possible value of 42.

The next group is made up from indicators of the underlying environment within the country: technical development level, expertise, access, and other national influences:

[(Technical Expertise (T) + Technological Development Level (TL) + Level of Telecomms Infrastructure (TI) + (Internet access (IA) × 2) + (GDP per Capita (G) to express the pervasive economic climate in the country)] + (Other Factors (Including Cultural Factors)) + (Government (Go)) which gives a range of indicators of the underlying environment. This gives a maximum possible value of 48.

The final group of influences are the indicators of active capability. These are made up of the history of relevant capability, with a significant weighting, known capability, with a moderate weighting, and other capability that could be inferred:

Table 5.2 Value Weightings of Nation State Threat Agents

Factor	Weighting Value					
	1	2	3	4	5	6
Adult population (P)	<1,000,000	1,000,001–5,000,000	5,000,001–10,000,000	10,000,001–50,000,000	50,000,001–100,000,000	>100,000,000
Literacy level (L)	<35%	35–50%	51–65%	66–80%	80–90%	>90%
Gross domestic product per capita (G)	<$1000	$1001–$2500	$2501–$5000	$5001–$10,000	$10,001–$20,000	>$20,000
Power consumption per capita (PC)	<500 kWh	501–1000 kWh	1001–2500 kWh	2501–5000 kWh	5001–10,000 kWh	>10,000 kWh
Telecommunications infrastructure: Number of phones per 1000 people (TI)	<50	51–100	101–250	251–500	501–750	751–1000
Internet access (IA)	Very low	Low	Low to medium	High to medium	High	Very high
Technological development level (TL)	Very low	Low	Limited	Medium	High	Very high

Table 5.2 Value Weightings of Nation State Threat Agents (continued)

Factor				Weighting Value		
	1	2	3	4	5	6
Technical expertise (T)	None	Minimal	Very limited	Limited	Adequate	High level
Indigenous information warfare capability (I)	None	Limited	Low	Medium	High	Very high
Allied nations capability (N)	None	Limited	Low	Medium	High	Very high
History of relevant activity (H)	None		Intermittent	Occasional	Regular	Regular and widespread
Other factors (AB)						Religious fundamentalism, support of international terrorism*
Government (Go)	Liberal democracy, monarchy			Junta, benign dictatorship	Dictatorship	

*This value is assessed to be of high weighting. This is not considered to be a value that would have a lesser importance expression.

61

((History of relevant activity (H)) × 4 gives equal weighting in importance to past activity + (Indigenous Information Warfare Capability (I) × 2) + (Allied Nation Capability (N)) to allow for potential support from allied nations gives a range of indicators of potential technical capability. This will give a maximum possible value of 42.

This allows a calculation to be constructed as follows:

$$\text{Threat capability} = \{[(P \times L) + PC] + [T + TL + TI + (IA \times 2)] \\ +G + AB + Go\} + (H \times 4) + (I \times 2) + N$$

This gives a total maximum value of 132, which can then be reduced to a percentage for ease of comparison.

TERRORISM

For terrorist organizations the metrics will comprise significantly different inputs, although there may be factors relating to nation states that will have an effect on the terrorist threat agent. Table 5.3 shows a set of open source factors that can be used to provide an indication of the potential threat from a terrorist threat agent. These factors could be modified or added to depending on the sources available. From the factors in Table 5.3 it can be determined that for any terrorist group, there should be indications in open source material of any history

Table 5.3   Terrorist Threat Agents

Factors	Terrorist Group
Group size (A)	
Level of education (E)	
Cultural factors (CF)	
Access to communications and Internet (CI)	
Technical expertise (T)	
History of activity (H)	
Sponsoring countries (SC)	
Funding (F)	

of the use of information technology to support the dissemination of the group aims and for communications or any history of the use of information systems as a vehicle for an attack. The level of access within the primary base country (or countries) and the likely education level and influencing cultural factors can also be derived.

To convert these values into a method that is of use and in which the different elements provide a suitable input into the metric and that can be replicated for all terrorist groups, it is necessary to allocate weightings that are applied to each part. This can be expressed as a metric as follows:

Number of supporters (activists)   (A)

Education level   (E)

For this information to be used as metrics for the terrorist threat agent, it is necessary to assign values to each of these elements, as shown in Table 5.4. As a result, it is now possible to derive a value for the terrorist threat agent that can be modeled with different values for each of the attributes.

To provide an appropriate and effective value to these diverse inputs, it is necessary to apply a range of weightings to them. The potential threat capability can be derived by applying the weightings, as follows. The threat capability can be broken down into three groups of influences. The first group relates to the personnel—their estimated numbers and their level of education—and provides an input to the overall assessment of approximately one-third:

$$(\text{Number of Activists (A)} \times 5) + (\text{Level of Education (E)}).$$
This gives a maximum possible value of 36.

The next group is made up from indicators of the underlying environment: the level of technical expertise, access, and funding:

$$[(\text{Technical Expertise (T)} \times 2) + (\text{Communications and Internet access}$$
$$(\text{CI}) \times 2) + (\text{Funding} \times 2) \text{ to express the resource availability}].$$
This gives a maximum possible value of 36.

The final group of influences are the indicators of active capability. These are made up of the history of relevant capability, with a significant weighting.

Table 5.4 Value Weightings of Terrorist Threat Agents

Factor	Weighting Value					
	1	2	3	4	5	6
Number of activists (A)	1–250	251–500	501–1,000	1,001–5,000	5,001–10,000	>10,000
Education level (E)	Extremely low	Very low	Low	Medium	High	Very high
Communications and Internet access (CI)	Extremely low	Very low	Low	Medium	High	Very high
History of relevant activity (H)	None	Limited	Intermittent	Occasional	Regular	Regular and widespread
Technical expertise (T)	None	Very limited	Limited	Adequate	Good	High level
Funding (F)	None	Very limited	Limited	Adequate	More than required	Unlimited

(History of relevant activity (H) × 6) gives equal weighting in importance to past activity. This will give a maximum possible value of 36.

This allows a calculation to be constructed as follows:

Threat capability = [(A × 5) + (E) + (T × 2) + (CI × 2) + (F × 2) + (H × 6)]. This gives a total maximum value of 108. This can then be reduced to a percentage for ease of comparison.

PRESSURE GROUP THREAT AGENTS

For pressure groups the metrics will, once again, comprise a significantly different set of inputs, although factors relating to nation states may have an effect on the pressure group threat agent. Table 5.5 shows a set of open source factors that can be used to provide an indication of the potential threat from a pressure group threat agent. Once again, these factors could be modified or added to, depending on the sources of information available. In themselves, pressure groups will vary in their purpose, size, popular support, cultural or religious influences, and financial backing. From those factors in Table 5.5 it can be determined that for any pressure group, there should be indications in open source material of any history of the use of information technology to support the dissemination of the group aims and for communications or any history of the use of information systems as a vehicle for an attack. The level of membership and the spread of support, together with indications of likely nation state or organizational sponsorship, can also be derived.

Table 5.5   Pressure Group Threat Agents

Factors	Pressure Group
Spread of membership (M)	
Number of activists (A)	
Funding (F)	
Types of target (D)	
Known attack characteristics (C)	
History of activity (H)	
Sponsor nations or organizations (S)	

To convert these values into a method that is of use and in which the different elements provide a suitable input into the metric and that can be replicated for all terrorist groups, it is necessary to allocate weightings that are applied to each part.

Spread of membership   (M)

Number of supporters (activists)   (A)

Funding   (F)

Types of target   (D)

Known attack characteristics   (C)

History of relevant activity   (H)

Sponsor nations or organizations   (S)

For this information to be used as metrics for this type of threat agent, it is necessary to assign values to each of these elements, as provided in Table 5.6. As a result, it is now possible to derive a metric value for the pressure group threat agent that can be modeled with different values for each of the attributes. It should be borne in mind that by the very nature of a pressure group, it will only become a threat when the target is in its sphere of interest, either directly or indirectly.

To provide an appropriate and effective value to these diverse inputs, it is necessary to apply a range of weightings to them. The potential threat capability can be derived by applying the weightings, as follows. The threat capability can be broken down into three groups of influences. The first group relates to the supporters—their estimated numbers and their spread of influence around the world—and provides an input to the overall assessment of approximately one third:

[(Number of Supporters (Activists) (A) $\times$ 5 + (Spread of Membership (M) $\times$ 2].
This gives a maximum possible value of 42.

The next group is made up from a range of indicators of the underlying environment: target types of the group, the typical attack characteristics, and the range of sponsorship and funding available:

Table 5.6 Value Weightings of Pressure Group Threat Agents

Factor		Weighting Value				
	1	2	3	4	5	6
Spread of membership (number of countries) (M)	1–5	6–10	11–15	16–20	21–30	>30
Number of members (activists) (A)	1–500	501–1000	1001–2,500	2,501–5,000	5,001–10,000	>10,000
Funding (F)	None	Very limited	Limited	Adequate	More than adequate	Unlimited
Target type (D)	Local interest	National, low profile	National	National, high profile	International	International, high profile
Attack characteristics (C)	None	Passive	Nondirect action	Limited direct action	Direct action	Violent direct action
History of relevant activity (H)	None	Limited	Occasional	Occasional	Regular	Regular and widespread
Sponsoring countries or organizations (S)	1–5	6–10	11–15	15–20	21–30	>30

(Target Type (D) × 2) + (Attack Characteristics (C)) + (Sponsorship (S)) +
(Funding (F)) × 2 to express the resource availability. This will give a
maximum possible value of 42.

The final group of influences are the indicators of active capability. These are
made up of the history of relevant capability, with a significant weighting.

(History of relevant activity (H) × 7) gives equal weighting in importance to
past activity. This will give a maximum possible value of 36.

This allows a calculation to be constructed as follows:

Target capability = [(A × 5) + (M × 2) + (H × 7) + (D × 2) + (C) + (S) + (F × 2)]
This gives a total maximum value of 120. This can then be reduced to a
percentage for ease of comparison.

COMMERCIAL THREAT AGENTS

For commercial groups the metrics will, once again, be significantly different,
and the factors that influence the potential of a commercial organization to initiate and sustain an attack will be different from those considered for a nation
state. Table 5.7 shows a set of open source factors that can be used to provide an
indication of the potential threat from a commercial threat agent. Once again,

Table 5.7   Commercial Organization Threat Agents

Factors	Organization
Market sector (V)	
Size (multinational/national/local) (Q)	
Target type (D)	
History of activity (H)	
Technical expertise (T)	
State of market sector (SM)	
Is target organization part of the Critical National Infrastructure (CN)	

these factors could be modified or added to, depending on the sources of information available. In themselves, the interests of commercial threat agents will tend to be highly focused against a specific organization or sector but most usually against another organization in its own sector. From those factors in Table 5.7 it can be determined that for any commercial threat agent, there may be indications in open source material of any history of the use of information technology. The size of the organization and the sector in which it operates will also be available.

To convert these values into a metric that is of use and in which the different elements provide a suitable input into the metric and that can be replicated for all commercial threat agent groups, it is necessary to adjust the weightings that are applied to each part.

For this information to be used as metrics for this type of threat agent, it is necessary to assign values to each of these elements, as shown in Table 5.8. As a result, it is now possible to derive a metric value for the commercial threat agent that can be modeled with different values for each of the attributes. It should be borne in mind that by the very nature of a commercial threat agent, it will only become a threat when the target is in its sphere of interest, either directly or indirectly. This will normally mean in the same commercial sector

To provide an appropriate and effective value to these diverse inputs, it is necessary to apply a range of weightings to them. The potential threat capability can be derived by applying the weightings, as follows. The threat capability can be broken down into a number of different groups of influences. The first group relates to the state of the market sector in which the organization operates and the size of the organization:

$$(\text{Market State (V)}) \times 4 \text{ (to give a weighting of up to a maximum of 24 to}$$
$$\text{market state)} + (\text{Organization Size (Q)}) \times 4 \text{ (to give equal weighting to}$$
$$\text{the size of the attacking enterprise)} + (\text{Target organization as part of}$$
$$\text{CNI (CN)}) \times 3.$$

The next group of influencing factors relate to any history that the commercial organization has of this type of activity and any indications of the likely technical capability of the organization. For instance, is the organization involved in a high technology industry?

$$(\text{History of Relevant Activity (H)}) \times 7 +$$
$$(\text{Technical expertise (T)})$$

Table 5.8 Value Weightings of Commercial Organization Threat Agents

Factor	Weighting Value					
	1	2	3	4	5	6
Market state (V)	Decline	Static	Volatile	Rising	Buoyant	Turmoil
Organization size (Q)	1–500	501–1000	1001–5000	1001–5000	5001–10,000	>10,000
Target type (D)	Local interest	National, low interest	National	National, high interest	International	International, high interest
History of relevant activity (H)	None	Rare	Intermittent	Occasional	Regular	Regular and widespread
Technical expertise (T)	None	Extremely limited	Very limited	Limited	Adequate	High level
Target organization part of the CNI (CN)	Not part of CNI	Marginally involved in CNI	Part of CNI	Important element of CNI	Significant part of CNI	Crucial part of CNI

The final grouping relates to the types of target that the commercial threat agent would find attractive:

$$(\text{Type of Target (D))} \times 2 \text{ (type of target of lesser importance than capability of attacker)}$$

This allows a calculation to be constructed as follows:

$$\text{Target capability} = (V \times 4) + (Q \times 4) + (CN \times 3) (H \times 7) + (T \times 3) + (D \times 2)$$
This gives a total maximum value of 138. This can then be reduced to a percentage for ease of comparison.

CRIMINAL GROUP THREAT AGENTS

For criminal groups the metrics will, again, be significantly different, although there may be factors relating to any of the other groups that will have an effect on the threat agent. Table 5.9 shows a set of open source factors that can be used to provide an indication of the potential threat from a criminal threat agent. Once again, these factors could be modified or added to depending on the sources of information available. In themselves, the interests of criminal threat agents will tend to be targeted against a specific organization or sector at any one time, although this will change as the opportunities become apparent. It is worth remembering that crime will follow the money, and this has been amply demonstrated by the arrest of three Russian nationals, who had been blackmailing the on-line gaming sites.[1] From the factors in Table 5.9 it can be determined that for any criminal threat agent, there may be indications in open source material of any history of the use of information technology for a group and the areas in which they have previously operated or are likely to operate in. The size of the organization and the sector in which it operates will also be available. The capability of a criminal threat agent to initiate an attack can be assumed as there is a history of them hiring or coercing people with the relevant skill sets as necessary.

   The values selected as indicative measures of the capability of the criminal threat agent represent the diversity and complexity of the criminal groups. The representation of the types of crime that they are involved in is intended to reflect the threat agents understanding and use of technology. To convert these values into a metric that is of use and in which the different elements provide a suitable input into to the metric and that can be replicated for all criminal threat agent groups, it is necessary to adjust the weightings that are applied to each part. This can be expressed as a metric as follows:

Table 5.9   Criminal Threat Agents

Factors	Criminal Group
Group range (international/ national/ local) (R)	
Size of group (Q)	
Type of crime (B)	
History of activity (H)	
Technical expertise (T)	

1. "Cyber blackmailers are nabbed in Russia." Article by Dmitri Kramarenko, 23 July 2004 in Computer Crime Research Center website *http://www.crime-research.org/news/23.07.2004/512/*

Group range (geographic)	(R)
Group size	(Q)
Type of crime	(B)
History of relevant activity	(H)
Technical expertise	(T)

For this information to be used as metrics for this type of threat agent, it is necessary to assign values to each of these elements, as shown in Table 5.10. As a result, it is now possible to derive a metric value for the criminal threat agent that can be modeled with different values for each of the attributes.

To provide an appropriate and effective value to these diverse inputs, it is necessary to apply a range of weightings to them. The potential threat capability can be derived by applying the weightings, as follows. The threat capability can be broken down into a number of different groups of influences. The first group relates to the size of the organization and its geographical spread:

(Group geographical range (R)) × 3 (to give 15 % weighting to internationalization) + (Group Size (Q)) × 3 (to give total value for organization of 36).

Table 5.10 Value Weightings of Criminal Threat Agents

Factor	1	2	3	4	5	6
				Weighting Value		
Group range (geographic) (R)	Local	Regional	National	More than one country	International	Global
Group size (Q)	1–500	501–1000	1001–5,000	5,001–10,000	10,001–20,000	>20,000
Type of crime (B)	Prostitution, usery, protection	Construction, debt collection	Fraud	Fraud	Money laundering, gambling, pedophilia	Industrial espionage, smuggling, extortion
History of relevant activity (H)	None	Rare	Intermittent	Occasional	Regular	Regular and widespread
Technical expertise (T)	None	Extremely limited	Very limited	Limited	Adequate	High level

The second group of influencing factors relate to the types of crime in which the group is involved that may be relevant, any known technical expertise, and any history of activity:

(Type of crime (B)) × 4 (type of crime relevant to capability) + (History of Relevant Activity (H)) × 7 + (Technical expertise (T)) × 3 (to give total value for capability of 84).

This allows a calculation to be constructed as follows:

Total capability = (R × 3) + (Q × 3) + (B × 4) + (H × 7) + (T × 3). This gives a total maximum value of 120. This can then be reduced to a percentage for ease of comparison.

HACKER GROUP THREAT AGENTS

For hacker groups the metrics that have been selected are again different, although there may be factors relating to a number of other groups that will have an effect on the threat agent. Table 5.11 shows a set of open source factors that can be used to provide an indication of the potential threat from a hacker threat agent. Once again, these factors could be modified or added to depending on the sources of information available. From the factors in Table 5.11 it can be determined that for any hacker threat agent, there are likely to be indications in open source material of any history of the use of information technology for a group and the areas in which they have previously operated or are likely to operate in. The sort of information available will be the news reports of detected hacking, websites that support hacking or hacker groups, and sites that report the exploits and successes of hackers.

Table 5.11   Hacker Threat Agents

Factors	Hacker Group
Size of group (Q)	
History of activity (H)	
Technical expertise of group (T)	
Prowess within community (Pr)	
Reason for target selection (U)	

The values of indicative measures of the capability of the hacker threat agent have been selected to represent the range and diversity of hackers' motives and affiliations. To convert these values into a metric that is of use and in which the different elements provide a suitable input into to the metric and that can be replicated for all hacker threat agent groups, it is necessary to adjust the weightings that are applied to each part.

For this information to be used as metrics for this type of threat agent, it is necessary to assign values to each of these elements, as provided in Table 5.12. As a result, it is now possible to derive a metric value for the hacker threat agent that can be modeled with different values for each of the attributes. To provide an appropriate and effective value to these diverse inputs, it is necessary to apply a range of weightings to them. The potential threat capability can be derived by applying the weightings, as follows. The threat capability can be broken down into a number of different groups of influences. The first group relates to the size of the group and its technical ability:

$$\text{(Group Size (Q)} \times 4) \text{ (the size of the group gives some measure of its ability to sustain an attack)} + \text{(Technical expertise (T)} \times 3) \text{ (to give total value for organization of 42).}$$

The second group of influencing factors relate to any history of activity by the hacker group and the known technical ability of the group:

$$\text{(History of Relevant Activity (H))} \times 7 + \text{(Target Selection (U))} \times 6 + \text{Prowess within community (Pr) (to give total value for capability of 84).}$$

This allows a calculation to be constructed as follows:

$$\text{Total capability} = (Q \times 4) + (T \times 3) + (H \times 7) + (U \times 6) + (Pr).$$ This gives a total maximum value of 126. This can then be reduced to a percentage for ease of comparison.

DISAFFECTED STAFF THREAT AGENT

For disaffected staff the metrics will be significantly different, but there is a potential for relationship to any or all of the other groups to have an effect on the threat agent. From Table 5.13 it can be determined that for a disaffected staff

Table 5.12 Value Weightings of Hacker Threat Agents

Factor			Weighting Value			
	1	2	3	4	5	6
Group size (Q)	1–25	26–50	51–100	101–200	201–300	>300
History of relevant activity (H)	None	Intermittent	Occasional	Occasional	Regular	Regular and widespread
Technical expertise (T)	None	Very limited	Limited	Limited	Adequate	High level
Prowess within community (P)	Not part of a group	Peripheral interest	Interest within group	Significant within group	Important within group	Very important within group
Reason for target selection (U)	Curiosity	Rebellion	Criminal gain	Criminal gain	Belief	Revenge, religion, racism, nationalism

Table 5.13 Disaffected Staff Threat Agents

Factors	Disaffected Staff
State of market sector (V)	
Changes taking place within organization (K)	
General morale (J)	
Technical expertise (T)	

member threat agent, there are likely to be indications, if any exist, in open source material of any previous attacks by disaffected members of staff. These will only be generic, because you are unlikely to find information relating to your own staff there. (If you did, it would indicate that you have significant problem with your security and staff selection!)

The values of indicative measures of the capability of the disaffected staff threat agent have been selected to represent the range and diversity of possible motives and affiliations and environmental issues that may have an impact. To convert these values into a metric that is of use and in which the different elements provide a suitable input into the method and that can be replicated for all disaffected members of staff threat agents, it is necessary to adjust the weightings that are applied to each part.

For this information to be used as metrics for this type of threat agent, it is necessary to assign values to each of these elements, as in Table 5.14. As a result, it is now possible to derive a metric value for the disaffected member of staff threat agent that can be modeled with different values for each of the attributes. The potential threat capability can be derived by applying the weightings, as follows. The threat capability can be broken down into two areas of influence. The first group relates to the market sector and the employing organization and the stability of the environment:

$$((\text{Market State } (V)) \times 5 \text{ (volatility of market gives indication of state)} +$$
$$(\text{Level of Organization Change } (K)) \times 5 \text{ (to give total value for}$$
$$\text{organization of } 60).$$

Table 5.14 Value Weightings of Disaffected Staff Threat Agents

Factor	Weighting Value					
	1	2	3	4	5	6
State of market sector (V)	Decline	Static	Volatile	Rising	Buoyant	Turmoil
Organizational change (K)	None	Rare	Intermittent	Occasional	Frequent	Widespread and erratic
Morale (general) (J)	Very high	High	Fairly high	Average	Low	Very low
Technical expertise (T)	None	Extremely limited	Very limited	Limited	Adequate	High level

The second group relates to the morale within the organization and the technical capability of the disaffected member of staff:

$$(\text{Morale (J)}) \times 5 + (\text{Technical expertise (T)}) \times 5 \text{ (to give}$$
$$\text{total value for capability of 60).}$$

Note: All influencing factors for the disaffected staff threat agent have been allocated equal weighting, because they were all considered of equal significance. This allows a calculation to be constructed as follows:

$$\text{Total capability} = (V \times 5) + (K \times 5) + (J \times 5) + (T \times 5). \text{ This gives}$$
$$\text{a total maximum value of 120. This can then be reduced to a percentage}$$
$$\text{for ease of comparison.}$$

OTHER INFLUENCES ON THREAT AGENTS

The groups of threat agents identified above are all affected by a range of influences that will have the effect of making an attack either more or less likely to occur or to be successful. The influencing factors given below cover a number of areas and have been referred to as threat amplifiers, inhibitors, catalysts, and motivators.

Threat Amplifiers

Threat amplifiers may have a direct or indirect relationship to a threat agent. They may have an effect on the general environment, the target, or the threat agent itself. As a result, some of the threat amplifiers apply to all threat agents, some apply to a number of threat agents, and some are specific to one threat agent. Others affect the general environment and some affect the target. Of the factors that amplify the likelihood of a threat agent conducting an attack or being successful in an attack, the factors in Table 5.15 have been selected as indicative. For this information to be used as metrics for threat amplifiers, it is necessary to assign values to each of these elements, as shown in Table 5.16.

Table 5.15 Threat Amplifiers

Factors	Environment	Target	Threat Agent
Peer pressure (PeP)		X	X
Peer perception (PP)			X
Public perception (PuP)	X	X	X
Search for recognition (fame) (Fa)		X	X
Access to information (AI)		X	X
Changing technologies (CT)	X	X	
Skills and education levels (SL)			X
De-skilling through scripting (DS)			X
Law enforcement activity (LE)	X		X
Target vulnerability (TV)		X	
Target profile (TP)		X	X

Table 5.16 Value Weightings for Threat Amplifiers

Factors	Environment	Target	Threat Agent
Peer pressure (PeP)			?
Peer perception (PP)			?
Public perception (PuP)	?	?	?
Search for recognition (fame) (Fa)		?	?
Access to information (AI)		?	?
Changing technologies (CT)	?	?	
Skills and education levels (SL)			?
De-skilling through scripting (DS)			?
Law enforcement activity (LE)	?		?
Target vulnerability (TV)		?	
Target profile (TP)		?	?

0, none; 1, weak; 2, strong, ?, Where ? is a value from 0 to 2

From this, it is now possible to derive a value for the threat amplifiers that can be modeled with different values for each of the attributes.

The potential threat amplification can be derived by applying the weightings, as follows. The threat amplification may be the result of one or more influences that fall into one or more areas. Threat amplification (TA) derives from the following:

- Total Value of Influences that affect the Environment (PuP + CT + LE/3)

- Total Value of Influences that affect the Target (PuP + Fa + AI + CT + TV + TP/6)

- Total Value of Influences that affect the threat agent (PeP + PP + PuP + Fa + AI + SL + DS + LE + TP/9)

Note: All influencing factors for threat agent amplification have been allocated equal weighting, because they are all considered of equal significance. This allows a calculation to be constructed as follows:

$$TA - (Environmental) (PuP + CT + LE/3)$$

$$TA - (Target) (PuP + Fa + AI + CT + TV + LE/6)$$

$$TA - (Threat Agent) (PeP + PP + PuP + Fa + AI + SL + DS + LE + TP/9)$$

This gives a total maximum value of 2 for each group. Note: Each of the areas should be considered separately, because the values may give an indication of which group would be most susceptible to countermeasures. These values can then be combined to give a single value for the threat amplifier. The threat amplifier combined score is (TA (Environmental) + TA (Target) + TA (Threat Agent))/3.

Threat Inhibitors

Influences that act to reduce the likelihood of an attack occurring or being successful are known as threat inhibitors and they may have a direct or indirect relationship to a threat agent. They may affect the general environment or the target or the threat agent. As a result, some of them will apply to all threat agents, whereas some are specific to a number of threat agents or an individual threat agent, and some will affect the environment or the target.

The range of inhibitors to the likelihood of an attack occurring or being successful will come from a number of sources. If the location from which the threat agent is intending to launch an attack or in which the target resides has strong, relevant, and enforced laws that are perceived to be effective, this will act as a deterrent. An environmental inhibitor might also be gained from the deterrence that is generated if the computer security organizations such as the Computer Emergency Response Teams and infrastructure are seen to be responsive and are known to take rapid and positive action. An inhibitor that affects the target organization could be what has a reputation for strongly enforced computer security and for taking action against attackers.

Of the factors that inhibit the likelihood of a threat agent conducting an attack or being successful in an attack, the factors listed in Table 5.17 have been selected as indicative.

Table 5.17   Threat Inhibitors

Factors	Environment	Target	Threat Agent
Fear of capture (FC)			X
Fear of failure (FF)			X
Level of technical difficulty (TD)	X	X	
Cost of participating (CP)			X
Public perception (PuP)		X	X
Law enforcement activity (LE)	X		X
Security of target (ST)		X	
Security of system (SS)		X	X

For this information to be used as metrics for a threat inhibitor, it is necessary to assign values to each of these elements, as provided in Table 5.18. From this, it is now possible to derive a value for the threat inhibitors that can be modeled with different values for each of the attributes.

Table 5.18   Value Weighting for Threat Inhibitors

Factors	Environment	Target	Threat Agent
Fear of capture (FC)			?
Fear of failure (FF)			?
Level of technical difficulty (TD)	?	?	
Cost of participating (CP)			?
Public perception (PuP)			?
Law enforcement activity (LE)	?		?
Security of target (ST)		?	
Security of system (SS)		?	?

0, none; 1, weak; 2, strong; ?, Where ? is a value from 0 to 2.

The potential level of threat inhibition can be derived by applying the weightings, as follows. The threat inhibition may be the result of one or more influences and they will fall into one or more of the areas. The threat inhibition (TIn) derives from the following:

- Total Value of Influences that affect the Environment (TD + LE/2)

- Total Value of Influences that affect the Target (TD + ST + SS/3)

- Total Value of Influences that affect the Threat Agent (FC + FF + CP + PuP + LE + SS/6)

Note: All influencing factors for threat agent inhibitors have been allocated equal weighting, because they are all considered of equal significance. This allows a calculation to be constructed as follows:

$$TIn - (Environmental)\ (TD + LE/2)$$

$$TIn - (Target)\ (TD + ST + SS/3)$$

$$TIn - (Threat\ Agent)\ (FC + FF + CP + PuP + LE + SS/6)$$

This gives a total maximum value of 2 for each group. Note: Each of the areas should be considered separately, because the values may give an indication of which group would be most susceptible to countermeasures. These values can then be combined to give a single value for the threat inhibitor. The threat inhibitor combined score is (TIn (Environmental) + TIn (Target) + TIn (Threat Agent)/3).

Catalysts

A catalyst may have a direct or indirect relationship with a threat agent or a target. The catalyst may have a direct effect on the threat agent (for example, a change in employment status or a direct instruction to take action) or may be an environmental effector (for example, the development of a new software tool that allows an attack not previously possible to be carried out). A catalyst that is related to the target may be a result of an action taken by the target organization, such as the release of information relating to activity being undertaken (such as a move into a new area of operations or the laying off of staff) by the organization or a change in status of the organization (Table 5.19).

Table 5.19   Threat Agent Catalysts

Factors	Environment	Target	Threat Agent
Change of personal circumstances (CC)			X
War or political conflict (WF)	X		
Significant events (SE)	X	X	X
Significant anniversaries (SA)	X	X	X
Commercial gain (Cg)		X	X

Table 5.20   Value Weighting for Threat Agent Catalysts

Factors	Environment	Target	Threat Agent
Change of personal circumstances (CC)			?
War or political conflict (WF)	?		
Significant events (SE)	?	?	?
Significant anniversaries (SA)	?	?	?
Commercial gain (Cg)		?	?

0, none; 1, weak; 2, strong; ?, . Where ? is a value from 0 to 2

For this information to be used as metrics for the catalysts, it is necessary to assign values to each of these elements, as in Table 5.20. From this, it is now possible to derive a value for catalysts that can be modeled with different values for each of the attributes.

The potential for a catalyst can be derived by applying the weightings, as follows. The catalyst may be the result of one or more influences that fall into one or more areas. The Catalyst (CA) will be derived from the following:

- Total Value of Influences that affect the Environment (WF + SE + SA/3)
- Total Value of Influences that affect the Target (SE +SA + Cg/3)
- Total Value of Influences that affect the Threat Agent (CC + SE + SA + Cg/4)

Note: All influencing factors for threat agent catalysts have been allocated equal weighting, because they are all considered of equal significance. This allows a calculation to be constructed as follows.

$$CA - (Environmental) (WF + SE + SA/3)$$

$$CA - (Target) (SE +SA + Cg/3)$$

$$CA - (Threat Agent) (CC + SE + SA + Cg/4)$$

This gives a total maximum value of 2 for each group. Note: Each of the areas should be considered separately, because the values may give an indication of which group would be most susceptible to countermeasures. These values can then be combined to give a single value for the catalyst. The catalyst combined score is (CA (Environmental) + CA (Target) + CA (Threat Agent)/3).

Motivation

The influencing factors that affect the motivation for an individual or a group to carry out an attack will vary considerably from group to group and are highly subjective. Something that would provide motivation to one individual or group may not affect another similar group in the same way. The elements identified in Table 5.21 are general indicators only. Although the motivational influences in some cases relate to only one or two groups, others may affect more than one group. It would not be realistic to try to derive a value for motivation through calculation, and the most effective way to gain a value for the strength of motivation would be through assessment, by the analyst, of the level of motivation at the present time. As a result, the value for motivation will be a percentage value estimated at the time of the analysis.

Table 5.21   Motivational Factors

Personal gain
Revenge
Financial gain
Knowledge or information
Peer recognition
Power
Curiosity
Influence
Political
Secular influence
Crime
Religious influence
Belief
Terrorism
National political/military objectives
Competitive advantage
Pressure group action

6

Example Threat Assessment

In this chapter we show a worked example of the threat assessment method for a fictitious organization. We look at the threat posed by a number of threat agents and show the areas where countermeasures can be implemented. We also show the potential for modeling different scenarios to allow for effective decision making.

For the purposes of this chapter, the Widget Aerospace Company is the organization on which we carry out the threat assessment; this organization develops and manufactures a range of light aircraft and unmanned autonomous vehicles (UAVs). The company is based in the United States with a number of facilities, mostly in the Midwest, and has a subsidiary in the United Kingdom. The company has a workforce of approximately 5000 staff and carries out both commercial and defense work. The company has spent the last 5 years developing a new ultralight UAV with a range that is expected to significantly outperform the currently available technologies. The new technologies underpinning the new UAV are also expected to be usable in commercial light aircraft that will be produced over the next few years.

What threat agents should be considered when creating the threat assessment for this company? Are there any from the list of potential threat agent sources that can be discounted? If we look at each in turn, it is possible to fairly quickly determine whether they should be included:

Nation state sponsored threat agent: Because the company is in the aerospace and defense sector, this type of threat agent cannot be discounted.

Terrorist threat agent: Again, because of the sector the company is operating in, this group cannot be discounted.

Criminal threat agent: Because of the nature of the business, there is currently no specific threat from the criminal threat agent.

Commercial threat agent: Because of the technology development and the defense contracts, there is likely to be a significant threat from competitors.

Hacker threat agent: Because of the nature of the business, there is a small potential threat from the hacker threat group.

Pressure groups threat agent: Because of the nature of the business and the recent national support for military "peace-keeping" actions, there is currently no specific threat from this group.

Disaffected employee: Because the company is known as a good caring employer and the business is expanding rapidly, a disaffected employee is not considered likely to pose a threat at the present time.

Having used our knowledge of the organization to discount threats we consider to be most unlikely, it is now possible to look at those threat agents we consider to be more likely to pose a threat. Why is it sensible to carry out this initial sift and exclude some of the potential threats? It makes sense to use the knowledge/intelligence you already have and then focus your resources on those areas that require it. Always remember that any form of assessment is expensive in terms of resources to carry out the investigation and assessment.

Now that we have a reduced list of threat agents to investigate, we can begin to gather the available information on them. The reduced set of threat agents now consists of nation state sponsored threat agent, terrorist threat agent, commercial threat agent, and hacker threat agent. Looking at each of these in turn, we deal with the nation state sponsored threat agent first.

Because the company is U.S. and U.K. based, the threat from this group is likely to come from either those countries that have companies competing with Widget Aerospace or from those countries known to collect information on these types of developments to advance their own national efforts. This list may be quite extensive and would be constructed from current intelligence, possibly supported by information from the respective governments. To test the model, we look at two countries: France, which has a significant aerospace industry and has stated it considers economic espionage to be a reasonable form of business, and China, where there is a history of gathering Western technologies to fuel its own defense industry.

The following values for France were taken, in the main, from the CIA World Factbook.[1] In the development stages of the method, a number of sources of information were explored. However, during research all the sources tested returned values within 1% or 2% of those given in the CIA World Factbook. As a result, after a period of testing a single source was used. Values inserted as the

---

1. CIA World Factbook. http://www.odci.gov/cia/publications/factbook/print/fr.html

result of research and that are subjective are the values for "history of relevant activity" and "other factors." There is no validated set of facts for these fields, but these types of influences are significant in determining a nation's capabilities.

FRANCE

This country is a European State that is a part of the European Union and a member of NATO. France is one of the few countries with a stated policy on the use of nation state intelligence capability for the benefit of its indigenous industries. The French attitude and doctrine to industrial espionage was reported as early as 1996.[2] France also has an active aerospace and defense manufacturing industry. There are reports that France has been active in the use of national assets to support its own defense and aerospace industries. The U.S. National Counterintelligence Centre[3] reported the following:

The September 1998 issue of the CIND (Counterintelligence, News and Developments publication) reported that France systematically listens in on the telephone conversations and cable traffic of many businesses based in the United States and other nations. Recent information from the Sunday Times reveals new insights into that activity, namely that French intelligence is intercepting British businessmen's calls from eight centers scattered across France.

Given this information, it is realistic to assume that France poses an active threat to the company for the theft of intellectual property (Tables 6.1 and 6.2).

As described in Chapter 5, these values can now be converted into a score as shown below:

((Adult Population (P) × (Literacy (L)) + (Power Consumption per capita (PC)) gives a maximum possible value of 42.
((Technical Expertise (T) + Technological Development Level (TL) + Level of Telecommunications Infrastructure (TI) + (Internet access (IA) × 2) + (GDP per Capita (G) to express the pervasive economic climate in the country) + (Other Factors (Including Cultural Factors)) + (Government (Go)) gives a range of indicators of the underlying environment.
This gives a maximum possible value of 48.

---

2. Conference paper for the 19th National Information Systems Security Conference, Baltimore, by Paul M. Joyal, the President of INTEGER Security Inc. http:// csrc.nist.gov/nissc/1996/papers/NISSC96/joyal/industry.pdf
3. The U.S. National Counterintelligence Centre, http://www.nacic.gov/nacic/news/2000/jun00.html#rtoc2

Table 6.1 French Nation State Sponsored Threat Agents

Factors	Country
Adult population (in millions) (P)	60,180,529
Level of literacy (L)	99%
Gross domestic product per capita (G)	$26,000
Power consumption per capita (PC)	6900 Kwh
Level of telecommunications infrastructure (TI)	34.86 million land lines and 11.078 million mobiles
Availability of Internet access (IA)	62 ISPs and 16.97 million users
Technological development level (TL)	Diverse industrial base, aerospace industry, and nuclear power generation
Technical expertise (T)	A diversity of technologies and high technical industries provide basis for technical expertise
Known indigenous information warfare capability (I)	Existence known but no evidence of its use
Allied nations capability (N)	United States, United Kingdom, and Germany all have developed capability
History of relevant activity (H)	Stated policy to use national assets to support the industrial base; several instances recorded
Other factors (AB)	
Government (Go)	Socialist Republic

Table 6.2 Value Weightings of French National Capability Threat Agent

Factor	Weighting Value					
	1	2	3	4	5	6
Adult population (P)	<1,000,000	1,000,001–5,000,000	5,000,001–10,000,000	10,000,001–50,000,000	50,000,001–100,000,000	>100,000,000
Literacy level (L)	<35%	35–50%	51–65%	66–80%	81–90%	>90%
Gross domestic product per capita (G)	<$1000	$1001–$2500	$2501–$5000	$5001–$10,000	$10,001–$20000	>$20,000
Power consumption per capita (PC)	<500 kWh	501–1000 kWh	1001–2500 kWh	2501–5000 kWh	5001–10,000 kWh	>10,000 kWh
Telecommunications infrastructure (number of phones per 1000 people) (TI)	<50	51–100	101–250	251–500	501–750	751–1000
Internet access (IA)	Very low	Low	Low medium	High medium	High	Very high
Technological development (TL)	Very low	Low	Limited	Medium	High	Very high
Technical expertise (T)	None	Minimal	Very limited	Limited	Adequate	High level
Indigenous information warfare capability (I)	None	Very low	Limited	Medium	High	Very high

Table 6.2 Value Weightings of French National Capability Threat Agent (continued)

Factor			Weighting Value			
	1	2	3	4	5	6
Allied nations capability (N)	None	Very low	Limited	Medium	High	Very high
History of relevant activity (H)	None	Intermittent	Occasional	Semiregular	Regular	Regular and widespread
Other factors (AB)						Active aerospace industry, stated government policy
Government (Go)	liberal democracy, monarchy, republic				Benign dictatorship	Dictatorship, communist state

((History of relevant activity (H)) × 4 gives equal weighting in importance to past activity + (Indigenous Information Warfare Capability (I) × 2) + (Allied Nation Capability (N)) to allow for potential support from allied nations gives a range of indicators of potential technical capability. This will give a maximum possible value of 42.

This allows a calculation to be constructed as follows:

$$\text{Threat capability} = (((5 \times 6) + 5) + (6 + 6 + 6 + (5 \times 2)) + 6 + 6 + 1) + (5 \times 4) + (5 \times 2) + 6$$

This gives score of 112 from a total maximum value of 132, which can then be reduced to a percentage for ease of comparison and gives us a figure of 85% for capability.

Having worked out the capability, we now need to look at each of the other factors to determine the level of threat.

Threat Amplifiers

Tables 6.3 and 6.4 show French nation state sponsored threat amplifiers and the value weighting for French nation state sponsored threat amplifiers, respectively. As shown Chapter 5, this can be converted into a score as shown below. Threat amplification (TA) is derived from

Total Value of Influences that affect the Environment (PuP + CT + LE)

Total Value of Influences that affect the Target (PuP + Fa + AI + CT + TV + + TP + LE)

Total Value of Influences that affect the Threat Agent (PeP + PP + PuP + Fa + AI + SL + DS + LE + TP)

This allows a calculation to be constructed as follows:

$$\text{TA} - \text{(Environmental)} \ (1 + 0 + 0)/3 = 0.333 \text{ of a potential}$$
$$\text{maximum of } 2 = 16.5\%$$
$$\text{TA} - \text{(Target)} \ (1 + 0 + 2 + 0 + 2 + 2)/6 = 1.165 \text{ of a potential}$$
$$\text{maximum of } 2 = 58\%$$
$$\text{TA} - \text{(Threat Agent)} \ (0 + 0 + 2 + 0 + 2 + 2 + 0 + 0 + 2)/9 = 0.889 = 44\%$$

Table 6.3   French Nation State Sponsored Threat Amplifiers

Factors	Environment	Target	Threat Agent
Peer pressure (PeP)			X
Peer perception (PP)			X
Public perception (PuP)	X	X	X
Search for recognition (fame) (Fa)		X	X
Access to information (AI)		X	X
Changing technologies (CT)	X	X	
Skills and education levels (SL)			X
De-skilling through scripting (DS)			X
Law enforcement activity (LE)	X		X
Target vulnerability (TV)		X	
Target profile (TP)		X	X

Table 6.4   Value Weighting for French Nation State Sponsored Threat
Amplifiers

Factors	Environment	Target	Threat Agent
Peer pressure (PeP)			0
Peer perception (PP)			0
Public perception (PuP)	1	1	2
Search for recognition (fame) (Fa)		0	0
Access to information (AI)		2	2
Changing technologies (CT)	0	0	
Skills and education levels (SL)			2
De-skilling through scripting (DS)			0
Law enforcement activity (LE)	0		0
Target vulnerability (TV)		2	
Target profile (TP)		2	2

0, none; 1, weak; 2, strong.

The threat amplifier combined score is (16.5 + 58 + 44)/3 = 39.5%.

Threat Inhibitors

Table 6.5 lists French nation state sponsored threat inhibitors. For this information to be used as metrics for a threat inhibitor, it is necessary to assign values to each of these elements (Table 6.6).

Table 6.5   French Nation State Sponsored Threat Inhibitors

Factors	Environment	Target	Threat Agent
Fear of capture (FC)			X
Fear of failure (FF)			X
Level of technical difficulty (TD)	X	X	
Cost of participating (CP)			X
Public perception (PuP)		X	X
Law enforcement activity (LE)	X		X
Security of target (ST)		X	
Security of system (SS)		X	X

Table 6.6   Value Weighting for French Nation State Sponsored Threat Inhibitors

Factors	Environment	Target	Threat Agent
Fear of capture (FC)			1
Fear of failure (FF)			2
Level of technical difficulty (TD)	0	2	
Cost of participating (CP)			0
Public perception (PuP)			2
Law enforcement activity (LE)	1		1
Security of target (ST)		2	
Security of system (SS)		2	2

0, none; 1, weak; 2, strong.

The Threat Inhibition (TIn) is derived from the following:

Total Value of Influences that affect the Environment (TD + LE)

Total Value of Influences that affect the Target (TD + LE + ST + SS)

Total Value of Influences that affect the Threat Agent (FC + FF + CP + PuP + LE + SS)

This allows a calculation to be constructed as follows:

TIn – (Environmental) $(0 + 1)/2 = 0.5$ of a potential maximum of 2 = 25%
TIn – (Target) $(2 + 2 + 2)/3 = 2$ of a potential maximum of 2 = 100%
TIn – (Threat Agent) $(1 + 2 + 0 + 2 + 1 + 2)/6 = 1.333$ of a potential maximum of 2 = 67%

The threat inhibitor combined score is $(25 + 100 + 67)/3 = 64\%$.

Catalysts

Table 6.7 lists the French nation state sponsored threat agent catalysts. For this information to be used as metrics for the catalysts, it is necessary to assign values to each of these elements (Table 6.8). It is now possible to create a numeric value for the catalyst. The Catalyst (CA) is derived as follows:

Total Value of Influences that affect the Environment ((WF + SE + SA)/3)

Total Value of Influences that affect the Target ((SE + SA + Cg)/3)

Total Value of Influences that affect the Threat Agent (CC + SE + SA + Cg/4)

Table 6.7   French Nation State Sponsored Threat Agent Catalysts

Factors	Environment	Target	Threat Agent
Change of personal circumstances (CC)			X
War or political conflict (WF)	X		
Significant events (SE)	X	X	X
Significant anniversaries (SA)	X	X	X
Commercial gain (Cg)		X	X

Table 6.8   Value Weighting for French Nation State Sponsored Threat Agent Catalysts

Factors	Environment	Target	Threat Agent
Change of personal circumstances (CC)			0
War or political conflict (WF)	2		
Significant events (SE)	0	2	2
Significant anniversaries (SA)	0	2	0
Commercial gain (Cg)		0	0

0, none; 1, weak; 2, strong.

This allows a calculation to be constructed as follows:

$$CA - (\text{Environmental}) \ (2 + 0 + 0)/3 = 0.667 \text{ of a potential maximum}$$
$$\text{of } 2 = 33\%$$
$$CA - (\text{Target}) \ (2 + 2 + 0)/3 = 1.333 \text{ of a potential maximum of } 2 = 66\%$$
$$CA - (\text{Threat Agent}) \ (0 + 2 + 0 + 0)/4 = 0.5 \text{ of a potential maximum}$$
$$\text{of } 2 = 25\%$$

The catalyst combined score is $(33 + 66 + 25)/3 = 41.33\%$.

Motivation

Table 6.9 lists the French nation state sponsored motivational factors. As a result, motivation is a percentage figure provided and inserted by the analyst. In this case the motivation could be either political or competitive advantage, an estimated value of 65%.

CHINA

China is communist state with an advance information warfare capability and a strong technical base. There have been reports over a long period of the Chinese collecting overseas research from developed countries to enhance their own military and industrial development. The United States has been the main target of Chinese Intelligence collection attacks.

Table 6.9   French Nation State Sponsored Motivational Factors

Personal gain
Revenge
Financial gain
Knowledge or information
Peer recognition
Power
Curiosity
Influence
Political
Secular influence
Crime
Religious influence
Belief
Terrorism
National political/military objectives
Competitive advantage
Pressure group action

Table 6.10 lists the Chinese nation state sponsored threat agents, and Table 6.11 shows the value weightings of those threat agents.

$$\text{Threat capability} = (((6 \times 5) + 3) + (6 + 6 + 3 + (1 \times 2)) + 3 + 0 + 6)$$
$$+ (6 \times 4) + (6 \times 2) + 4$$

This gives a total of 95 from a maximum value of 132, which can then be reduced to a percentage for ease of comparison to give us a figure of 72% for capability.

Table 6.10   Chinese Nation State Sponsored Threat Agents

Factors	Country
Adult population (in millions) (P)	1287
Level of literacy (L)	86%
Gross domestic product per capita (G)	$4700
Power consumption per capita (PC)	1019 kWh
Level of telecommunications infrastructure (TI)	135 million land line and 65 million mobiles
Availability of Internet Access (IA)	3 ISPs and 45.8 million users
Technological development level (TL)	Major producer of microchip technologies, active space and missile research, nuclear power
Technical expertise (T)	A wide range of technologies from microchip fabrication to ballistic missiles provides the basis for technical expertise
Known indigenous information warfare capability (I)	Research and development of the concepts; army has three information warfare battalions that have been exercised
Allied nations capability (N)	Not as well developed as the indigenous capability
History of relevant activity (H)	Extensive history of industrial and defense espionage, particularly against the United States
Other factors (AB)	Major trans-shipment point for heroin produced in the Golden Triangle; growing domestic drug abuse problem; source country for chemical precursors and methamphetamine
Government (Go)	Peoples Liberation Army (communist)

Table 6.11   Value Weightings of Chinese National Capability Threat Agent

Factor	Weighting Value					
	1	2	3	4	5	6
Adult population (P)	<1,000,000	1,000,001–5,000,000	5,000,001–10,000,000	10,000,001–50,000,000	50,000,001–100,000,000	>100,000,000
Literacy level (L)	<35%	35–50%	51–65%	66–80%	81–90%	>90%
Gross domestic product per capita (G)	<$1000	$1,001–$2,500	$2,501–$5,000	$5,001–$10,000	$10,001–$20,000	>$20,000
Power consumption per capita (PC)	<500 kWh	501–1,000 kWh	1,001–2,500 kWh	2,501–5,000 kWh	5001–10,000 kWh	>10,000 kWh
Telecommunications infrastructure (number of telephones per 1000 people) (TI)	<50	51–100	101–250	251–500	501–750	751–1,000
Internet access (IA)	Very low	Low	Low medium	High medium	High	Very high
Technological development (TL)	Very low	Low	Limited	Medium	High	Very high

Table 6.11 Value Weightings of Chinese National Capability Threat Agent (continued)

Factor	Weighting Value					
	1	2	3	4	5	6
Technical expertise (T)	None	Minimal	Very limited	Limited	Adequate	High level
Indigenous information warfare capability (I)	None	Limited	Low	Medium	High	Very high
Allied nations capability (N)	None	Limited	Low	Medium	High	Very high
History of relevant activity (H)	None	Intermittent	Occasional	Semiregular	Regular	Regular and widespread
Other factors (AB)						
Government (Go)	Liberal democracy, monarchy				Benign dictatorship	Dictatorship communist

Threat Amplifiers

Table 6.12 gives the value weighting for Chinese nation state sponsored threat amplifiers.

Table 6.12 Value Weighting for Chinese Nation State Sponsored Threat Amplifiers

Factors	Environment	Target	Threat Agent
Peer pressure (PeP)			0
Peer perception (PP)			0
Public perception (PuP)	1	1	1
Search for recognition (fame) (Fa)		0	0
Access to information (AI)		2	2
Changing technologies (CT)	0	2	
Skills and education levels (SL)			2
De-skilling through scripting (DS)			0
Law enforcement activity (LE)	0		0
Target vulnerability (TV)		2	
Target profile (TP)		2	1

0, none; 1, weak; 2, strong.

This allows a calculation to be constructed as follows:

$$TA - (Environmental)\ (1 + 0 + 0)/3 = 0.333 \text{ of a potential}$$
$$\text{maximum of } 2 - 16.6\%$$
$$TA - (Target)\ (1 + 0 + 2 + 2 + 2 + 2)/6 = 1.5 \text{ of a potential}$$
$$\text{maximum of } 2 = 75\%$$
$$TA - (Threat\ Agent)\ (0 + 0 + 1 + 0 + 2 + 2 + 0 + 0 + 1)/9 = 0.666$$
$$\text{of a potential maximum of } 2 - 33\%$$

The threat amplifier combined score is $(16.6 + 75 + 33)/3 = 41.53\%$.

Threat Inhibitors

For this information to be used as metrics for a threat inhibitor, it is necessary to assign values to each of these elements (Table 6.13). This allows a calculation to be constructed as follows:

TIn – (Environmental) $(1 + 1)/2 = 1$ of a potential maximum of $2 = 50\%$
TIn – (Target) $(2 + 2 + 2)/3 = 2$ of a potential maximum of $2 = 100\%$
TIn – (Threat Agent) $(2 + 2 + 0 + 1 + 1 + 0)/6 = 1$ of a potential
maximum of $2 = 50\%$

The threat inhibitor combined score is $(50 + 100 + 50)/3 = 66.67\%$.

Table 6.13   Value Weightings for Chinese Nation State Sponsored Threat
Inhibitors

Factors	Environment	Target	Threat Agent
Fear of capture (FC)			2
Fear of failure (FF)			2
Level of technical difficulty (TD)	1	2	
Cost of participating (CP)			0
Public perception (PuP)			1
Law enforcement activity (LE)	1		1
Security of target (ST)		2	
Security of system (SS)		2	0

0, none; 1, weak; 2, strong.

Catalysts

For this information to be used as metrics for the catalysts, it is necessary to assign values to each of these elements (Table 6.14). This allows a calculation to be constructed as follows:

CA – (Environmental) $(2 + 1 + 1)/3 = 1.333$ of a potential maximum
of $2 = 66.65\%$
CA – (Target) $(0 + 0 + 0)/3 = 0$ of a potential maximum of $2 = 0\%$
CA – (Threat Agent) $(0 + 2 + 1 + 0)/4 = 0.75$ of a potential
maximum of $2 = 37.5\%$

The catalyst combined score is $(66.65 + 0 + 37.5)/3 = 34.75\%$.

Table 6.14 Value Weighting for Chinese Nation State Sponsored Threat
Agent Catalysts

Factors	Environment	Target	Threat Agent
Change of personal circumstances (CC)			0
War or political conflict (WF)	2		
Significant events (SE)	1	0	2
Significant anniversaries (SA)	1	0	1
Commercial gain (Cg)		0	0

0, none; 1, weak; 2, strong.

Motivation

Motivation is a percentage figure provided and inserted by the analyst. The motivation for the Chinese to carry out an attack on a foreign aerospace or a defense company could be either political or commercial gain, an estimated value of 85%.

TERRORIST THREAT AGENT

Most threat agents can be discounted as not operating effectively in the countries in which the company is based and not having a direct interest in the products of the business. In light of activity by Al Qaeda and their use of aircraft and hostility to both of the countries in which the company is based, this group should be assessed.

Table 6.15 lists terrorist threat agents, whereas Table 6.16 gives the value weighting those threat agents. These values can now be converted into a score:

(Number of Activists (Q) × 5) + (Level of Education (E)). This gives a maximum possible value of 36.

(Technical Expertise (T) × 2) + (Internet access (IA) × 2) + (Funding × 2) to express the resource availability). This gives a maximum possible value of 36. (History of relevant activity (H) × 6) gives equal weighting in importance to past activity. This will give a maximum possible value of 36.

Table 6.15 Terrorist Threat Agents

Factors	Terrorist Group
Group size (Q)	Over 1000 active members (estimated)
Level of education (L)	Good when based in host countries; poor when based in primary locations
Access to telecommunications and Internet (IA)	Limited in main operating areas; good for members located in host countries
Technical expertise (T)	Limited numbers with relevant education, training, and experience
History of activity (H)	Regular history of attacks on U.S. and Western interests; limited information on computer based attacks
Cultural factors (CF)	Islamic fundamentalists
Sponsoring countries (S)	Afghanistan, Pakistan?, Saudi Arabia?
Funding (F)	Osama Bin Laden, the head of Al Qaeda, reputed to have a personal fortune in excess of $300 million

This allows a calculation to be constructed as follows:

$$\text{Threat capability} = ((4 \times 5) + (4) + (3 \times 2) + (1 \times 2) + (5 \times 2) + (5 \times 6))\text{ gives}$$
value of 72 from a total maximum value of 108.

This can then be reduced to a percentage for ease of comparison and gives us a figure of 66% for capability.

Threat Amplifiers

Table 6.17 lists the terrorist threat amplifiers, whereas Table 6.18 gives the value weighting for those threat amplifiers. Threat Amplification (TA) is derived from the following:

Total Value of Influences that affect the Environment (PuP + CT + LE)/3

Total Value of Influences that affect the Target (PuP + Fa + AI + CT + TV + TP)/6

Total Value of Influences that affect the Threat Agent (PeP + PP + PuP + Fa + AI + SL + DS + LE + TP)/ 9

Table 6.16 Value Weighting of Terrorist Threat Agent

| Factor | | Weighting Value | | | | |
	1	2	3	4	5	6
Number of activists (Q)	1–250	251–500	501–1,000	1001–5,000	5,001–10,000	>10,000
Education level (E)	Extremely low	Very low	Low	Medium	High	Very high
Internet access (IA)	Extremely low	Very low	Low	Medium	High	Very high
Technical expertise (T)	None	Very limited	Limited	Adequate	Good	High level
History of relevant activity (H)	None	Limited	Intermittent	Occasional	Regular	Regular and widespread
Funding (F)	None	Very limited	Limited	Adequate	More than required	Unlimited

Table 6.17 Terrorist Threat Amplifiers

Factors	Environment	Target	Threat Agent
Peer pressure (PeP)			X
Peer perception (PP)			X
Public perception (PuP)	X	X	X
Search for recognition (fame) (Fa)		X	X
Access to information (AI)		X	X
Changing technologies (CT)	X	X	
Skills and education levels (SL)			X
De-skilling through scripting (DS)			X
Law enforcement activity (LE)	X		X
Target vulnerability (TV)		X	
Target profile (TP)		X	X

Table 6.18 Value Weighting for Terrorist Threat Amplifiers

Factors	Environment	Target	Threat Agent
Peer pressure (PeP)			0
Peer perception (PP)			1
Public perception (PuP)	1	0	2
Search for recognition (fame) (Fa)		0	2
Access to information (AI)		0	0
Changing technologies (CT)	1	1	
Skills and education levels (SL)			1
De-skilling through scripting (DS)			1
Law enforcement activity (LE)	1		0
Target vulnerability (TV)		1	
Target profile (TP)		2	2

0, none; 1, weak; 2, strong.

This allows a calculation to be constructed as follows:

$$\text{TA} - \text{(Environmental)} \; (1 + 1 + 1)/3 = 1 \text{ of a potential maximum of } 2 = 50\%$$
$$\text{TA} - \text{(Target)} \; (1 + 0 + 0 + 1 + 1 + 2)/6 = 0.83 \text{ of a potential}$$
$$\text{maximum of } 2 = 42\%$$
$$\text{TA} - \text{(Threat Agent)} \; (0 + 1 + 2 + 2 + 0 + 1 + 1 + 0 + 2)/9 = 1 \text{ of a potential}$$
$$\text{maximum of } 2 = 50\%$$

The threat amplifier combined score is $(50 + 42 + 50)/3 = 47.33\%$.

Threat Inhibitors

Table 6.19 lists the terrorist threat inhibitors. For this information to be used as metrics for a threat inhibitor, it is necessary to assign values to each of these elements (Table 6.20). The Threat Inhibition (TIn) is derived from the following:

Table 6.19 Terrorist Threat Inhibitors

Factors	Environment	Target	Threat Agent
Fear of capture (FC)			X
Fear of failure (FF)			X
Level of technical difficulty (TD)	X	X	
Cost of participating (CP)			X
Public perception (PuP)		X	X
Law enforcement activity (LE)	X		X
Security of target (ST)		X	
Security of system (SS)		X	X

Total Value of Influences that affect the Environment $(\text{TD} + \text{LE})/2$

Total Value of Influences that affect the Target $(\text{TD} + \text{ST} + \text{SS})/3$

Total Value of Influences that affect the Threat Agent $(\text{FC} + \text{FF} + \text{CP} + \text{PuP} + \text{LE} + \text{SS})/6$

This allows a calculation to be constructed as follows:

$$\text{TIn} - \text{(Environmental)} \; (2 + 1)/2 = 1.5 \text{ of a potential maximum of } 2 = 75\%$$

Table 6.20   Value Weighting for Terrorist Threat Inhibitors

Factors	Environment	Target	Threat Agent
Fear of capture (FC)			0
Fear of failure (FF)			1
Level of technical difficulty (TD)	2	2	
Cost of participating (CP)			0
Public perception (PuP)			2
Law enforcement activity (LE)	1		2
Security of target (ST)		1	
Security of system (SS)		2	1

0, none; 1, weak; 2, strong.

TIn − (Target) $(2 + 1 + 2)/3 = 1.67$ of a potential maximum of 2 = 83%.
TIn − (Threat Agent) $(0 + 1 + 0 + 2 + 2 + 1)/6 = 1$ of a potential maximum of 2 = 50%.

The threat inhibitor combined score is $(75 + 83 + 50)/3 = 69.33\%$.

Catalysts

Table 6.21 lists the terrorist threat agent catalysts. For this information to be used as metrics for the catalysts, it is necessary to assign values to each of these elements (Table 6.22).

Table 6.21   Terrorist Threat Agent Catalysts

Factors	Environment	Target	Threat Agent
Change of personal circumstances (CP)			X
War or political conflict (CF)	X	X	X
Significant events (SE)	X	X	X
Significant anniversaries (SA)	X	X	X
Commercial gain (Cg)		X	X

Table 6.22 Value Weighting for Terrorist Threat Agent Catalysts

Factors	Environment	Target	Threat Agent
Change of personal circumstances (CP)			0
War or political conflict (CF)	2	2	2
Significant events (SE)	1	2	2
Significant anniversaries (SA)	1	2	2
Commercial gain (Cg)		0	0

0, none; 1, weak; 2, strong.

The Catalyst (CA) is derived from the following:

Total Value of Influences that affect the Environment (CF + SE +SA)/3

Total Value of Influences that affect the Target (CF + SE + SA +Cg)/4

Total Value of Influences that affect the Threat Agent (CP + CF + SE + SA + Cg)/5

This allows a calculation to be constructed as follows:

CA – (Environmental) (2 + 1 + 1)/3 = 1.33 of a potential maximum of 2 = 66.7%

CA – (Target) (2 +2 +2 + 0)/4 = 1.5 of a potential maximum of 2 = 75%

CA – (Threat Agent) (0 + 2 + 2 + 2 + 0) /5 = 1.2 of a potential maximum of 2 = 60%

The catalyst combined score is (66.7 + 75 + 60)/3 = 67.23%.

Motivation

Motivation is a percentage figure provided and inserted by the analyst. In this case, because of the history of activity by Al Qaeda against Western targets, particularly those from the United States and the United Kingdom, and the aspirations of the group, the threat is assessed as being high and the motivation level is estimated to be 90%.

COMMERCIAL THREAT AGENT

Competing commercial organizations pose a significant potential threat. This is based partially on the high cost of development of products in this market and partially on the aggressive nature of the industry, compounded by the high technical nature of the industry. For the purposes of this book, we invent two such companies—one will be a U.S. based company that trades under the name of "Boring Aerospace and Defense," and the other will be a company based in France that is called "Aerospaciale France."

Boring Aerospace and Defense

Boring Aerospace is a multinational company with a large number of subdivisions that range in their interests from commercial aerospace to defense aerospace, telecommunications and satellite, and software development. They have a history of aggressive activity against competitors and have been taken to court in the past for industrial espionage activities. They also have a history of take-overs of competitors that threaten their market share in any of the sectors in which they operate.

Table 6.23 lists the commercial organization threat agents, and Table 6.24 gives the value weighting for Boring Aerospace and Defense threat agents. The threat capability can be broken down into a number of different groups of influences:

Table 6.23 Commercial Organization Threat Agents

Factors	Organization
Market sector	Defense and aerospace
State of market sector (V)	Volatile due to increasing defense contracts but canceled civil commercial work
Size (multinational/national/local) (Q)	Multinational
History of activity (H)	The corporation has been named on a number of occasions with regard to industrial espionage; currently one case under litigation
Is target organization part of the CNI? (CN)	Yes
Technical expertise (T)	Highly technically competent staff

Table 6.24 Value Weighting for Boring Aerospace and Defense Threat Agent

Factor		Weighting Value				
	1	2	3	4	5	6
Market state (V)	Decline	Static	Volatile	Rising	Buoyant	Turmoil
Organization size (Q)	1–250	251–500	501–1,000	1,001–5,000	5,001–10,000	>10,000
History of relevant activity (H)	None	Rare	Intermittent	Occasional	Regular	Regular and widespread
Target type (D)	Local interest	National, low interest	National	National, high interest	International	International, high interest
Technical expertise (T)	None	Extremely limited	Very limited	Limited	Adequate	High level
Target organization part of the CNI (CN)	Not part of CNI	Marginally involved in CNI	Part of CNI	Important element of CNI	Significant part of CNI	Crucial part of CNI

(Market State (V)) × 4 (to give a weighting of up to a maximum of 24 to market state) + (Organization Size (Q)) × 4 (to give equal weighting to the size of the attacking enterprise)
(History of Relevant Activity (H)) × 7 + (Technical expertise (T))
(Type of Target (D)) × 2 (type of target of lesser importance than capability of attacker) + (Target organization part of the CNI (CN))

This allows a calculation to be constructed as follows:

Threat capability = $(3 \times 4) + (6 \times 4) + (4 \times 7) + (6 \times 3) + (4 \times 2) + (3)$ gives a total of 93 from a maximum potential value of 126.

This can then be reduced to a percentage for ease of comparison to give us a figure of 74% for capability.

Threat Amplifiers

Table 6.25 shows the commercial threat amplifiers, whereas Table 6.26 gives the value weighting for those threat amplifiers. Threat Amplification (TA) is derived from the following:

Total Value of Influences that affect the Environment (PuP + CT + LE)/3

Total Value of Influences that affect the Target (PuP + Fa + AI + CT + TV + LE)/6

Total Value of Influences that affect the Threat Agent (PeP + PP + PuP + Fa + AI + SL + DS + LE + TP)/ 9

This allows a calculation to be constructed as follows:

TA − (Environmental) $(2 + 1 + 2)/3 = 1.67$ of a potential maximum of 2 = 83%
TA − (Target) $(2 + 0 + 2 + 2 + 2 + 2)/6 = 1/67$ of a potential maximum of 2 = 83%
TA − (Threat Agent) $(0 + 0 + 2 + 0 + 2 + 2 + 0 + 2 + 2)/9 = 1.11$ of a potential maximum of 2 = 55%

The threat amplifier combined score is $(83 + 83 + 55)/3 = 73.67\%$.

Table 6.25 Commercial Threat Amplifiers

Factors	Environment	Target	Threat Agent
Peer pressure (PeP)			X
Peer perception (PP)			X
Public perception (PuP)	X	X	X
Search for recognition (fame) (Fa)		X	X
Access to information (AI)		X	X
Changing technologies (CT)	X	X	
Skills and education levels (SL)			X
De-skilling through scripting (DS)			X
Law enforcement activity (LE)	X		X
Target vulnerability (TV)		X	
Target profile (TP)		X	X

Table 6.26 Value Weighting for Boring Aerospace and Defense Threat Amplifiers

Factors	Environment	Target	Threat Agent
Peer pressure (PeP)			0
Peer perception (PP)			0
Public perception (PuP)	2	2	2
Search for recognition (fame) (Fa)		0	0
Access to information (AI)		2	2
Changing technologies (CT)	1	2	
Skills and education levels (SL)			2
De-skilling through scripting (DS)			0
Law enforcement activity (LE)	2		2
Target vulnerability (TV)		2	
Target profile (TP)		2	2

0, none; 1, weak; 2, strong.

Threat Inhibitors

Table 6.27 lists commercial threat inhibitors. For this information to be used as metrics for a threat inhibitor, it is necessary to assign values to each of these elements (Table 6.28).

Table 6.27   Commercial Threat Inhibitors

Factors	Environment	Target	Threat Agent
Fear of capture (FC)			X
Fear of failure (FF)			X
Level of technical difficulty (TD)	X	X	
Cost of participating (CP)			X
Public perception (PuP)		X	X
Law enforcement activity (LE)	X		X
Security of target (ST)		X	
Security of system (SS)		X	X

Table 6.28   Value Weighting for Boring Aerospace and Defense Threat Inhibitors

Factors	Environment	Target	Threat Agent
Fear of capture (FC)			2
Fear of failure (FF)			1
Level of technical difficulty (TD)	1	2	
Cost of participating (CP)			1
Public perception (PuP)			2
Law enforcement activity (LE)	1		2
Security of target (ST)		2	
Security of system (SS)		2	2

0, none; 1, weak; 2, strong.

The Threat Inhibition (TIn) is as follows:

Total Value of Influences that affect the Environment (TD + LE)/2

Total Value of Influences that affect the Target (TD + ST + SS)/3

Total Value of Influences that affect the Threat Agent (FC + FF + CP + PuP + LE + SS)/6

This allows a calculation to be constructed as follows:

$$TIn - (Environmental) \; (1 + 1)/2 = 1 \; of \; a \; potential \; maximum \; of \; 2 = 50\%$$
$$TIn - (Target) \; (2 + 2 + 2)/3 = 2 \; of \; a \; potential \; maximum \; of \; 2 = 100\%$$
$$TIn - (Threat \; Agent) \; (2 + 1 + 1 + 2 + 2 + 2)/6 = 1.67 \; of \; a \; potential \; maximum \; of \; 2 = 83\%$$

The threat inhibitor combined score is (50 + 100 + 83)/3 = 77.67%.

Catalysts

Table 6.29 lists the commercial threat agent catalysts. For this information to be used as metrics for the catalysts, it is necessary to assign values to each of these elements (Table 6.30).

Table 6.29 Commercial Threat Agent Catalysts

Factors	Environment	Target	Threat Agent
Change of personal circumstances (CP)			X
War or political conflict (CF)	X		X
Significant events (SE)	X	X	X
Significant anniversaries (SA)	X	X	X
Commercial gain (Cg)		X	X

The Catalyst (CA) is derived from the following:

Total Value of Influences that affect the Environment (CF + SE + SA)/3

Total Value of Influences that affect the Target (SE + SA + CG)/3

Total Value of Influences that affect the Threat Agent (CP + CF + SE + SA + CG)/5

Table 6.30 Value weighting for Boring Aerospace and Defense Threat Agent Catalysts

Factors	Environment	Target	Threat Agent
Change of personal circumstances (CP)			0
War or political conflict (CF)	1		2
Significant events (SE)	1	2	1
Significant anniversaries (SA)	0	0	0
Commercial gain (CG)		2	2

0, none; 1, weak; 2, strong.

This allows a calculation to be constructed as follows:

CA – (Environmental) $(1 + 1 + 0)/3 = 0.67$ of a potential maximum of 2 = 33%
CA – (Target) $(2 + 0 + 2)/3 = 1.33$ of a potential maximum of 2 = 66%
CA – (Threat Agent) $(0 + 2 + 1 + 0 + 2)/5 = 1$ of a potential maximum of 2 = 50%

The Catalyst combined score is $(33 + 66 + 50)/3 = 50\%$.

Motivation

Motivation is a percentage figure provided and inserted by the analyst. In this case the motivation is for commercial gain and market position. With the volatility of the market and low margins being suffered in the industry, motivation is estimated at 70%.

Aerospaciale France

Aerospaciale France is a part state owned aerospace company that has wide ranging civil and defense interests. It forms part of the European Aerospace consortium that is currently developing a new long haul commercial aircraft that has a potential for use as a military cargo aircraft and mid-air refueler. They also have a strong research and development and production facility for unmanned aerial vehicles and are a major competitor for overseas sales.

Table 6.31 gives the value weighting for Aerospaciale France commercial threat agents.

Table 6.31 Value Weighting for Aerospaciale France Commercial Threat Agent

Factor	Weighting Value					
	1	2	3	4	5	6
Market state (V)	Decline	Static	Volatile	Rising	Buoyant	Turmoil
Organization size (Q)	1–250	251–500	501–1,000	1,001–5,000	5,001–10,000	>10,000
Target type (D)	Local interest	National, low interest	National	National, high interest	International	International, high interest
History of relevant activity (H)	None	Rare	Intermittent	Occasional	Regular	Regular and widespread
Technical expertise (T)	None	Extremely limited	Very limited	Limited	Adequate	High level

This allows a calculation to be constructed as follows:

$$\text{Threat capability} = (3 \times 4) + (6 \times 4) + (5 \times 7) + (6 \times 3) + (4 \times 2) \text{ gives a total of 97 from a maximum potential value of 120.}$$

This can then be reduced to a percentage for ease of comparison to give us a figure of 81% for capability.

Threat Amplifiers

Table 6.32 gives the value weighting for Aerospaciale France threat amplifiers.

Table 6.32 Value Weighting for Aerospaciale France Threat Amplifiers

Factors	Environment	Target	Threat Agent
Peer pressure (PeP)			0
Peer perception (PP)			0
Public perception (PuP)	2	1	2
Search for recognition (fame) (Fa)		0	0
Access to information (AI)		2	2
Changing technologies (CT)	2	2	
Skills and education levels (SL)			2
De-skilling through scripting (DS)			0
Law enforcement activity (LE)	2		2
Target vulnerability (TV)		2	
Target profile (TP)		2	2

0, none; 1, weak; 2, strong.

This allows a calculation to be constructed as follows:

$$\text{TA} - \text{(Environmental) } (2 + 2 + 2)/3 = 2 \text{ of a potential maximum of } 2 = 100\%$$

$$\text{TA} - \text{(Target) } (1 + 0 + 2 + 2 + 2 + 2)/6 = 1.5 \text{ of a potential maximum of } 2 = 75\%$$

$$\text{TA} - \text{(Threat Agent) } (0 + 0 + 2 + 0 + 2 + 2 + 0 + 2 + 2)/9 = 1.1 \text{ of a potential maximum of } 2 = 55\%$$

The threat amplifier combined score is $(100 + 75 + 55)/3 = 76.67\%$.

Threat Inhibitors

For this information to be used as metrics for a threat inhibitor, it is necessary to assign values to each of these elements (Table 6.33).

Table 6.33   Value Weighting for Aerospaciale France Threat Inhibitors

Factors	Environment	Target	Threat Agent
Fear of capture (FC)			2
Fear of failure (FF)			1
Level of technical difficulty (TD)	1	2	
Cost of participating (CP)			1
Public perception (PuP)			2
Law enforcement activity (LE)	2		2
Security of target (ST)		2	
Security of system (SS)		2	2

0, none; 1, weak; 2, strong.

This allows a calculation to be constructed as follows:

$$\text{TIn} - \text{(Environmental)} \ (1 + 1)/2 = 1.5 \text{ of a potential maximum of } 2 = 75\%$$
$$\text{TIn} - \text{(Target)} \ (2 + 2 + 2)/3 = 2 \text{ of a potential maximum of } 2 = 100\%$$
$$\text{TIn} - \text{(Threat Agent)} \ (2 + 1 + 1 + 2 + 2 + 2)/6 = 1.66 \text{ of a potential maximum of } 2 = 83\%$$

The threat inhibitor combined score is $(75 + 100 + 83)/3 = 86\%$.

Catalysts

For this information to be used as metrics for the catalysts, it is necessary to assign values to each of these elements (Table 6.34).

Table 6.34 Value Weighting for Aerospaciale France Catalysts

Factors	Environment	Target	Threat Agent
Change of personal circumstances (CC)			0
War or political conflict (WF)	1		1
Significant events (SE)	0	2	1
Significant anniversaries (SA)	0	0	0
Commercial gain (Cg)		2	2

0, none; 1, weak; 2, strong.

This allows a calculation to be constructed as follows:

$$CA - (\text{Environmental}) \ (1 + 0 + 0)/3 = 0.33 \text{ of a potential maximum of } 2 = 16.7\%$$
$$CA - (\text{Target}) \ (2 + 0 + 2)/3 = 1.33 \text{ of a potential maximum of } 2 = 66\%$$
$$CA - (\text{Threat Agent}) \ (0 + 1 + 1 + 0 + 2)/5) = 0.8 \text{ of a potential maximum of } 2 = 40\%$$

The catalyst combined score is $(16.7 + 66 + 40)/3 = 41\%$.

Motivation

Motivation is a percentage figure provided and inserted by the analyst. In the case of the threat from Aerospaciale France, in France it is considered an acceptable form of gaining knowledge and a reasonable way in which to conduct business. Because they operate in the same market sector and suffer the same pressures, the level of motivation is estimated at 85%.

HACKER THREAT AGENT

Because military and government organizations are a priority "prestige" target for the hacker, a company in the aerospace industry with connections to the military is a potential target. The hacker may target the company as a result of identifying the link to the military from a successful intrusion into one of the military systems or as a potential route into military systems.

The fictitious organization detailed below has been created to make the point. This is a group of hackers that have been active in "Hacktivist" actions in the past. They have a history of over 200 denial of service attacks and at least

30 successful intrusions where they have gained access to and published sensitive information. The group is currently against Western military involvement in the Middle East and has attacked a number of government and military establishments to gain information and to disrupt operations. They have threatened to take action against anyone involved in the facilitation of the government's "oppression" of the local populations.

Table 6.35 lists the hacker threat agents, whereas Table 6.36 gives the value weighting for these hacker threat agents.

Table 6.35 Hacker Threat Agents

Factors	Hacker Group
Size of group (Q)	Over 60
Technical ability of group (T)	High; widespread reporting of their attacks on a number of military systems
History of activity (H)	Widespread reporting of their attacks on a number of military systems
Reason for target selection (U)	History of attacking defense and related systems

The threat capability can be derived from the following:

(Group Size (Q) × 4) (the size of the group gives some measure of its ability to sustain an attack) + (Technical expertise (T) × 3) (to give total value for organization of 42)
(History of Relevant Activity (H)) × 7 + (Target Selection (U)) × 6 (to give total value for capability of 78)

This allows a calculation to be constructed as follows:

Threat capability = (3 × 4) + (6 × 3) + (6 × 7) + (5 × 6) gives a total of 102 out of a possible maximum value of 120

This can then be reduced to a percentage for ease of comparison and gives us a figure of 85% for capability.

Threat Amplifiers

Table 6.37 lists threat amplifiers, and Table 6.38 gives the value weighting for those threat amplifiers. Threat Amplification (TA) is derived from the following:

Table 6.36 Value Weighting for Hacker Threat Agents

Factor	Weighting Value					
	1	2	3	4	5	6
Group size (Q)	1–25	26–50	51–100	101–200	201–300	>300
Technical expertise (T)	None	Very limited	Limited	Adequate	Moderate	High level
History of relevant activity (H)	None	Intermittent	Occasional	Semiregular	Regular	Regular and widespread
Reason for target selection (U)	Curiosity	Rebellion	Criminal gain	Belief	Exert pressure	Revenge, religion, racism, nationalism

Table 6.37 Threat Amplifiers

Factors	Environment	Target	Threat Agent
Peer pressure (PeP)			X
Peer perception (PP)			X
Public perception (PuP)	X	X	X
Search for recognition (fame) (Fa)		X	X
Access to information (AI)		X	X
Changing technologies (CT)	X	X	
Skills and education levels (SL)			X
De-skilling through scripting (DS)			X
Law enforcement activity (LE)	X		X
Target vulnerability (TV)		X	
Target profile (TP)		X	X

Table 6.38 Value weighting for Hacker Threat Amplifiers

Factors	Environment	Target	Threat Agent
Peer pressure (PeP)			2
Peer perception (PP)			2
Public perception (PuP)	2	1	1
Search for recognition (fame) (Fa)		1	1
Access to information (AI)		2	1
Changing technologies (CT)	0	1	
Skills and education levels (SL)			2
De-skilling through scripting (DS)			1
Law enforcement activity (LE)	2		2
Target vulnerability (TV)		2	
Target profile (TP)		1	1

0, none; 1, weak; 2, strong.

Total Value of Influences that affect the Environment (PuP + CT + LE)/3

Total Value of Influences that affect the Target (PuP + Fa + AI + CT + TV + LE)/6

Total Value of Influences that affect the Threat Agent (PeP + PP + PuP + Fa + AI + SL + DS + LE + TP)/ 9

This allows a calculation to be constructed as follows:

$$TA - (Environmental) \ (2 + 0 + 2)/3 = 1.333 \ of \ a \ potential \ maximum$$
$$of \ 2 = 66\%$$
$$TA - (Target) \ (1 + 1 + 2 + 1 + 2 + 1)/6 = 1.333 \ of \ a \ potential \ maximum$$
$$of \ 2 = 66\%$$
$$TA - (Threat \ Agent) \ (2 + 2 + 1 + 1 + 1 + 2 + 1 + 2 + 1)/9 = 1.44$$
$$of \ a \ potential \ maximum \ of \ 2 = 72\%$$

The threat amplifier combined score is ((66 + 66 + 72)/3 = 68%).

Threat Inhibitors

Table 6.39 lists the hacker threat inhibitors. For this information to be used as metrics for a threat inhibitor, it is necessary to assign values to each of these elements (Table 6.40).

The Threat Inhibition (TIn) is derived as follows:

Total Value of Influences that affect the Environment (TD + LE)/2

Table 6.39 Hacker Threat Inhibitors

Factors	Environment	Target	Threat Agent
Fear of capture (FC)			X
Fear of failure (FF)			X
Level of technical difficulty (TD)	X	X	
Cost of participating (CP)			X
Public perception (PuP)		X	X
Law enforcement activity (LE)	X		X
Security of target (ST)		X	
Security of system (SS)		X	X

Table 6.40 Value Weighting for Hacker Threat Inhibitors

Factors	Environment	Target	Threat Agent
Fear of capture (FC)			2
Fear of failure (FF)			1
Level of technical difficulty (TD)	2	2	
Cost of participating (CP)			1
Public perception (PuP)			2
Law enforcement activity (LE)	2		2
Security of target (ST)		1	
Security of system (SS)		2	2

0, none; 1, weak; 2, strong.

Total Value of Influences that affect the Target (TD + LE + ST + SS)/3

Total Value of Influences that affect the Threat Agent (FC + FF + CP + PuP + LE + SS)/6

This allows a calculation to be constructed as follows:

TIn − (Environmental) (2 + 2)/2 = 2 of a potential maximum of 2 = 100%
TIn − (Target) (2 + 1 + 2)/3 = 1.66 of a potential maximum of 2 = 83%
TIn − (Threat Agent) (2 + 1 + 1 + 2 + 2 + 2)/6 = 1.66 of a potential maximum of 2 = 83%

The threat inhibitor combined score is (100 + 83 + 83)/3 = 88.67%.

Catalysts

Table 6.41 shows the hacker threat agent catalysts. For this information to be used as metrics for the catalysts, it is necessary to assign values to each of these elements (Table 6.42).

The Catalyst (CA) is derived from the following:

Total Value of Influences that affect the Environment (WF + SE +SA)/3

Total Value of Influences that affect the Target (SE +SA + Cg)/3

Total Value of Influences that affect the Threat Agent (WF + CC + SE + SA + Cg)/5

Table 6.41   Hacker Threat Agent Catalysts

Factors	Environment	Target	Threat Agent
Change of personal circumstances (CC)			X
War or political conflict (WF)	X		X
Significant events (SE)	X	X	X
Significant anniversaries (SA)	X	X	X
Commercial gain (Cg)		X	X

Table 6.42   Value Weighting for Hacker Threat Agent Catalysts

Factors	Environment	Target	Threat Agent
Change of personal circumstances (CC)			0
War or political conflict (WF)	2		2
Significant events (SE)	1	2	1
Significant anniversaries (SA)	1	1	1
Commercial gain (Cg)		0	0

0, none; 1, weak; 2, strong.

This allows a calculation to be constructed as follows:

$$CA - \text{(Environmental) } (2 + 1 + 1)/3 = 1.33 \ 1.66 \text{ of a potential maximum of } 2 = 66\%$$
$$CA - \text{(Target) } (2 + 1 + 0)/3 = 1 \text{ of a potential maximum of } 2 = 50\%$$
$$CA - \text{(Threat Agent) } (0 + 2 + 1 + 1 = 0)/5 = 0.8 \text{ of a potential maximum of } 2 = 40\%$$

The catalyst combined score is $(66 + 50 + 40)/3 = 52\%$.

Motivation

In the case of the Hacktivist group, the motivation is to put pressure on governments and the boards of directors. Motivation is estimated to be 60%.

SUMMARY

Having derived values for all factors that contribute to the potency of the threat agent, it is now possible to look at them all together as shown in Table 6.43. At all times the person reading these figures must grasp that they remain subjective and should not be directly compared against each other. What the figures do provide is an insight into the areas of greatest concern and the direction in which effort should be directed.

Table 6.43 Comparison of All Threat Agents

	Capability	Motivation	Amplifier	Inhibitor	Catalysts
France nation state	85	65	39.5	64	41.33
China nation state	72	85	41.53	66.67	34.75
Al Qaeda	66	90	47.33	69.33	67.23
Boring Aerospace	75	70	73.67	77.67	50
Aerospaciale France	81	85	76.67	86	41
Hacker	85	60	68	88.67	52

Table 6.43 shows a comparison of all the threat agents discussed in this chapter.

From the figures generated in the scenarios earlier in the chapter, it would be reasonable to draw the conclusions that effort (and resources) could beneficially be directed, reducing the effect of amplifiers that influenced commercial and hacker threat agents and reducing the motivation of state sponsored and terrorist threat agents. The results of the threat assessment give the user a guide as to where the most potent threats may originate and also allows the user to model the effect of the difference that changing the values of any of the factors will have on the potency of that threat.

When you have an understanding of the problem, you can start to make effective decisions on the actions you need to take to reduce the level of threat an organization is exposed to. Always remember that understanding the threat, although enlightening and informative, is of no value in isolation and is only a process that informs the risk assessment process.

Section III
Vulnerability Issues

7

Operating System Vulnerabilities

In this chapter we give examples and details of the types of vulnerabilities that exist in systems and the problems they cause. If the fact that there are potential vulnerabilities in the software and hardware and firmware that we use in our information systems is news to you, then you are probably reading the wrong book. Vulnerabilities in software are largely well documented, and a number of organizations, such as the Computer Emergency Response Team (CERT),[1] Computer Incident Advisory Capability (CIAC),[2] and Microsoft,[3] produce and maintain comprehensive databases that address not only the vulnerabilities that have been made public, but also the actions that need to be taken to "fix" the problem. In the case of hardware and firmware, the situation is less transparent and vulnerabilities tend not to be publicized to any great extent.

What is not so well understood is that these vulnerabilities fall into a number of categories. The vulnerabilities everyone knows about have made their way into the public domain. In the main these are vulnerabilities that have been discovered and for which a "patch" has been written and been made available to counter the problem. These vulnerabilities have a life cycle that precedes this point. One scenario (the best case) is that a vulnerability that exists in a piece of software is discovered and the person who identifies it is a "responsible" member of the community or a "cracker" who wishes to gain acknowledgment for their prowess by being named as the discoverer of the problem. For either of the above, they will normally notify the relevant manufacturer to allow them to produce a suitable patch and notify their customers of the problem and the fix before the problem becomes public knowledge. Another scenario is that the vulnerability is

---

1. Computer Emergency Response Team. http://www.cert.org/
2. Computer Incident Advisory Capability. http://www.ciac.llnl.gov/
3. The Microsoft Corporation. http://www.microsoft.com/

discovered by someone who will either attempt to exploit it or to gain credibility among their peers, who may exploit the flaw, and the vulnerability will be known among the "cracking" community and be used to break into systems for a period of time before the manufacturer becomes aware of it and a patch is produced. A third scenario is that a flaw in the software, hardware, or firmware is discovered in a research laboratory and remains there and is not released to the public or the manufacturer. Why would any responsible research laboratory take such an apparently unethical line? In probability, depending on the ownership of the research laboratory, it is either for commercial advantage or to allow the continuation of a piece of research that would be affected if the manufacturer produced a patch to address the problem. It must be pointed out that this last group of vulnerabilities pose no threat to the normal user, because for a flaw in a piece of software, firmware, or hardware to become a vulnerability there must be someone who knows and exploits it.

The areas where vulnerabilities cause the end user the most problems fall into four groups. The first group are those flaws that are discovered and notified to the manufacturer for which no fix can be created. Although this is a fundamental flaw in the system, there are times when these flaws are discovered in systems that have been in use for a considerable time and for which there are no obvious alternatives. The only things that can be done in this case are for the manufacturers and the research community to continue to address the problem and try to discover a fix. Although this may take some time, it is a moral obligation for the responsible manufacturer. It may be that the fix is actually a next generation of software that uses a different approach to achieve the functionality that is required.

The next group are those flaws that have been discovered and notified to the manufacturer. In the past, a considerable time gap was common between the notification of a flaw in software to the manufacturer and the production of a patch that addresses the problem. Responsible manufacturers have, in recent years, addressed this issue and now try to produce patches within a reasonable period; however, there is a period of days, weeks, or months during which a vulnerability is known about and for which no patch is available. Interestingly, this change in approach was in part forced by responsible crackers, who, having discovered flaws in the systems, were disappointed by the response of the manufacturers, who were taking an inordinate amount of time to produce and disseminate the patches. As a result, in a number of cases, the manufacturers were told they had a finite period of time to produce and deploy the patch before the cracker groups would publicize the flaw to the wider community.

It is normal during this period that the end user will not be informed of the problem, and this is, in the main, a reasonable approach. To do otherwise would increase the number of people who are aware of the problem and who may try to exploit it, while at the same time doing nothing to improve the situation, because there is no patch available to fix it. The problem here is that, during this period, there are a limited number of people who know about the problem, but these numbers are likely to grow as the knowledge seeps out. With the increased numbers of people in the know and the possibility that other groups will independently discover the same problem, the likelihood increases throughout the period that someone will exploit the flaw.

The next group is the one that probably causes the greatest problem and is the group of vulnerabilities for which patches have been developed and deployed. An example of this problem is shown in the details of the Solar Sunrise[4] case that affected the U.S. Department of Defense in which two teenagers from Cloverdale, California, accessed and broke into more than 200 systems as a result of patches for a well-known vulnerability in the Solaris operating system that had been available for several months but were not applied. If this sounds appalling, it is, but remember that the Department of Defense has a very well-structured system management and security organization and is better managed than most organizations. In the commercial sector the problem is much worse. If you want to get some idea of the scope of the problem, look at sites like Zone-H[5] or Security.nl[6] for some idea of the number of sites that are broken into on a daily basis and the types of attack that are carried out on them.

Another group are those "undocumented features" that are programmed in when the software is developed, either for the amusement of the programmers (Easter eggs) or to enable them to carry out recovery of the system during development (back doors).

EASTER EGGS

Easter eggs have been found in software for a number of years. As the software has become more complex, so have the types of Easter eggs that can be found in them. Some excellent examples of these can be found at sites such as the Easter

---

4. Article by Kevin Poulsen of SecurityFocus, "Solar Sunrise Attacks Panicked Top U.S. Officials." Jan. 9, 2001. http://www.securityfocus.com
5. Zone-H. http://www.zone-h.net/ accessed 2 March 2004.
6. Security.nl. http://www.security.nl/ accessed 2 March 2004.

Egg Archive at http://www.eeggs.com, which in March 2004 listed 2925 Easter eggs for software hardware and electronic systems, of which 162 are for operating systems, or Egg Heaven 2000 at http://www.eggheaven2000.com, which lists and categorizes a wide range of Easter eggs.

Examples of the types of Easter eggs that appear in even the most modern of operating systems are described below. In the first edition of the Windows 2000 operating system, a video of Bill Gates and a number of software developers is embedded. It can be found by doing the following:

Right click on the mouse and then going to Properties and Backgrounds. From there, select clouds and tiled for your background. From there, select Apply and then OK and return to the main screen. Select "My Computer" and then change the name to my Microsoft and keep the mouse still. The video clip will appear.

Another Easter egg in Windows 2000 carried over from Win95 and NT are the teapots in the 3D Pipes screen saver. To find this, change your screen saver to the 3D Pipes and click on Settings, and then change the settings to multiple pipes and traditional joints, with the mixed joint type. Then set the resolution to maximum and click OK and watch to see what happens. Every so often, a teapot is displayed instead of the standard ball joint at the corner of a pipe.

Another Easter egg in Windows 2000 that has migrated from Windows 95 and Windows 98 is the "Volcano" screen saver. To find this Easter egg, right click on "Properties" on the desktop and then select the "Screensaver" menu. Go to the 3D text screen saver and open the properties tag. In the text box, type the word "volcano" (without quotes).

To show that Easter eggs still exist even on the most advanced of operating systems, the next example is from the Windows XP Professional operating system. There is a secret file in the Windows XP operating system called "quotes." To access it, open up "My Computer" and double click on your main drive (normally C:\) then go to (Drive:\)WINDOWS\SYSTEM32\DRIVERS\etc. This is where the quotes file is located. Open the file "quotes" with your text editor (notepad, Word) and you will see the quotes that have been put there by the Microsoft developers!

As a final example, the following Easter egg is from Linux Version 2.2.1 that has bidirectional printer support. To see the Easter egg, generate a print from the network and force a printer jam (by folding the paper or wrinkling it up), then give the print command and observe the message that appears on the console (Lp0 printer on fire).

Although they may be amusing to find, it raises the fundamental question of how these pieces of code could have managed to escape any reasonable quality control procedure. As a user, you may ask yourself if large blocks of code, including video clips, can remain undetected, what else is hidden in the software?

BACK DOORS

Back doors are "features" purposely inserted into the software, normally at the software development stage. They are normally written into the code by the development engineers to help them while they are writing the code and to help them recover when they encounter problems. You might expect that in a professional software development environment these back doors would be removed once the software was completed and fully tested and, if not, the software quality review stage would identify it, but you would be wrong for at least two reasons.

The first is that back doors can be very difficult to detect, and in large and complex pieces of software they may escape detection. Even in safety critical systems, once you exceed around a hundred lines of code, it is very difficult to mathematically prove that the software does what it is supposed to and nothing more or less. The second reason is that the back doors may be deliberately left in by the developer to allow them the means to recover a customer's system once they have been delivered and are in use.

One of the authors has personal experience of this, when working on a critical system that was in use by a government department. This system was based on custom-made software that had been created to fulfill a specific role. The software had been developed under controlled conditions and had been externally validated by a third party. In the early hours of one Saturday morning, the system failed and, despite using all the skills and knowledge available and following all the documented procedures, it could not be restored. As a result of a good relationship with the developers of the system, one of the development engineers was awakened at about 4 o'clock in the morning, and once he had gathered his thoughts and got a cup of coffee, he checked to be sure all the procedures that were available had been followed. When it was apparent they had been and this had failed, he then talked the system manager through a start up sequence, with a totally unknown and undocumented set of keystrokes that recovered the system at the first attempt. Remember, this was a government system in a critical role that had been externally validated and this back door still existed!

HARDWARE VULNERABILITIES

When we talk of vulnerabilities, we normally think in terms of software, but don't forget that some hardware has processors embedded in them and firmware may also contain vulnerabilities. Most of us remember the year 2000 scares and the cost of ensuring that systems did not shut down or malfunction at the end of the last century. In the investigations that were undertaken to determine the extent of the problem, one issue that became significant was the number of embedded processors that were in use in systems nobody could remember or knew about. They carried out simple functions and functioned well and people had, over time, forgotten they existed.

An example of a hardware vulnerability can be seen from the Cisco Security Advisory on Multiple Vulnerabilities in Cisco IP telephones,[7] which reported that several vulnerabilities had been identified and repaired in Cisco IP phones. One vulnerability was reported to allow unauthorized modifications to be made to the configuration of the phones, whereas others caused the phone to restart when certain types of network traffic are received. The range of equipment affected by these vulnerabilities included, and was reported to be limited to, Cisco IP phone models 7910, 7940, and 7960.

The vulnerability was created because the Cisco IP phones store their configuration information locally and most configuration information is accessible through the "Settings" button on the phone. By default, these settings are locked (shown by a padlock icon in the title bar when viewing them) to prevent them from being accidentally changed. These settings can be changed via the trusted path key combination: (**#). Once unlocked, however, several fields can be reconfigured and any change to the phone's configuration is unlikely to be detected, because a user never normally has to use the configuration menu where these changes were made.

The effect of these vulnerabilities was that Cisco IP phones could be forced to restart by an attacker using a wide range of commonly available and well-known denial of service programs if they could successfully transmit packets to the phone. The phone could also be restarted if it received a crafted HTTP request with invalid arguments. Any current call on the phone would be disconnected and the IP phone would be unusable until it had finished restarting and could resume normal operation. This attack can be repeated indefinitely.

Another example of a hardware vulnerability can be found in the CIAC Advisory I-038 notice on the Ascend Routing Hardware Vulnerabilities that reported two vulnerabilities had been discovered on the Ascend Pipeline (version 5.0A) and MAX (version 5.0Ap42) router. The first vulnerability was with regard to UDP packets sent to the router and the second was with regard to SNMP

---

7. Cisco Security Advisory: Multiple Vulnerabilities in Cisco IP Telephones, Document ID: 23849, 22 May 2002.

"read" and "write" community passwords. If the first of these vulnerabilities was exploited, an attacker could cause a system lock-up, causing a denial of service. If the second was exploited, an attacker could possibly gain root access if the attacker could guess the community password.

SYSTEM CONFIGURATION

Despite any vulnerabilities the software or hardware developers may have either purposely or accidentally created, by far the biggest problem with security is the user. Systems are complex and require a good knowledge by the user to ensure they are safe and secure to use. Most home and small business users do not have the knowledge, inclination, or time to make sure their systems are configured properly and maintained in that state. After all, who wants to spend time on that boring stuff when you can be surfing the net or downloading your favorite MP3s?

A good example of the types of vulnerability that can occur if systems are not configured correctly can be seen in the example illustrated by the CIAC advisory notice[8] regarding the Oracle 9iAS Default Configuration Vulnerability in which a vulnerability was reported in the Oracle Database Server version 9iAS configuration that could potentially allow remote users to view the "globals.jas" file. If this vulnerability was exploited, an attacker could obtain information that may contain Oracle user names and passwords.

The Microsoft range of operating systems were, in the past, delivered in a totally insecure state, with all the security features turned off. People have been strong in their criticism of the company, but the fault, in reality, lies not with Microsoft but with the user. People wanted an operating system that would work "out of the box" and that was set up to allow them to do whatever they wanted, and that is exactly what Microsoft delivered. In the most recent versions of the operating system, this policy has changed and the new versions are being delivered in a more secure configuration.

The CERT Coordination Center in the United States provides advice and guidelines for the configuration of UNIX systems,[9] and as part of this guidance, 6 of 14 sections are dedicated to "inappropriate" settings and entries. The document describes the most commonly exploited UNIX system configuration problems and recommends practices that can be used to help deter several types

---

8. CIAC Advisory Notice M-048: Oracle 9iAS Default Configuration Vulnerability, February 27, 2002.
9. CERT® Coordination Center, UNIX Configuration Guidelines, June 2003 Version. http://www.cert.org/tech_tips/
unix_configuration_ guidelines.html

of break-ins. Some of the main configuration issues identified in this document are poor password security, accounts with default passwords, reusable and shared passwords, inappropriate network configuration file entries, inappropriate file and directory protections, old versions of system software in use, and vulnerable protocols and services

SOCIAL ENGINEERING ATTACKS

It is worth noting even a well-configured and secure system is vulnerable to a social engineering attack. This type of attack does not exploit a vulnerability in the system but instead persuades the user to subvert the system. The attack may be in the form of a direct attack, in which the user's log-on ID and password are gained by shoulder surfing, or by the receipt of an e-mail that the user opens, thereby allowing rogue codes to execute, or that the user responds to and reveals information that can be exploited. Help desks are operated to assist people, so it is not surprising that they can be persuaded to help an attacker and provide the attacker with useful information.

Examples of some of the vulnerabilities to social engineering attacks are detailed below. It is interesting to note that even though this is not a technical issue, the CERT® Coordination Center issues incident notes to warn users of the potential problem. A CERT® Incident Note[10] published information about incidents to the Internet community relating to social engineering attacks via Internet relay chat and instant messaging. The report stated that intruders had tricked unsuspecting users into downloading and executing malicious software. In doing this the user had made it possible for the intruder to use the user's systems to act as platforms from which distributed denial of service attacks could be launched. The report went on to state that it had good indications that tens of thousands of systems had been compromised in this manner in the recent past. The report went on to give an example of the type of message that had been sent: "You are infected with a virus that lets hackers get into your machine and read ur files, etc. I suggest you to download [malicious url] and clean ur infected machine. Otherwise you will be banned from [Internet relay chat network]."

Another example of vulnerabilities that can be created through social engineering is an experiment carried out in the United Kingdom and published in *The Register*.[11] In this experiment, it was reported that in the second annual

---

10. CERT® Incident Note IN-2002-03 issued by the CERT Coordination Center on 19 March 2002.
11. Article by John Leyden for *The Register,* " Office Workers Give Away Passwords for a Cheap Pen," posted 17 April 2003.

survey into office scruples carried out by the organizers of InfoSecurity Europe 2003: "Workers are prepared to give away their passwords for a cheap pen." According to the report, 90% of the office workers interviewed at London's Waterloo Station gave away their computer password in return for a cheap pen. This compared with a figure of 65% in 2002. It also revealed that men were slightly more likely to reveal their password (95%) than women (85%). The survey also revealed that some 80% of those interviewed would take confidential information with them when they changed jobs. Survey results showed the most common password was "password" (12%) and the most popular type of password was the user's own name (16%) followed by their favorite football team (11%) and date of birth (8%).

SUMMARY

It is normal to think of vulnerabilities as being relevant to the software we use on our systems. It is hoped that this chapter broadened the perception of where vulnerabilities can exist, because in reality they can be in the hardware, the firmware, the operating system software, the application software, or the user. Any risk assessment must take all these into account.

8

Application Vulnerabilities

In this chapter we give examples and details of the types of vulnerabilities that exist in the applications we use and the problems they cause. Chapter 7 concentrated on the problems that may exist in the platforms we use, looking at the hardware, firmware, and operating systems. Here we look at the vulnerabilities that exist in the applications we load onto the system to make it useful to us. There are applications that enable the system to do just about anything the user can think of, from the best known applications such as word processing packages, databases, and spreadsheets to much less obvious and well-known packages such as those that can be used for on-line gambling or peer-to-peer file sharing such as Kazaa or one that utilizes the spare processing cycles on your computer as part of a cooperative effort to interpret the signals that the SETI (Search for Extra Terrestrial Intelligence) intercept from space. As with operating systems, applications are written by a wide range of interested parties; in some cases these are teams of software engineers who are working for the same company that produced the operating system, such as in the case of the Microsoft® Office suite, which provides an integrated word processing facility, a spreadsheet, and a database program. Other companies produce applications for specialist areas or interest, such as the games producers and specialist packages for the financial sector and stock exchanges and hackers who produce tools that make it easier or quicker for them to achieve their aims by automating some of the repetitive processes.

Realistically, it is less likely that applications produced by a company such as Microsoft will undermine any security features built into the operating system; however, this has occurred but largely as a result of the complexity of the software and the interaction between the application and the operating system.

An example of this is the exploit[1] "WINMAIN.EXE" that was discovered by the spywareinfo.com team. This represented an entirely new attack method

---

1. Privacy Software Corporation Security Advisory. Tuesday, July 29, 2003. HTA DOWNLOAD EXPLOIT

against systems, with the offending executable activating a dangerous piece of Internet Explorer and exposing a significant new risk to systems, because the executable runs for an entire Windows session. The exploits drop a file called "C:\WINLOG.HTML"; however, future exploits will be able to generate other files. This exploit is the first of its kind and is likely to be a whole new approach to trojans.

"Winmain.exe" was the first version of "HTASPLOIT" that was discovered and was apparently loaded as a form of "spyware" on a number of systems and was probably installed with freeware or shareware trial software. This is now a common practice and uses advertising software, "adware," to subsidize free software. Unfortunately, the HTASPLOIT goes far beyond an advertising "downloader" and exposes a new realm of risk. The HTASPLOIT operates by loading Microsoft's vulnerable "MSHTA.EXE" program, the "HyperText Application" interpreter. Because this is a Microsoft product, it is not blocked by a firewall. Once downloaded, the "Winmain" immediately loads the MSHTA.EXE and places it on "hot standby"; once it is running, "Winmain" exits. The MSHTA program then runs for the remainder of the system session until Windows itself is shut down. Once the system is restarted, it is automatically run again. Another example can be found in the FrontPage Personal web server, which is reported[2] to allow an attacker to view any file on the system with the use of a bug known as doubledot.

Increasingly, the major operating system and application manufacturers are collaborating to ensure that the different software packages do not conflict and cause problems. Although they may be in competition for market share, bad publicity benefits no one, and the professionalism of the whole industry affects them all.

At the other end of the scale, those "applications" produced by hackers will normally be trying to achieve exactly the opposite aim—to undermine any security features that exist in either the application or the operating system by exploiting flaws in the logic or overpowering the security measures that have been implemented, for example, through the use of password crackers. It is a strange world where we can visit a website of a legitimate software producer and then, if you know the URL, go straight from there to a hacker website where you can obtain the tools that you need to undermine the software produced by that manufacturer. There are many thousands of hacker sites and "warez" sites where you can obtain the information and tools you need to break into systems. A few examples of hacker sites that hold a good selection of this information and software are

---

2. http://www.pestpatrol.com/pestinfo/d/doubledot_bug_in_ frontpage_frontpage_personal_web_server.asp

- Hideaway.net[3]
- The Underground News[4]
- The Cult of the Dead Cow[5]
- WWW.HACKER.AG[6]
- The Hacker Index[7]

If life was simple, one could visit a manufacturer's site for the professionally built and legitimate applications and visit a hacker site to obtain software to undermine it. Unfortunately, it is not, and although many of the hacker sites are clearly identified, we move into murky areas when we download that "must have" freeware or shareware program. Unless you have used software from the site and the author in the past and have gained confidence that it is well written and does not contain flaws or malicious code, you are effectively buying a ticket in a lottery. If you are one of the bad guys and you want to distribute a piece of software to a large number of normal users, is it more sensible to put it on a hacker's site or on a freeware site? So when you download the freeware "must have" from the Internet that looks so promising, how do you actually know what effect it is having on your system?

If we were all good honest citizens with unlimited funds and we were prepared to pay for the software we use, there would be less of a problem, but the reality is very different. A large number of reports from a range of sources inform us that the a large proportion of the software that is in use is illegal. This is obviously a major concern for the manufacturers, who are losing significant revenue, but it is also a major problem for the users because the illegal software has been copied and redistributed countless times.

In 2001 The Business Software Alliance (BSA) reported that globally around 40% of all software is pirated and that the proportion is increasing. The losses to the software industry are now calculated as being in the region of $11 billion per annum. In the BSA's 2001 annual survey report,[8] the 10 countries with the highest piracy rates were identified:

---

3. The Hideaway.net website, http://www.hideaway.net/
4. The Underground News website, http://www.undergroundnews.com/
5. Cult of the Dead Cow website, http://www.cultdeadcow.com/
6. The Hacker.AG website, http://www.warez-crackz-serialz.de/
7. The Hackers Index website, http://www.hackerindex.com/
8. BSA 2001 Annual Software Piracy Report, http://global.bsa.org/usa/press/newsreleases/2002-06-10.1129.phtml? CFID= 2211323&CFTOKEN=67588729

Vietnam:	2000, 97%; 2001, 94%
China:	2000, 94%; 2001, 92%
Indonesia:	2000, 89%; 2001, 88%
Ukraine/Other members of the Commonwealth of Independent States (CIS):	2000, 89%; 2001, 87%
Russia:	2000, 88%; 2001, 87%
Pakistan:	2000, 83%; 2001, 83%
Lebanon:	2000, 83%; 2001, 79%
Qatar:	2000, 81%; 2001, 78%
Nicaragua:	2000, 78%; 2001, 78%
Bolivia:	2000, 81%; 2001, 77%

Although a culture exists where it is acceptable to use pirated software, users should not be surprised if they get what they paid for. In fact, for anyone with malicious intent, if users of the software happen to work for a government agency or a targeted company, what better way to insert modified software onto their system?

In Chapter 7 the issue of Easter eggs, found within operating systems, was raised. For consistency, detailed below is a small selection of the Easter eggs that can be found hidden in software applications:

- Microsoft Excel 2000, Spy Hunter9: To activate this Easter egg, open Excel and then in a blank worksheet select "Save as" and choose "Save as web page." Next, click on Publish and Add interactivity and save as any name you like. Then, load in the page with MS Internet Explorer, and Excel appears in the webpage. Go to row 2000, Column WC, and highlight all of row 2000 and press Tab to make column wc the active column, then hold the keys Ctrl, Alt, Shift and click on the Office Icon. Once the Easter egg starts, use the arrow keys to drive your car and the "0" key to drop paint slicks. The spacebar is used to fire and the "H" key is used for the headlights. (Note: DirectX needs to be loaded for this to work.)

- Adobe Acrobat 4.0, Whale Sounds: To get to this Easter egg, open Adobe Acrobat and go to Help, About Plug-ins, Acrobat Annotations, and then

9. http://www.eggheaven2000.com/detailed/148.html

hold down Ctrl and left click on Credits. You will hear the sound of a whale, see the Plug-in logo change to a whale, and see the Credits button change to Harpoon.

- Windows 95 or later, Norton System Doctor development team[10]: To get to this Easter egg, open Norton System Doctor and click HELP, ABOUT NORTON SYSTEM DOCTOR, then hold down the N and U keys simultaneously. Move the mouse over the developers' heads, and you will see some of the developers pictures by clicking the buttons.

- Outlook Express, the Outlook Express development team details: To view this Easter egg, click the Compose Message button and select Format, Rich Text, then click in the main body to make the formatting bar come to life. Click on Font and type in "athena" and then press enter. Return to the main Outlook Express program and click on "Outlook Express" in the folders list and then click on an empty space on the page that appears. Next type "about" to see the names of the Outlook Express development team appear on the screen.

- SimCity 2000 Version 1.0: When running SimCity 2000, type the word "porn" and you should hear a voice singing "can't get enough." Alternatively, type the word "damn" while you are playing and a dialog box should come up with the words "Same to you pal." There is also another one that appears after a large section of forest has been cleared, when the "citizens" will protest. If this happens repeatedly, you will be asked if you want to hear the call of the moose, who are the inhabitants of the forest you're destroying. If you click "Yes," you will hear it.

SUMMARY

This chapter has followed the theme of the previous chapter and has hopefully highlighted the fact that whatever the source of your software, no matter how reputable, you will almost certainly be getting more than you paid for. Although most of the "undocumented code" is benign, some of it is not. It brings home quite forcefully that even when you have a tight control of your systems, you cannot eliminate risk—all you can do is minimize it.

---

10. http://www.eeggs.com/items/797.html

9

Public Domain or Commercial Off-the-Shelf Software?

In this chapter we compare and contrast public domain and commercial off-the-shelf (COTS) software and the merits and disadvantages of each. We also examine the place within the market that is held by custom-made software and hardware. We cover a range of issues, including hardware, firmware, operating systems, applications, and the network infrastructure.

COMMERCIAL OFF-THE-SHELF SOFTWARE

In the past when serious computing power was the domain of government agencies, corporations, and academic institutes, most software in use was custom-made, that is, purpose written for a specific implementation. In addition, because processing power and storage were so limited, there was huge benefit in ensuring that any code produced was efficient in terms of both the processing power it required and the amount of storage space it occupied. Systems were also, in the main, discrete and not widely connected. If they were connected outside the building in which the computer hall was located, it tended to be via privately owned communications infrastructures.

As the technology developed and started to converge with communications technologies, this changed. Where, in the past, the opportunity to access the computers of an organization was restricted to those who could gain direct access to the closely guarded and precious facilities, as computers became more widely used and the unthinkable happened, the home computer, access and connectivity became easier, and as a result the threat from external influences increased. With the increasing use of computers came the rise of commonly used equipment and software. People started to use the same software at home they used in the office, and COTS products had arrived.

The rationale for the use of COTS software is that first it provides a common platform, so that organizations can easily exchange information and staff do not have to relearn how to use the software and hardware for each organization or department. Second, COTS goods provide good capabilities at a reasonable cost, because the cost of development has been shared over a large number of users. COTS products tend to be upgraded, and updated versions of products are frequently delivered. The timeline (the life cycle) of a product continues to shorten, with the hardware life cycles now at around 9 months and software life cycles at around 18 months.

One of the main shortcomings of COTS software is that it is commercially driven and is produced in a competitive environment where the constant drive is to increase its functionality and provide all the features the user could ever dream of (and a lot that the average user will never use). There is also a requirement to maintain the profitability of the product and that normally means an "updated product" every couple of years. When these factors together with the need to create the product in a cost-effective manner are combined, a situation is created where, particularly in the software industry, the programs are increasingly "feature rich" and complex but are produced to a timescale. Inevitably this results in products being put onto the market in a flawed state, where in effect users become the "beta testers," and it is only when version 1.1 or 1.2 of the product is released that it is actually in a marketable quality.

It is not unusual these days for a software product to be developed in a number of countries or even continents in which there are, or may be, technological competitors to the United States. Why would any technology or software developer expose themselves to this potential for the theft of their intellectual property rights? The answer is simple—it is much cheaper to have electronic devices fabricated in the Far East than in either Europe or the United States. It also allows for an extended software development day, because the software can be worked on in the United States for the normal working day and then the development can be moved to the Indian subcontinent or the Far East for another working day before being shipped back to the original site for the next working day.

Security features are increasingly being built into modern software to meet the demands of the consumer in a changing environment. For example, in Windows NT there are at least 300 security features that can be turned on as required. Although this is admirable, it is unfortunately the case that most users do not have the skill, knowledge, or inclination to use them. Modern software is increasingly complex, and it takes just one weakness that has not been detected and resolved in one system to create a vulnerability that makes all users vulnerable to exploitation and attack.

As systems have become more interconnected, the concept of trust relationships between systems has become necessary. It is because of these relationships between systems and networks that a weakness in one system can cause problems to all other systems that "trust" it.

COTS Software Development Process

A number of prominent COTS operating systems are widely used today, including the Microsoft Windows family (95, 98, NT, 2000, and XP), the Macintosh operating system, and Novell. Although each of these groups is different in the way it works, they all have to achieve similar functionality to meet the requirements of interconnection and the expectations of the users.

All these operating systems are developed in a competitive market where the commercial drivers to maintain and gain market share are achieved by delivering new feature-rich operating systems that meet the current technologies (that is, they can handle developments like ADSL and wireless connectivity) to market at the right time. The market for operating systems demands that each generation of the software is more feature laden than its predecessor or its competitors. In their attempt to achieve this, software developers have been forced to incorporate ever more and more features into each release. This has meant that the size of the operating system has consistently grown with each generation of the software. Through this, although the developers are keeping pace with the demands of the market and to maintain their market share, they are also aiming to meet the requirements of a wide range of users—in essence, to be all things to all people. The result of this is that operating systems have now become so large and complex it is no longer possible to verify in a formal manner whether they are functioning in the way they are supposed to or operating in a way that is "safe."

This development of large, complex, and feature-rich operating systems has a direct relationship with the platforms for which it is developed. If we were still using 8086 processors on motherboards that could take 8 or 16 kilobytes of RAM and, if you were very lucky, 10 megabytes of storage and with the removable media capacity of a 5 ¼" floppy disk (360 kilobytes), it would not be possible to store or run them. Imagine how many floppy disks you would need to load Windows XP.

The Microsoft Windows family of operating systems currently holds by far the highest share of the personal computer operating system market, within the region of 86% of the market.[1] It has recently been acknowledged that

---

1. *PC World Magazine*, July 1998.

approximately 600 Mb of the Windows source code has been stolen in a hacking attack. However, apart from the prestige of "hacking Microsoft," the benefit gained from stealing this code is not as obvious as it may at first appear, because the Windows 2000 operating system is reputed to consist of more than 40 million lines of code. Just having access to the code will not greatly benefit the thief, because the amount of time it takes to understand 600 Mb of code means it will probably be obsolete before it can be used.

OPERATING SYSTEMS

Modern operating systems now have a significant number of security features built into them. Why is it that when the products have this functionality, they are delivered with them all switched off? Unfortunately, most users do not have the skill or knowledge they need to set the appropriate security features and achieve the appropriate security for their system. Also, they do not have the time or inclination to learn how to use them or to maintain them. Security has always been seen as a nonproductive and obstructive feature that gets in the way of people doing what they want and need to do. The reality is that if an operating system was to be delivered with all of its security functionality enabled, it would not allow most users to use it in the way they wish. This would mean the next time they went to purchase a product, they would look elsewhere, so we should not be too critical of commercial software developers who provide us with what we want.

This situation is likely to change in the near future. Microsoft has announced in recent years that it now considers security to be a major issue and has expended considerable effort into making its products more secure in a "user friendly" manner. The versions of their software that are due to be delivered in the near future will be delivered with a significant set of security features enabled, making it possible for more systems to be protected "out of the box."

The Windows NT based operating systems, which, as mentioned above, have in excess of 300 security settings that can be selected, are delivered with them all set to off. In this way, it is easily loaded and is fully functional as soon as it is loaded. Few people have the skills and knowledge to configure the system in a secure manner and the only way, in the present environment, this will change is through the education of the users. Although this is a superb idea, who would pay for it? After all, the average home user has no interest and believes it has no impact on them. People have a commonly held view that their home computers hold nothing of importance and, with the exception of annoying viruses, that they have never had a problem. This would be bad enough if it were to be constrained to the home environment, but these are the same people that work in our businesses and for our government departments.

Even if these people do care, there is little chance they have the capability to configure the system in a secure manner. Once securely configured, there is a considerable cost in maintaining the security of the system to deal with fresh vulnerabilities as they are discovered, which happens on an almost daily basis. The reality is that most users do not care about security and want the out of the box full functionality they have become used to. From the developer's point of view, commercial prudence says that you will deliver the product in a state that is acceptable to most of your users. For some users that require enhanced security, you provide the means to enable them to do it. The fact that most of the Internet is totally insecure is the fault not just of the developers, who we are quick to blame, but mainly of the consumer.

APPLICATIONS

Having established that most users cannot and will not install and configure their operating systems in a secure manner, it must be remembered that it is the applications we load on top of the operating system that make the system do what we actually want it to do. There are applications that will enable you to do just about anything you can think of, from word processing packages and spreadsheets to less commonly known applications, such as packages for interactive betting on the Internet or mathematical modeling applications. We also load onto our computers software that we gain pleasure from but which provide no specific functionality, for example, screen savers. The range of people who develop these applications is hugely varied, from professional development teams to academic groups to hackers. It is unfortunately true that we all want something for nothing, so if software that appeals to us appears on the Internet for free, how many people will refuse it? As a result, if someone wants to insert malicious software on your system, it is not difficult to persuade a large number of users to do the job for them.

It would be reasonable to assume that applications developed by Microsoft or one of the major manufacturers with whom they collaborate do not undermine any of the security features built into their operating systems. Although this would be true in a perfect world, it does still happen. One example of this is a vulnerability to a denial of service that was discovered in the NetMeeting application.[2] This denial of service vulnerability can be activated when a malicious client

---

2. Microsoft Security Bulletin (MS00-077), 14 November 2000.

sends a malformed string to a port on which the NetMeeting service is listening when the Remote Desktop Sharing is enabled. With the Windows NT4 operating system, the application has to be downloaded separately, but with Windows 2000 it has been incorporated into the operating system.

As mentioned above, it is not only legitimate software development houses that produce and make available software. When we look at some of the applications produced by hackers (yes, hackers do produce software—visit any of the good hacker sites to see the software available), a lot of these applications are designed to undermine security features by exploiting flaws in the logic of the operating system or legitimate applications. One information system's security professional has maintained a database of in excess of 6000 such hacker websites, and this is by no means a comprehensive list.

It would be easy to say that if we were all good sensible citizens and we were all prepared to pay for the software we use, the problem would disappear. This, however, is a simplistic, and untrue, view. The case for public domain software is discussed below and has a great deal of validity. It is also true that software is available that can be downloaded at no cost (freeware) or for a small cost on a "try before you buy" basis (shareware) that has no commercial equivalent but that provides functionality that cannot be found elsewhere. In reality, a large proportion of the software that is in use, particularly on home systems, is illegal. It has been copied and redistributed countless times. (How many people have a copy of the software that is licensed for their work environment loaded on their home system?)

A few years ago in Hong Kong it was the norm that if you had a system built, you would tell the person building it what software you wanted on it and it would be delivered with it installed, at no additional charge. Although the police and authorities in Hong Kong tried to stop it, they were singularly unsuccessful for a number of years. On one occasion in 1998, customs officials in Hong Kong seized more than 100,000 suspect compact disks (worth U.S.$244,000) from just one shopping arcade. It was also common that when you received your system, you had not only the software you asked for, you also got a cocktail of viruses and other malicious software, as the "computer hygiene" of the system builders was not high. If you believe this a dated example and that the problem is confined to the Far East, then you are mistaken; in 2002 a group of individuals in the United States, Australia, and the United Kingdom were arrested for counterfeiting software on a massive scale. The group, known as "Drink or Die,"[3] was

---

3. Dan Bell, "Alleged Aussie Drink or Die Co-Leader May Face US Piracy Charge." *News.com.au*, 14 March 2004.

reported to have plundered in the region of U.S.$50 million worth of music, film, game, and software products. Although there is no indication they were careless or in any way contaminated the material they plundered, the scale of their operation is larger than many legitimate organizations.

A recent report from Microsoft[4] stated that in Vietnam 97% of the software in use is not legitimately purchased and that in Russia and Indonesia 92% of all software has been pirated. Interestingly, this is not just a problem in the East. The United States, Japan, Germany, France, Italy, the United Kingdom, and Canada are in the top 10 countries for the piracy of software.

IMPROVING THE SITUATION

As with the manufacture of most products, the people who write software are largely anonymous. You can equate this to the manufacture of a car—you will probably never get to meet the people who made it, but you will certainly gain first-hand experience of their skill and level of interest in its production the first time it breaks down. It is natural for developers to be proud of their achievements and to make their mark, especially when they have invested vast amounts of effort to the task of developing the product. Their ability to leave their mark on the final product has been facilitated by the complexity and very richness in features of the software currently being developed and the availability of storage space and memory. In addition, with such large and complex software packages, it is difficult to predict the interaction of one part of software on another, and it is often the case that even when security patches are applied, their interaction with some applications is not that which was anticipated.

The software currently in use and under development is, in the main, not produced by individuals or by small teams. The complexity and size of the software suites means they are normally produced by large teams. In this environment, quality control of the software becomes increasingly difficult to manage, because the interaction of the individual elements can have unexpected outcomes. In addition, the main driver in the commercial market is to get the product to market at the right time for a realistic investment to maintain or increase market share.

It has become common practice to get the product to market and to use the purchasers of the software to act as the testers of the product and, when there are a sufficient number of reported problems, to produce a patch. If the users were

---

4. The Microsoft Corporation website, http://www.Microsoft®.com/piracy/basics/worldwide

less interested in getting all the latest features they will probable never use and were more concerned with the quality of the delivered product, then the software developers might be pressured into delivering to the market a higher quality product.

DEVELOPMENT OF OPEN SOURCE SOFTWARE

The open source development of software is the production of the software source code in a way that means it is open for inspection by anyone who chooses to look at it. As a result, the software is normally in public ownership. The advantage is that the software is exposed to input and review by a wide peer group, and, as a result, at the end of the review process the software has been thoroughly tested and should be as close to perfect as possible.

Although having the software in the public arena has the advantages described above, among the disadvantages of this approach is that the software does not belong to any organization or individual. This means there is no direct economic benefit to be gained from the software. With no direct commercial benefit, the development time of open source software is likely to extend far beyond that of a commercial software package. Another disadvantage of open source software is that the source code is available to anyone who has the skill and would like to spend time in analyzing the software to identify any shortcomings to identify potential vulnerabilities.

A project, named GNU, was launched in 1984 to develop an open source UNIX-like operating system that would be available at no cost to anyone who wanted it. The GNU system (GNU is a recursive acronym for "GNU's Not Unix") and variants of the GNU operating system, which use the Linux kernel, are now widely used; however, although these systems are often referred to as "Linux," they should more accurately be called GNU/Linux. The GNU project had the advantages that the contributors to the project came from all types of backgrounds and were prepared to work for the common good to produce software that is free for use by everyone.

Linux

Linux is a free UNIX-like operating system that was originally created by Linus Torvalds, who has gained huge support for the project from like-minded software developers around the world. The operating system was developed under the GNU General Public License, and the source code for Linux is freely available to anyone who wishes to download a copy of it. Linux is hugely popular with the more technically capable users of the Internet, and despite the growth in the number of features that it contains, the code tends to be developed in a modular form. Because problems are solved rather than "patched," it tends to be much cleaner and more compact than a commercially available operating system.

Freeware

Not all open source software that is made available at no cost to the user is offered through the GNU project. There is a huge range of software that has been developed by anyone from individuals to groups with specific interests that is made available. Much of this software is excellent and has been hand crafted by experts who developed it to meet a specific need. Unfortunately, because there is no commercial benefit to be directly derived from it, it is unlikely to have gone through rigorous quality control or to have been tested against the functionality of the operating systems to ensure it does not undermine it.

Shareware

Shareware is a hybrid that lies between freeware and commercial software. The concept behind shareware is that you make it available free, normally on the Internet, for people to download and evaluate. The developer then invites anyone who likes it and wishes to continue to use it to pay a nominal sum and, in some cases, to receive updates of the software and support from the developer. The problem, as with freeware, is that the level of quality control and testing will be low; also, because the source of the software can be hidden, there is the potential for malicious software to be inserted. There is truth in the adages that "there is no such thing as a free lunch" and "buyer beware."

Issues with Open Source Software

Most software developed under the open source philosophy is produced in this way by people who believe that the software should be freely available or do not have the commercial infrastructure to market it through the mainstream commercial avenues. Most groups that develop this type of software are individuals, like-minded groups, and academic or research institutes. By releasing the source code for the software for inspection by the wider Internet community, many of whom are highly skilled and have relevant knowledge, it is possible to develop good free software that has been subject to widespread peer review and testing and to agreed improvements. Unfortunately, the downside of this concept is that, in most cases, no one "owns" the development and there is no commercial drive to turn the software into a marketable quality product. An additional issue is that when the source code has been made available to all who want to see it, it can be modified and have unwanted features added by anyone who so desires.

Most of the people who use open source software download a compiled version that is ready to run. Despite the fact that it is possible to download the source code and to inspect it and compile it, most users do not have the knowledge or desire to check that the source code only does what it is supposed to and to compile it. There are a number of notable exceptions to this generalization, and operating systems such as LINUX have established a huge following and an excellent reputation and have been commercialized by organizations that will provide compact disks of variants of the operating system and also support. But what of the other operating systems and applications that we see? The best advice is to obtain your freeware or shareware from a reputable source where the provider has taken reasonable care. Some examples of well-respected sites that are repositories for freeware and shareware are

- Ziff Davis website[5]

- Tucows website[6,7]

- Shareware.com[8]

CUSTOM SOFTWARE

Custom-made software is developed for a specific customer or for a specific purpose. Historically, governments and the military have been the main customer for custom-made systems, because the main military powers need state of the art equipment rather than "off the shelf" defense systems. In the past, it has effectively only been governments and a small number of multinational corporations that could afford the cost of the development of custom-made systems or could justify that expense.

Although this approach should provide the perfectly tailored solution to a specific requirement, it does have disadvantages: the systems are hugely expensive, take a long time to develop, and rarely meet the requirements of the user by the time they are delivered. None of this is really surprising when you consider

---

5. Ziff Davis website, http://downloads-zdnet.com.com.
6. The Tucows website, http://www.tucows.com/
7. Alternate Tucows website, http://tucows.blueyonder.co.uk/
8. The Shareware.com website, http://www.shareware.com/

that if someone is going to invest in a custom-made system, they are trying to go where no one has been before; otherwise, there would be a COTS solution. Another disadvantage is that with the long development cycles for custom-made systems, by the time the system is delivered it may be obsolete or the requirement may have changed. To counter these problems, it is more normal in the current environment to take a COTS product and to modify it to meet the specific needs of the organization. In its simplest form, this may take the form of producing templates for spreadsheets for use in a finance department or the development of a specific database application. This is a much lower cost and lower risk option than a fully custom-made system and will allow a shorter development cycle and more modern technologies to be introduced. The main shortcoming of this approach is that by taking a COTS product and modifying it, you have inherited all the additional functionality that is built into the product. As a result, you will be exposed to all the problems inherent in those features.

In summary, in a custom-made system the only functionality that should exist in the system is that which it is designed to have and the production of the system should be more tightly controlled. This assumes that the developer is building the product for you from scratch and is not reusing software modules that have previously been produced for another customer with a similar requirement.

The Dilemma

With custom-made software, the main issues are the cost of obtaining and main-taining it and the time taken to develop it. You would expect that a reputable developer would have taken effort to ensure the quality of the product and also that it did not interfere with any of the functionality of other software that may be in use on the system. If one organization bears the total cost of developing a system, it will need to have very deep pockets, as opposed to the use of commercial software, where the development costs are spread across the whole popula-tion of users who buy it, so the cost of its development may be shared across millions of purchases. Another disadvantage is that any software developer undertaking the development of a custom-made system for a client will do so based on the experience that it has gained from similar projects that it has under-taken in the past. Given the opportunity, the developer will adopt a software reuse approach because this is cost effective for them and allows them to be more competitive. After all, if the code has been developed in the past for another proj-ect and has been tested with an existing client and proved to be effective, why reinvent the wheel? Unfortunately, the problem is that the code will probably not be implemented in exactly the same way as it was designed for use by the last client, and this may result in it being less than perfect for the current project. The benefit to the developer is that he or she will have shortened the project development period and that the reused elements will have already have been tested.

The only way in which problems with custom-made system can be reduced is by greater vigilance on the part of the customer in ensuring that the developer undertakes the level of quality control that is appropriate. Although the reuse of code is in many ways sensible and cost effective, it must be done in a way that ensures it is totally suitable for the product currently under development.

HARDWARE

In these days of convergent technologies, it is increasingly difficult to determine what we mean by the term "computer hardware". Even in the recent past we would have assumed it meant the computer, input devices such as keyboard and mouse, and output devices such as the monitor or printer. Now, we have to broaden our thinking to decide whether we include the infrared or wireless connected hand-held microcomputer. Does it include the mobile phones such as the Nokia Communicator, with its own full (if somewhat miniaturized) keyboard and screen that can be used as a network browser in one mode or as the modem for a laptop in another? In general, we tend to consider the system hardware as those bits of plastic, metal, wire, printed circuits, and integrated circuits.

It is reasonable to assume that the hardware we purchased is benign and only carries out the functions for which it was designed. Unfortunately, there is increasing evidence that a piece of hardware could have been modified to carry out one or more functions not advertised. There were a number of reports, both supporting the possibility[9,10] and debunking it[11] as a hoax, that during the first Gulf War 1990 and 1991, an attempt was made to ensure that printers that had been modified were delivered to Iraq. The story contends that a shipment of printers from a French source was intercepted and fitted with modified chips by the U.S. government. The most commonly held belief is that the purpose of the modified chips was to inject a virus into the systems being used by the Iraqi Air Defense. To date, no report has ever been circulated indicating how the virus was to be activated or how the coalition forces would know that the target systems had been disabled so that they could exploit the failure.

9. *The Next World War*, James Adams, 1998.
10. Center for Strategic Studies report, "Cybercrime, Cyberterrorism, Cyberwarfare."
11. Crypt Newsletter, "A Good Year for the Gulf War Virus Hoax," 1999.

More recently, there have been a number of reports[12] that in 1982 the U.S. Central Intelligence Agency, under the presidency of Ronald Regan, attempted to sabotage the Soviet economy through the covert insertion of malicious software that caused a natural gas pipeline in Siberia to be destroyed. If this report is correct, then this is very probably the first implementation of information warfare, and it took place long before a term had been devised to describe it. It is of note that although both of these are within the bounds of possibility, neither of them has been confirmed.

An attack of this type should not be of concern to the average home user, but what if the hardware that we are all using had been modified so that on some predetermined command or at a prespecified time, they would carry out a specific operation or even cease to function altogether? Can we really be certain of the hardware we are using? I think it is reasonable to assume that in most cases nobody except governments will care, but if you look at the labels on printed circuit boards and chips located in your computer, you can see where they were made. Most Western nations do not produce their own printed circuit boards or the chips that are located on them. In the main they are fabricated in the Far East. In the event of a global conflict or a natural disaster, this leaves the Western nations vulnerable to blackmail or to market shortages. This was demonstrated in the global shortage of random access memory (i.e., RAM) that occurred as a result of the earthquake in Kobi, Japan.

FIRMWARE

Firmware has been included in this chapter because of the relationship with hardware. Firmware is best described as special-purpose modules of low level (either hexadecimal or machine code) software that coordinates the function of the hardware during normal operation. An example of this is a typical modem, in which the firmware is used to establish the modem's data rate, command set recognition, and special feature implementation.

Firmware is a type of memory chip that does not lose its memory when the power is removed or lost. This is known as *nonvolatile* memory and is classified as read-only memory (i.e., ROM) because the user, during normal operation, does not have the ability to change the information stored on it. The basic type of chip is known as a programmable read-only memory (PROM) and can be programmed by anyone who has the skill and a programming console with the

---

12. Article by D. E. Hoffman, *Washington Post* Foreign Service, 27 February 2004.

appropriate equipment. This basic PROM can only be programmed with one set of instructions, and when the code is "burned in" to the PROM it cannot be modified at a later date. To update the firmware, the PROM must be replaced with a new chip. A more versatile version of the basic PROM is the erasable programmable read-only memory (i.e., EPROM), and this type of chip can be updated through reprogramming.

The problem here is that the instruction sets that are programmed onto a chip cannot be read by the average user and can only be accessed with specific equipment, which leaves the potential open for anyone who has access to the hardware to replace the existing chip with one that carries out additional functionality. In most circumstances this would be totally undetectable.

SUMMARY

In this chapter we attempted to examine the strengths and weaknesses of the different sources of the hardware and software that we all depend on. COTS products provide the users with what they are prepared to pay for and to tolerate and normally provide a level of after sales support. The shortcomings of the products are those that the users are prepared to accept in their rush to obtain the extended capability the packages offer. The manufacturers provide us with the software in the state that most of their customers prefer—with all the security features switched off and with the package ready to run when you take it out of the box. The users who want to achieve a higher level of security normally have to reconfigure the software to turn on the security features built into the software.

The manufacturers are capable of providing the users with products that are inherently far more secure and have now started to deliver them in this state in response to the changing requirements of the users and the changing environment. If users are prepared to continue to accept delivery of software in the state that it is currently offered, which is not as fully tested as possible, the manufacturers will continue to sell it to them. The situation is improving as the environment changes and users are becoming more aware they have a responsibility to protect their systems and the infrastructure they rely on. We are now seeing the results of public pressure to influence the manufacturers, who are responding.

With open source software, programs such as the GNU public license aim to provide good quality free software, and one particular endeavor merits mention. There has been collaboration between the developers of LINUX and the U.S. National Security Agency to produce a secure version of the LINUX operating system. The very idea of a government security agency collaborating with and supporting an open source venture is a demonstration of the changing environment and would have been inconceivable in the past. There is some degree of truth in the saying that you get nothing for nothing. With few exceptions, the level of support for freeware products is normally lower, if it exists at all, but this is hardly surprising when there is no commercial gain to be made from the product.

10

Connectivity and Dependence

In this chapter we look at the effects of the use of the Internet and the increasing reliance of most organizations on an infrastructure over which they have no influence.

HISTORY OF THE INTERNET

Before it is possible to understand the effect the Internet has had, it is perhaps helpful to take a short look at its history. The way in which it has grown and the speed with which this has occurred have both had a significant effect on the infrastructure we have come, increasingly, to rely on. Some of the most significant events in the development of the Internet are as follows:

- In 1967 the first packet switched network was developed at the National Physical Laboratory in Middlesex in the United Kingdom.

- In 1969 the ARPANET was introduced in the United States.

- In 1970 the first "real" e-mail system was introduced.

- In 1972 the File Transfer Protocol (i.e., FTP) was developed.

- In 1973 the first overseas connection to ARPANET was introduced, when a connection was established via a satellite link and then land line to University College London, and then to Brighton.

- In 1991 the WorldWide Web was developed and introduced.

From its very limited use at the beginning, when the ARPANET connected just four systems together, growth has been truly phenomenal. The estimated number of users at the start of 2004, according to one of the Nua Surveys[1] Internet Surveys, is 605,600,000.

From these early beginnings and its use by the U.S. Government and academic institutions, we saw a move to home usage, and in the last 10 years we have seen a major shift in the use of the Internet. The business sector identified, initially, that the use of the Internet could reduce their costs and also, potentially, increase their market visibility. With the take-up of the Internet by the early adopters, it increasingly became essential to have a web presence to show a prof. in the market. Also, as more home users became used to the information available on the Internet, they increasingly wanted to interact with suppliers on-line and to use the facility to compare different suppliers in a way that was not previously possible. Today we have e-commerce, the electronic shopping mall, and e-business, which give us the infrastructure to enable businesses to communicate both with their suppliers and their customers and to conduct business 24 hours a day. We now also have m-commerce, which provides the ability to carry out business on the move and allows us to do such things as buying an airline ticket from a mobile phone.

The last decade of the twentieth century and early part of the twenty-first century saw the rise, the fall, and the rebirth of the dot com revolution, where entrepreneurs tried to change the buying habits of the public. Although most of these have yet to show a significant profit, there have been many high profile failures. The initial failure of the majority of the dot com companies has, in the main, been caused by a lack of confidence by the buying public, who are still not convinced of the safety of on-line monetary transactions or of the probity of the companies. As more of the conventional "bricks and mortar" companies have started to develop their web presence and as public confidence continues to rise, the amount they are prepared to spend on on-line purchases has also continued to increase.

The Internet has developed and migrated in a number of ways in its very short history. The growth in the number of users has been phenomenal. Where in the past we were used to an "industrial age" concept of time, where change took place in terms of decades and years, we now have the term "Internet time" to describe the speed that must be achieved from concept to delivery for organizations to remain competitive in today's electronic market place. The developments that have taken place have led to what is now referred to as the global information infrastructure (GII).

---

1. Nua Surveys, http://www.nua.com/surveys/analysis/index.html

THE GLOBAL INFORMATION INFRASTRUCTURE

The term "global information infrastructure" was coined to describe the result of the converging telecommunications and computing technologies. What it really highlights is the systems and networks that are now essential to the well-being and continuing development of national and global commerce and politics. The effects of this highly connected world are that we can instantly communicate with any organization or individual anywhere in the world at an affordable cost. In addition, everyone now has access to more information than ever before, and the uses and benefits that can be gained are ever increasing. Before global connectivity, the communities that we belonged to tended to be more geographic and locally based. Services that we relied on were provided by local suppliers. As globalization has increased, businesses have become increasingly international to optimize the cost effectiveness of their operations. The GII is the result of a large number of different influences, with the main ones as follows:

- The convergence of a number of technologies
- The diversity and availability of communications
- Information technology
- Information
- People

Perhaps one of the best and most useful descriptions of the GII has come from the U.S. National Institute of Standards and Technology, which describes it as follows:

Governments around the globe have come to recognize that the telecommunications, information services, and information technology sectors are not only dynamic growth sectors themselves, but are also engines for the development and economic growth through the economy . . . The United States is but one of many countries currently pursuing national initiatives to capture the promise of the Information Revolution. Our initiative shares with others an important, common objective: to ensure that the full potential benefits of advances in information and telecommunications technologies are realized for all citizens.

The GII is an outgrowth of that perspective, a vehicle for expanding the scope of these benefits on a global scale. By interconnecting local, national, regional, and global networks, the GII can increase economic growth, create jobs, and improve infrastructures. Taken as a whole, this worldwide "network of networks" will create a global information marketplace, encouraging broad-based social discourse within and amongst all countries.[2]

NATIONAL INFORMATION INFRASTRUCTURE

The national information infrastructure (NII) is the term used to describe the set of information systems and networks on which an individual nation state depends to function effectively. Individual NIIs come together to form the basis of the GII. An NII belongs to a nation state and comes under the legislative control and the protection and authority of that nation's government. If we accept that individual countries have NIIs, then those elements of that infrastructure that are essential to the well-being of the nation have been termed the critical national infrastructure (CNI).

THE INCREASED RELIANCE OF BUSINESSES ON THE ELECTRONIC INFRASTRUCTURE

As the business benefits of increased access to a global customer base and reduced costs are realized, the ability of organizations to revert to the systems that were used before they adopted the technologies is reduced. Commercial organizations have benefited hugely from the available technologies and communications. To give an example of just some of the benefits, let us look at a typical enterprise. Information technology has allowed companies to automate their stock taking and reordering system, and as a result they need to carry less stock and are more reactive to the purchasing patterns of the customers. Instead of high investment in large warehouses to hold the stock they used to need, they now have systems that are linked directly from the point of sale to their suppliers. Now instead of paper orders that took time to put together and then possibly days to reach the supplier, who would then make up the order and deliver it, as soon as the electronic point of sale equipment indicates sufficient sales to require a restock, the computers create the order and transmit it directly to the supplier. The supplier can use the same set of electronic data to create the delivery note and the invoice and to make up the manifest for the loading of the truck. The suppliers warehouse stock levels will also be decremented—all with the same set of data. The

---

2. "What is the GII?" National Institute of Standards and Technology. 1996. http://nii.nist.gov/gii/whatgii.html

downside is that having come to rely on this information being available, if it is not, very few organizations now have the staff levels or the infrastructure to manage without them (remember, part of the saving was getting rid of the warehouse space). Also, a system failure would lead to delays in orders being made and then filled, with the result that shops could end up with no stock for a period. When all the systems are working as they are supposed to, there is another issue that is mostly ignored. Most commercial organizations have a number of suppliers to which their systems are connected, and each supplier provides goods to a number of customers, so you have a customer with many suppliers connected to a supplier with many customers. The result is that neither party has any idea of just who is indirectly connected to them. Take this a step further and imagine that you are a government that is trying to identify all the systems that are critical to the national well-being (known as the CNI) and the systems to which they, in turn, are connected or are dependent on and you start to get some idea of the complexity of the problem..

CRITICAL NATIONAL INFRASTRUCTURES

The United States was the first nation to identified a CNI. Given that the United States is the most developed country in the world, it is not surprising that it should be the first to recognize its dependence on certain essential systems. Since the United States first identified that it had a CNI, a number of other countries, including the United Kingdom and most of the European countries, have also identified that they have CNIs. Unfortunately, none of them can identify what these infrastructures actually consist of or what the dependencies and interdependencies of these critical systems are. In this globally connected world with a large number of multinational companies, it is not unusual for a company that is providing critical elements of a nation's infrastructure to be owned and controlled by a company that is based in another country. Efforts are currently underway in several countries to identify the elements of their CNIs and to identify measures that can be taken to either protect these systems or to reduce their importance, for example, by building alternative systems that give diversity of supply or redundancy.

The United Kingdom established an organization known as the National Infrastructure Security Co-ordination Centre (NISCC). The role of this organization is more conservative than that of the U.S. National Information Protection Center (now part of the Department of Homeland Security) but has a similar task of providing protection for the CNI against electronic attack. The NISCC was established in 1999 with an announcement by the Right

Honourable Tom King MP that was reported in the U.K. Intelligence and Security Committee Annual Report for 1999–2000[3] that stated the following:

> . . . A single point access to the Government's Critical National Infrastructure Protection (CNIP) arrangements. The NISCC, which is largely resourced by the existing Security Service and CESG baselines, acts as an umbrella organization co-ordinating relevant activities in several departments and Agencies, including the Security Service, CESG, Cabinet Office, Home Office, MoD, DERA, DTI, and the Police.

The main role of the U.K. NISCC is the coordination of activities in support of the government's aim to achieve an effective level of protection from electronic attacks against critical systems within the United Kingdom. As has also been identified in the United States, this task requires the development of partnerships with the owners of the infrastructure and an exchange of information, particularly of material relating to threats to the systems. This poses a problem for governments, because the organizations that own the elements of the infrastructure may not be nationals of the country, and it will potentially involve the dissemination of sensitive information on threats to information systems.

The U.K. government is keen to create an electronic infrastructure that is viewed as a safe and desirable place to conduct electronic business. As businesses move toward the e-economy, the business case for information security is easy to make as it becomes clear that it is vital to successful transactions in the new environment.

REAL AND POTENTIAL BENEFITS OF THE INTERNET

The development of the Internet has come about as the result of advancements and a convergence of technologies that have been adopted in a number of areas. One of the first areas to adopt this new capability was the academic arena. The opportunity to share what had been, until then, rare research resources and knowledge and the chance to undertake collaborative studies in real time were quickly identified and taken up. Also, the opportunity to access that portion of the population that had previously been excluded as quickly taken up and developed. One disadvantage that was not initially noticed was the phenomenon that new developments in research are now published and debated over the Internet rather than in papers published in academic circles. The result of this development is that debate is now temporal, and in most cases there is no permanent

---

3. Intelligence and Security Committee Annual Report 1999-2000. HM Stationary Office.

record of the comments made as a result of the peer review. One early example of a potential benefit was the use of the radio networks in Australia to provide access to education to school-aged children who lived in areas too remote from the nearest school to be able to attend.

With the advent of the Internet, the radio school concept that worked so well in Australia has been updated to on-line distance learning programs that are global in their reach, such as the Open University in the United Kingdom and distance learning programs that are based in Thailand, now produced by many countries.

Government, non-government, and international agencies also realized the potential benefits that could be gained from the use of these resources. A number of governments have now initiated programs to allow their citizens easier and greater access to their government departments and resources. For example, in the United Kingdom there has been the Modernizing Government program, commonly known as "joined up government," that has mandated that all dealings with government departments, by citizens, should be achievable electronically by no later than 2008 and that public services will be available at any time of the day or night, every day of the year.[4]

As the numbers of users of the Internet have escalated, so has the interest of the commercial sector. The financial markets around the world can now operate and communicate with each other 24 hours a day, and as the market in one part of the world closes, another one opens. The consumer can now trade in their preferred market around the globe, whereas in the past they had no option but to trade in their local market. Examples of this are on-line stores such e-buyer, lastminute.com, and Amazon.com, the on-line bookstore. It is now as easy for a buyer in Europe or Asia to log on to a U.S. based on-line store and benefit from the U.S. prices as it is for them to order from their local store. Delivery has proven to be reliable, and the times for receipt of goods from these on-line stores are now sufficiently short to be realistic.

As the communications infrastructure has expanded and speeds have increased, it has become realistic now to achieve contact, either by voice or by data, to and from almost anywhere in the world. Along with this expansion has come the necessary redundancy so that even after a major disaster, it is almost certain that some of the communications paths will have survived. Alternatively, as was demonstrated in the wake of the 9/11 attacks, it is possible to establish alternative systems quickly and on demand.

---

4. U.K. Government White Paper, "Modernising Government." March 1999.

THE DOWNSIDE

Organizations have come to realize that with all the benefits that are gained, there are also penalties. Because of its very nature, there is no nation or organization that has overall responsibility and control of the infrastructure. In times of international tension or conflict, one or more nations involved may try to use the infrastructure itself to launch an attack on another nation. With the globalization of the infrastructure has come new risks and threats. With the vastly increased number of users has come an increased exposure to potential harm of each of the individual elements as the vulnerabilities that exist in each of the separate infrastructures are enhanced by their easy accessibility via the Internet by anyone who wishes to cause them harm. The interdependency of systems means that an attack on one element of the infrastructure may well have an impact on another that nobody had predicted or foreseen.

INTERNET CRIME

The access of the individual to the Internet was followed, very quickly, by crimes that are related to its use. With the commercialization of the Internet, the types of crime involved increased, as crime will always follow the money. When a new technology is introduced, criminals will quickly adapt to take advantage if it. Described below are a number of the types of crime that have been identified in the interconnected environment.

In a bulletin entitled *How Techno-Criminals Operate*, Carter[5] defined a number of types of computer crime, where with the computer as a target, included

- Hacking
- Denial of service attacks
- Intellectual property theft
- Spying
- Industrial espionage

In this group of crimes, most are a variant of pre-high-technical crimes, but others could not exist before the advent of the computer. Crimes such as intellectual

---

5. D. L. Carter, *How Techno-Criminals Operate*. School of Criminal Justice, Michigan State University.

property theft, spying, and industrial espionage predate the computer and have been adapted to make use of the new environment, whereas hacking and denial of service attacks rely on the use of computers.

An example of a distributed denial of service (DDoS) attack was reported in the InfoWorld News[6] in March 2003 on the Arab satellite television network Al-Jazeera. The network was reported to have suffered a second day of sustained DDoS attacks against its English and Arabic language websites. The attacks were reported to have driven the Doha, Qatar, based network off the web for a period and forced them to increase their bandwidth for the sites and upgrade security in an effort to get back online. During the attacks, the traffic rates were reported to be in excess of 200 megabits per second and up to 300 megabits per second.

The next group identified is when the computer is used as an instrument of the crime and includes

- Terrorism – Communications
- Phishing
- Fraud
- Cyber stalking
- Pornography and pedophilia

All these crimes predated the computer, but again the perpetrators of the crimes have adapted to use the new environment.

An example of this type of crime can be found in a Department of Justice press release[7] regarding the conviction of a Maryland man on charges of "cyber stalking" in April 2000. Warren Gray, a 19-year-old man from Upper Marlboro, Maryland, pleaded guilty to five counts of sending threatening e-mails to a Largo High School administrator. In addition to sending five threatening e-mails, Gray also admitted that during a 2-week period in November of the previous year, he also twice slashed the victim's car tires at Largo High School and left a hatchet in the victim's school office. The e-mails, which were placed into the federal court record, included graphic threats to kill the victim, harm his family, and to burn down his home. Gray pleaded guilty to five counts of violating Title 18, U.S. Code, Section 875, which criminalizes threats sent through the interstate wires.

---

6. P. Roberts, *Al-Jazeera Hobbled by DDOS Attack, News Site Targeted for Second Day*, Infoworld News, http://www.infoworld.com/article/ 03/03/26/HNjazeera_1.html, accessed March 26, 2003.
7. U.S. Department of Justice Press Release, *Internet "Cyber Stalker" Pleads Guilty to Federal Charges*. April 19, 2000.

The next group is where the computer is incidental to other crimes and includes

- The storage of criminal information on computers (details of planned and actual crimes, fraudulent accounts, trade secrets)

- Pornography and pedophilia

Crimes in this group do not necessarily directly involve computers. The computer or computer media has, in many cases, just replaced paper as the storage medium for the record of the crime.

The next group is crimes associated with the prevalence of computers:

- Computer theft

- Software piracy

- Copyright violations

- Counterfeit software

This group of crimes has increased in prevalence as a direct result of the massive increase in the number of home computers and their components and the difficulty in tracing them. This type of computer crime is illustrated by the case reported by the Department of Justice of a Richmond, Virginia, man who was sentenced to 70 months in prison and charged $1.7 million in restitution for illegal distribution of counterfeit Microsoft software. The report[8] stated that the U.S. Attorney's Office had worked closely with special agents with the Bureau of Immigration and Customs Enforcement and piracy investigators with Microsoft Corporation to bring about the successful prosecution of Mr. B. J. Barbot in 2004. The report stated that between early 2001 to December 3, 2002, Barbot had been engaged in the illegal distribution of counterfeit Microsoft software through multiple Internet-based stores that he had created. He had primarily distributed compact disks of counterfeit Microsoft Office Professional 2000, although he had also distributed smaller numbers of other counterfeit Microsoft products. Most of the software that he had distributed was high quality counterfeits produced and imported in Asia. The report stated that Barbot had distrib-

---

8. U.S. Department of Justice Press Release, Richmond, Virginia, *Man Sentenced to 70 Months and $1.7 Million Restitution for Illegal Distribution of Counterfeit Microsoft Software*. March 23, 2004.

uted well over $7 million retail value of counterfeit Microsoft Office Professional 2000 computer software during the relevant period.

Other examples from this group are the theft of computers. In the United Kingdom, the Ministry of Defence is reported[9] to have admitted to "losing" more nearly 600 laptops over a 5-year period. It would appear that in all, a total of 1354 government-owned computers could not be accounted for over the same period. The Ministry of Defence, which was the worst offender, had lost 594 laptops, followed by the Department of Work and Pensions, which reported 419 computers as either lost or stolen. On the other hand, in the United States the Federal Bureau of Investigation (FBI) was reported[10] to have lost hundreds of laptops and guns. An audit of the FBI revealed that it was missing hundreds of laptop computers, many of which were believed to have been stolen. FBI officials admitted that 184 computers were unaccounted for and that three of them were believed to contain sensitive material, one known to hold classified data. To make matters worse, 449 weapons, including a number of submachine guns, were missing from the Bureau's armory, of which 265 were lost and 184 stolen, according to officials.

The report went on to say that the State Department admitted that in 2000 it had "misplaced" a laptop containing highly classified information. The same report also said that agents of the United Kingdom's security services had been reported to leave laptops in tapas bars after a night of partying. The FBI losses reportedly took place over a period of 11 years and were attributed a variety of causes, including retiring agents retaining weapons and the loss of laptops as they were been transferred around the different offices that shared them.

The advances in computer and related technologies together with the dependence on them of organizations in the developed world has, in the case of some crimes, changed either the target of the crime, the perpetrator of that crime, or the vehicle used to carry out the crime. The levels of reported crime and the impact that these crimes are having in terms of financial cost has varied over time. In 1998 Rapalus[11] reported that the annual cost of computer crime has risen to $136 million, a rise of 36% on the 1997 reported figure. In 2001 the CSI/FBI Survey[12] gave the cost of cyber crime in the United States in 2000 at $378 million, a rise of nearly 300% in a period of only 2 years. However, in the 2003 report, the same organization reported that although attacks were continuing, the level of losses was down, with a total of $201,797,340, down from the

---

9. John Leyden, *Ministry of Defence loses 594 laptops*, http://www.theregister.co.uk/2003/07/30/whitehall_laptop_theft_prompts_security/, 14th January 2002.
10. J. Leyden , *FBI "Loses" Hundreds of Laptops and Guns*, http://www.theregister.co.uk/2001/07/18/fbi_loses_hundreds_of_laptops/, July 18, 2001.
11. P. Rapalus, *Issues and Trends: 1998 CSI/FBI Computer Crime and Security Survey*. Computer Security Institute.
12. FBI/CSI 2001 Survey. http://www.gocsi.com/prelea_000321.htm

peak of $455,848,000 the previous year. The survey reported that in a shift from previous years, the second-most expensive computer crime was now denial of service attacks, with an estimated cost of $65,643,300, a rise of 250% from the previous year's losses.

THE PROBLEM TODAY

Since the general public has gained both easy and affordable high speed access to the Internet, the level of computer related crime increased, and the legal systems and law enforcement bodies have struggled to develop and enforce laws that are capable of dealing with the new environment. Given the speed of change in the environment, it is not surprising that the legal system has not been able to keep pace with the changes effectively police the environment.

One of the major problems for law enforcement is the lack of international laws and the time it takes to create and ratify them. With the increase in connectivity, it is now possible for a person in one country to carry out a crime in another country without ever physically entering that country. It may also be the case that they can do this without breaking any of the laws in the country from which they carried out the crime. One of the few exceptions to this situation is the United Kingdom, where the act of undertaking a computer crime is a crime in the United Kingdom, even if the target machine is in another country.

Even within a country, there may be a problem with jurisdiction. Depending on the type of crime, different agencies may have responsibility. For example, one organization may be responsible for dealing with terrorism and another for financial crime and yet another for organized crime. The result is that law enforcement agencies may not have enough staff with the technical skills required to deal with the crimes that come within their jurisdiction. Within local police forces there is little incentive to become involved in policing the Internet for crime that does not directly concern their geographical area. Local police forces are normally under pressure from the local authority (that, in some countries, may have elected them) to address issues that affect the people who fund the police service. This often leads to them being given priorities such as addressing the local drug or prostitution problem or reducing street crime, burglary, or car theft.

Another problem increasingly encountered in the prosecution of computer crimes is that when the evidence is presented to a court, neither the judges nor the juries have sufficient technical knowledge to understand the complex details of the evidence. Even if they do understand the technical detail, computer crimes are often viewed as a victimless crime, and the penalties that are awarded are far lower than for other crimes that have a similar monetary value.

THE EFFECT OF NEW TECHNOLOGIES ON CRIME

Three main types of crime have come about as a result of new technologies: technology supported terrorism, on-line fraud, and on-line pornography.

Terrorism

It has been suspected for some time that terrorists have been using the Internet to exchange encrypted messages. Given the availability of anonymous accounts on the Internet and the potential to use proxy servers, establishing a chain of continuity for a message from the originator to the recipient is very difficult. There are now a number of documented cases where terrorist groups have used the Internet to publicize their cause to anyone who is interested, but on a global basis. One good example of this was the web presence of the Irish Republican Army in the form of the site AN PHOBLACT.[13] Another extremely effective example of the use of the Internet by a terrorist group to apply global public pressure to prevent or minimize the reaction of a government to incidents was demonstrated by the Mexican Zapatista group.[14] There is now also concern[15] that terrorist groups have the knowledge and access to the required technology they need to initiate attacks on the infrastructure of a nation and create disruption and put pressure on governments to further their causes.

On-Line Fraud

The use of the Internet by criminals to carry out frauds is well documented. The recent past has seen a new generation of crimes; phishing, the 419 scams, identity theft, and blackmail are becoming increasingly widespread. Phishing is an attack using "spoofed" e-mails and fraudulent websites designed to fool the recipient into divulging personal financial data such as credit card numbers, bank account user names and passwords, or social security numbers. By hijacking the trusted brands of well-known banks, on-line retailers, and credit card companies, phishers are able to convince around 1 in 20 of the recipients to respond to them.

The trend in this type of attack is an increasing number of incidents, with some 282 cases reported in February 2004. Some of the organizations recently affected by phishing scams include e-Bay, Citibank, Paypal, Wells Fargo, and AOL. In fact, any organization is likely to be a target.

---

13. http://www.utexas.edu/students/iig/archive/aprn/95/ July06/index.html.
14. http://flag.blackened.net/revolt/zapatista.html.
15. A. Jones, Warfare and extortion. *Journal of Financial Crime.* Volume 6, Number 2, October 1998. Henry Stewart Publications.

The 419 scams were initially all attributed to Nigeria (Nigerian 419s) but have been around for a while and do not seem to be decreasing in numbers. The example shown below would appear to have originated in the United Kingdom, and I am sure the gentleman who sent it to me will not object to it being reproduced here:

From: p_440adams@tiscali.co.uk [mailto:p_440adams@tiscali.co.uk]
Sent: Wednesday, April 07, 2004 8:51 PM
Subject: Compliments [Please Read carefully & reply soon]
MR. PETER ADAMS
United Kingdom
Dear Sir,

My name is Peter Adams, I am the credit manager in a bank here in the United Kingdom. I am contacting you of a business transfer, of a huge sum of money from a deceased account. Though I know that a transaction of this magnitude will make any one apprehensive and worried, but I am assuring you that everything has been taken care off, and all will be well at the end of the day. I decided to contact you due to the urgency of this transaction.

PROPOSITION;

I am the account officer of a foreigner named Gerald Welsh who died in an air crash along with his wife in 31st October 1999 an Egyptian airline 990 with other passengers on board. you can confirm this from the website below http://www.cnn.com/US/9911/02/egyptair990.list/index.html Since his death, none of his next-of-kin are alive to make claims for this money as his heir, because they all died in the same accident (May his soul rest in peace). We cannot release the fund from his account unless someone applies for claim as the next-of-kin to the deceased as indicated in our banking guidelines. Upon this discovery, I now seek your permission to have you stand as a next of kin to the deceased, as all documentations will be carefully worked out by me for the funds (US$9,000,000.00) to be released in your favor as the beneficiary's next of kin. It may interest you to know that we have secured from the probate an order of mandamus to locate any of the deceased beneficiaries. Please acknowledge receipt of this message in acceptance of our mutual business endeavour by furnishing me with the following information if you are interested.

1. A Beneficiary name?. In order for me to prepare the document for transfer of the funds in your name.

2. Direct Telephone and fax numbers??. For our personal contact and mutual trust in each other. Upon your acceptance I shall send you a copy of my international passport and drivers license for more confidentiality and trust.

I shall be compensating you with a million dollars ($3 Million dollars) on final conclusion of this project for your assistance, while the balance $6 million dollars shall be for me for investment purposes. If this proposal is acceptable by you, please endeavor to contact me immediately. Do not take undue advantage of the trust I have bestowed in you, I await your urgent mail to my personal email address:

Regards,

PETER ADAMS

This 419 is considerably more believable than many of the fairly primitive early versions, and without doubt even more sophisticated versions will be produced as time goes by.

The blackmail of on-line gambling establishments through the use of denial of service attacks has increased in the recent past. This is largely due to the large sums of money that are involved and the cost to the on-line casinos in lost revenue if they are "off line" for any period of time. A good example of this is illustrated by the Commission Exchange.com[16] in November 2003. The article was titled "Russian Mafia target online gambling sites" and reported that, according to law enforcement agencies, there had been a greater number of reports of organized crime gangs conducting DDoS attacks against on-line gambling and e-commerce websites to blackmail them. The article referred to attacks on the WorldPay system that had crippled its operations. The DDoS attacks were reported to have affected thousands of the on-line casinos that rely on WorldPay for their on-line transactions and payment services. The article went on to report that in a similar incident, Wordplay.com and at least six other on-line businesses had been targeted by attackers who had demanded £50,000. It is reputed that a number of organizations have actually paid up on these blackmail demands, as the cost is less than the revenue they would lose if an attack was successful, but none is admitting it. At least one crime gang has been arrested after a multinational law enforcement effort.

The passage of credit card numbers across the Internet and the storage of these and personal details on computers that are accessible from the Internet have become commonplace as trade over the Internet has increased. Unfortunately, the lack of adequate security and encryption and the failure by some on-line traders to thoroughly check purchases that are made by credit cards have led to exploitation by criminals, making the customer cautious. The reduction and detection of this type of crime remains in the hands of the commercial sector and the banking community with the need for improved verification and checking

---

16. CommissionExchange.com.

systems to improve customer confidence and ensure the continued growth of this area of business.

On-Line Pornography

The Internet has provided the ability for large numbers of people to access information and to communicate with others who have similar interests, without having to meet in person. In most cases this has been beneficial, but in cases such as the trading in pornographic material, it has increased the level of this type of crime, because the participants perceive that the risk of being caught is reduced. The Internet removes the need for an individual to visit a shop or have the "brown paper parcel" delivered to their home. Now they can easily visit a vast number of websites, anonymously, and access their preferred type of pornography. The globalization of communications and the span of the Internet also mean that material illegal in one country can be stored and accessed in another country where it is legal or where, perhaps, the law is not strictly enforced.

ACTIONS TAKEN TO ADDRESS THE PROBLEMS

As information technology has developed, the efforts of governments and law enforcement agencies have been focused on creating and implementing new laws that answer the problems that emerge. Unfortunately, international agreements and national laws, by their very nature, take a long time to bring into effect, and there is a resultant "gap" in the laws until they can be used. Detailed below are just some of the international efforts taken over the last decade to address the fast changing world of information technology:

- In 1995 the Council of Europe resolution on the lawful interception of telecommunications looked at ways of harmonizing law within Europe to facilitate the detection of computer related crime.
- In 1996 the United Nations highlighted Internet crime in relation to international terrorism, organized crime, and drug trafficking.
- In 1997 the First European Conference on Combating Violence and Pornography on the Internet convened.
- In 1997 the Group of Eight (G8) developed a strategy to defeat Internet crimes.
- In 1998 the INTERPOL initiative addressed the need for international cooperation in the fight against organized crime.

At the time of writing, some 37 separate countries[17] have enacted specific computer crime laws or are in the process of creating the relevant legislation. Other countries, such as the Philippines, have relied on existing legislation to successfully deal with computer crimes.

If the Internet is to become a safe place to carry out business in the twenty-first century, it will require the efforts and influence of the Internet community. The community are the people who see the problems first and, in most cases, have the best understanding of the implications. They are also likely to be the group with the best knowledge and equipment to deal with the problems. There are already groups on the Internet that take action against certain types of activity—at the simplest form, flaming wars—but also, where other unacceptable behavior is detected, by groups who feel strongly enough to take action. The concept of vigilantism, although dangerous, does have some merit when there is no other recourse; however, the type of person to take action may likely be a zealot who does not represent the broad spectrum of the community.

Corporate entities that have, or are likely to, suffer financial losses have already started to take action to protect their investment—to do otherwise would not be good management. They have taken action to improve the security of their systems and make crimes against them more difficult, and they have also formed associations and groups with similar interests and problems to share knowledge and prevent others from suffering from a known type of crime.

SUMMARY

The Internet has developed as the result of many separate influences, affecting governments, commerce and industry, academia, and the individual. The main issue of concern is developing a method to accurately predict what the impact on the confidentiality, availability, and integrity of the interconnected systems will be. Systems that may be critical to a nation's CNI may be owned or managed by organizations that have differing priorities for their management and use to that of the government to which they are critical. The use of the Internet by criminal interests and the lack of ownership and effective international laws or law enforcement bodies means that the identification and prosecution of "network criminals" is difficult.

---

17. The Legal Framework-Unauthorized Access to Computer Systems. Penal Legislation in 37 Countries. Stein Schjolberg. January 2001.

Section IV

The Risk Process

11

What Is Risk Assessment?

A central part of understanding risk and making sure it works for us is in being able to align it with business strategy. This involves looking outside as well as inside the organization, making the most of business opportunities but in a controlled evaluated way in the fast-moving business environment. It is also important to consider that risk can be positive in the business environment and that organizations increasingly have to take more risks in an effort to become proactive rather than reactive in their activities to achieve a competitive advantage. The information security risk manager needs to find a balance between the advances offered by information systems and the security necessary to minimize the risk to which systems, processes, and people are vulnerable.

In this chapter we consider the risk assessment process and the issues that must be addressed from a corporate perspective if risk is to be addressed holistically. We also discuss why the risks are greater now than ever before.

Security requirements come out of risk assessments, statutory and contractual requirements, business principles and objectives, and requirements for information processing that form part of an organization's culture. Generally, it is accepted that information security will address the areas of confidentiality, integrity, availability, and non-repudiation:

- Confidentiality means that information is protected from being read or copied by anyone who does not have the permission of the owner of that information.

- Integrity means that information is not deleted or altered in a way that will cause damage or disruption.

- Availability means that information should be protected so that it is not degraded or made unavailable without authorization.

- Non-repudiation means that an individual should not be able to deny having received or having sent information.

First, we need to go back to basics. Risk is defined as the possibility of a threat exploiting a vulnerability and thereby causing harm to an asset. The threat will exploit the vulnerability to compromise one of the principles detailed above. This is a generally accepted definition of risk in the information security environment, and the formula given below is one way of measuring risk:

$$\text{Risk} = \text{threat} \times \text{vulnerability} \times \text{impact (asset value)}$$

In this definition risk is a function of asset value, threat, and vulnerability. The key terms are risk, threat agent, vulnerability, and impact. Without either a threat agent, a vulnerability, or an impact, there is no risk. There must be a threat agent to exploit a vulnerability, and this exploitation must cause an impact for there to be a risk to the organization. It is easy to see how the key terms are interconnected. Organizations that are becoming more mature in their approach to risk are becoming more skillful at understanding their vulnerability and the impacts that these could cause. They are becoming better at looking inward at the organizations' processes and practices. Unfortunately, they are not so good at looking outward at their environment, and they need to be if they are to get a true measure of risk.

As we have already seen, the threats that information security must protect against are diverse. It is interesting to note that emerging technologies bring about a set of problems not typically associated with the physical domain. Although it is possible to estimate the capability and intent of an attacker, relationships are increasingly asymmetrical. A phenomenon has been noted, called the empowered small agent.[1] As technology becomes more sophisticated, it is possible for small pressure groups to wreak havoc on the systems of entire nations.

Just as threats can take many forms, so too can vulnerabilities. A vulnerability is anything that allows a threat to exploit or compromise an information system or process. Vulnerabilities can be human failings (within the user community, the organization in general, or external to the organization), weaknesses in physical security, or flaws in technology that can be exploited.

---

1. J. Macintosh, *Empowered Small Agents*. Presentation given to U.S. Department of Defense as part of U.S./U.K. military liaison, 1997.

Threat and vulnerability can be used to assess risk when they are set against the value of an information asset that needs to be secured. Assets can be physical, consist solely of information, or be functions that may enable a business process to be carried out. The value of an asset often is more than merely the capital costs or operational costs. Value can lie in the embarrassment that would be suffered by an organization if that asset was lost, the danger that would be posed to national security, or the loss of business in a commercial organization.

Companies will have different appetites for risk. Some companies will be risk averse, whereas others won't. It will depend on the culture of the organization, the success of the company, and the industry sector in which they operate. The way they prioritize confidentiality, integrity, availability, and non-repudiation also depends on these factors. The outcome of a risk that is realized, whether the purpose is to degrade information, destroy it, or deny access to it, depends on the type of information affected. The impact of a risk varies. For some organizations, for example, hospitals, degrading the quality of information could pose a threat to human life, whereas leakage of information (although unacceptable from the patient's perspective) would not necessarily have an impact of the same magnitude. Would the identification of both attacks be considered risks of equal importance? The first case seems obviously to signify a high risk. The second might be difficult to weight the same way unless it happened as a result of hacking. If it occurred, however, as a result of staff inadvertently revealing confidential information, it could be difficult to persuade hospital officials of its importance. On the other hand, any patient whose information had been revealed might legitimately see the event as a high priority risk. In either case threatening the quality of information and leaking information would likely provoke very different responses from a hospital. In the first attack a successful defeat would be achieved when there was certainty that information had been returned to its original state, whereas in the event of the second attack a successful defeat would be achieved when security holes had been plugged and appropriate action taken against the perpetrator (whether hacker or staff member). This example demonstrates that defining a risk is not straightforward, and the level of risk does not remain static within an organization but is always in flux.

Similarly, the destruction of information, perhaps designs or plans, could cause a business to fail, whereas degrading this information might not have an impact of the same magnitude and could be treated differently. For the military, denying access to information could have a devastating impact on the outcome of an engagement, whereas the impact of inadvertently revealing information could have a range of possible impacts depending on the life span of the information. As a result, the risks facing information networks would be handled differently according to the circumstances. As you can see from these examples, different information networks will have different priorities, and these should be reflected in any risk assessments undertaken.

Because there are many different approaches to understanding risk within organizations, the difficulties of aligning processes for risk management in an organization are complicated further by the usual concerns. These encompass issues of lack of time and money and scarce resources in general as well as the need for business cases for security spending. There are also company issues to consider; these can be important when a large part of a company's assets are tied up in its reputation. There may also be political considerations surrounding third party connectivity. For example, the relationship is determined by whether it is taking place upstream or downstream in the value chain. It may be easier to impose risk management techniques downstream in the value chain but harder to achieve upstream. Organizations may not put confidentiality as a priority, but they will still have to comply with legal and regulatory issues that address the area of personal data. Finally, there is a need to align business strategy with information technology—to ascertain what will work best for the organization and how to balance the two.

When risk has been measured, it must be decided whether the risk should be transferred, avoided, accepted, or managed. The transferal of risk means that it is passed on to someone else; thus, insurance is a form of transferring risk. Transferring risk may not always be possible or acceptable. Risk avoidance generally requires that the asset is not subject to human contact or that all the vulnerabilities have been mitigated. In general, this can only be achieved by not undertaking the task for which the information system was designed. It is accepted that this approach is usually impractical and that risk management should be used. By managing a risk, the risk is quantified and brought down to an acceptable level by the deployment of security techniques and tools. Thus, risk assessment is an important measure in determining the requirements and effectiveness of security.

So how can organizations help themselves? They need to understand what information security risks might look like. They could be computer network attacks, and hopefully the risk from this can be mitigated by security activities such as penetration testing and compliance with good practice such as ISO 17799. At worst they will be detected through the employment of security aware staff and the deployment of intrusion detection systems. Either way the impact of a computer network attack is mitigated by a thorough understanding of technical vulnerabilities. However, other information security risks could include media manipulation (misuse of images, brand names, and logos) and inadvertent or purposeful leakage of proprietary information (such as business plans or strategies).

Organizations need to develop comprehensive asset registers of their hardware and to understand and document the value of the information that this hardware supports. This needs to be thought through carefully and dispassionately. The information security risk manager needs to be aware that project managers frequently either overvalue their information assets (on the basis that their project is the most important in the organization) or undervalue them (to try to deflect attention from the risk manager).

The assessment of the threat level is more difficult for many organizations than the valuation of information assets, but as we saw in the last section this is a vital part of the risk assessment process. In the past, risk assessment has tried to play down the importance of the level of threat. The attitude of many risk managers was that this was something that was too difficult to tackle successfully, so it was either left out of the risk assessment process or, as is the case in many risk assessment software tools, was left to a discrete number of generic threat categories. But as we have seen, there is no reason why the mature organizations cannot carry out their own assessment of the threat using open source material and supplementing this with other forms of information where appropriate.

It has to be accepted that vulnerabilities are not always technical in origin. There are just as likely to be vulnerabilities in processes and procedures. Technical vulnerabilities can be uncovered by keeping abreast of news groups and information supplied by vendors. Alternatively, organizations can use network discovery tools to map networks and ascertain the vulnerabilities. The key to finding vulnerabilities in processes and procedures is to ensure that they are thoroughly documented and to perform walk-throughs on a regular basis.

The final issue to consider is how the assessments for asset value, threat, and vulnerability are combined to give a measure of risk, and this is dealt with in detail in Chapter 12. So what kind of risk assessment process should we put in place to address risk holistically? Well, we probably need to think again about risk assessment, where it happens in the organization and how it is communicated if we are to develop a joined-up approach. When it comes to deciding between a quantitative or qualitative approach, the popular tendency to look for quantitative data at the expense of qualitative data is often going to be fruitless. There needs to be much more work on information security metrics before we can go too far down this route. Furthermore, business risk is not always a quantitative measurement but relies heavily on qualitative data, and the risk manager needs to consider the benefits of talking about information security risk in the language of business. We return to a discussion of the relative benefits of qualitative and quantitative approaches to risk assessment in Chapter 14.

Another issue to consider when aiming to address risk holistically is whether to include physical security and personnel security with information security. This can be the first step in being able to produce a risk assessment that will appeal to a broader cross-section of roles within the organization. These three areas are frequently addressed separately despite obvious interdependencies. One other area that is frequently omitted is business continuity planning, although it seems clear this relies on the risk assessment process for physical, information, and personnel security if it is going to deliver workable plans.

A range of tools can be used to support the risk assessment process. Some of the current ones include CRAMM, COBRA, OCTAVE, and the tools produced by the Information Security Forum such as FIRM, SARA, and SPRINT. Most of these tools follow a similar method and tend to use qualitative data to produce relative measures that are useful in prioritizing risks. These tools are considered in greater detail in Chapter 16. Ultimately, however, it does not really matter which tool you use or whether you develop your own process; the risk manager should use whatever suits the organization best as long as it is a method that is transparent, repeatable, auditable, and rigorous. One of the most important aspects to consider is how risk is communicated.

These are the basic ideas that need to be considered if the risk manager is to address risk holistically, but there are still gaps that need to be filled. Tools and techniques do not tend to help address the risks from the environment in any detail because they oversimplify aspects outside the organization either at an industry, national, or international level. Allied to this is the need to understand the threat environment. As we noted earlier, this is a fundamental part of managing the risk. There is a need to be able to prove good use of resources and to produce effective business cases to ensure that security spending is approved. In addition, in a fast paced environment businesses need to be proactive. Ultimately, there is a need to think strategically about information security risk, and to achieve this a range of approaches is needed.

A further issue for the information security risk manager to consider is the way that technology is changing. Developments that are on the horizon at the current time and those that are likely to occur in the coming years are likely to have an impact on the requirements for risk assessments. Distributed systems, pervasive computing, and agent technology mean that there is likely to be a move toward more open flexible systems and networks with more connectivity and a greater need to negotiate to minimize information security risks. Examples of pervasive computing can be seen with the advances in grid technology, and this will enable many systems to interact more widely. Other examples include wearable computing devices. One of the issues with pervasive computing is the recognition that with networks interconnecting on an ad hoc flexible basis there will never be a complete understanding of the system as a whole; therefore, risk assessments need to be undertaken based on a partial and dynamic appreciation of the system. Agent-based technology allows autonomous software entities to interact with each other, and this involves some kind of negotiation in security terms for software agents to establish trust in their relationships. Overall boundaries and responsibilities will become blurred and the outcome of actions increasingly unknowable. The Cyber Trust and Crime Prevention[2] project recently completed for the Department for Trade and Industry in the United Kingdom has explored the implications of these technologies and the impact on public perceptions and expectations. A review of the conclusion of this project suggests a need to develop a lightweight risk assessment processes that can cope with changing system boundaries. These processes also need to take into account new channels for distributing information such as televisions and mobile communications. Users will need to be educated as information becomes available from many sources, and the risks involved in relying on this information or contributing to it will need mechanisms for assessing the provenance of information. Risks to privacy will occur as data are decentralized and more widely distributed. Although the Cyber Trust and Crime Prevention project primarily considered the public's role in these advances, new technology will be used by business, and the information security risk manager will need to take into account the business user and employee.

Accompanying this new technology is an increase in governance requirements, particularly with regard to transactions that cross borders. This will be particularly relevant to the information security risk manager in an international business. Overall, we are likely to see an entanglement of systems (both public and private, national and international), and it is the role of the risk manager to disentangle the information security implications of this situation.

The primary issues for the forward-thinking risk manager to consider are the scale and complexity of these new systems. Boundaries will become blurred between systems and responsibilities, and systems development will be evolutionary. Risk assessments should address aspects such as self-configuration of networks, self-healing networks, and flexible adaptation as systems connect, disconnect, and reconnect according to demand in dynamic environments.

For most organizations the value of a documented method for information security risk assessment comes from providing evidence of the decision-making

---

2. M. Botterman, J. Cave, J. P. Kahan, N. Robinson, R. Shoob, R. Thomson, and L. Valeri, *Cyber Trust and Crime Prevention: Gaining Insight from Three Different Futures.* Prepared for the Foresight Directorate, Office of Science and Technology, United Kingdom, 29 April 2004.

process that has taken place. As with threat assessment, the aim is to provide a process that is traceable and auditable, and this is particularly relevant with regard to the increased focus on corporate governance issues from the Turnbull Report in the United Kingdom to the Sarbanes Oxley Act in the United States. A simple but rigorous information security risk assessment process provides a methodical way of thinking through security issues, explaining relevant issues across the organization, and providing evidence for business cases.

What follows is a walk-through of a very basic information security risk assessment that is expanded in detail in Chapter 12.

STEP 1: IDENTIFY ASSETS

There may already be a series of asset registers in existence in the organization, and, if so, these can be used as the basis for this first step. Assets to be considered should include people, information (as opposed to the technology supporting the information), processes, and physical assets such as building and technology. The usual criteria used to assess the value of assets are as follows:

- Confidentiality: What would be the impact on the business if the confidentiality of the asset was breached?

- Integrity: What would be the impact on the business if the integrity of the asset was breached?

- Availability: What would be the impact on the business if this asset was no longer available?

- Non-repudiation: What would be the impact on the business if it could not be proved that a transaction had taken place?

This could be particularly relevant in the future with the rise of dynamic interconnected systems that we alluded to earlier in this chapter.

STEP 2: VULNERABILITY ASSESSMENT

A vulnerability assessment works from inside the organization to consider the weaknesses in the asset classes (people, processes, information, and physical assets) that could be exploited. Scenario analysis is particularly useful for considering the vulnerabilities in processes. When it comes to understanding technical vulnerabilities, there is a strong argument for using penetration testing or, failing that, network scanning tools. This gives a technical appreciation of specific hardware and software vulnerabilities in an organization and should be used to complement the information gathered through scenario analysis.

STEP 3: THREAT ASSESSMENT

Threat assessment has already been discussed in some detail in previous chapters. This is an area where the organization starts to look outside its own boundaries and to understand the threat agents or actors that choose to exploit a vulnerability. The consideration of threat agents should be broken down into the areas of motivation, capability, inhibitors, amplifiers, and catalysts.

STEP 4: RISK ASSESSMENT

This is the point where the information gathered during the last three steps is brought together. In its simplest form the output could be a probability impact grid based on an assessment of the impact (using the information from step 1) assessed against the probability or likelihood that the impact will occur, bringing together the information gathered at steps 2 and 3. A traffic light system can be used to highlight whether the risks are assessed as high (red), medium (amber), or low (green). This provides a purely qualitative and subjective assessment based on the opinions of those involved in the risk assessment mediated by the information security risk manager.

STEP 5: DEFINE COUNTERMEASURES

The final step in the iteration is to define and select suitable countermeasures to mitigate the risk. These countermeasures need to be suitable for the culture of the organization and mitigate the risk to a level where the organization is comfortable with the residual risk that remains after the implementation of countermeasures. Countermeasures may include technical measures such as an up-to-date patching policy or a new access control mechanism, but equally they should be viewed within the context of people, processes, and technology and could include changes to processes or to human resources practices.

It should be noted that the risk assessment process is iterative and needs to be kept up to date. The results should be revisited on a regular basis to see whether any significant changes take place. Defining countermeasures should not be the end of the risk assessment process. Countermeasures should be selected and a project plan drawn up to assist implementation. It is only by tracking the results of the risk assessment that it will be possible to ascertain how the risk has been mitigated. It is too often the case that organizations go through the risk assessment process only to fail to follow through the results in a thorough manner. Where it is decided that selected countermeasures will not be implemented (either due to not being appropriate or for reasons of cost or complexity) this should be documented and signed off. It is sometimes difficult to keep the momentum of the risk assessment process going right through to the end, and expectations need to be set at the beginning of the process that the risk will not be fully managed until this final stage is completed.

In its simplest form risk assessment is the probability that a threat will exploit a vulnerability and cause harm to an asset. It is generally accepted that information security risk is assessed against confidentiality, integrity, availability, and non-repudiation, and these risks could involve any type of information within the organization and should not limited to those involving technology. The risk assessment should not be considered complete until the selected countermeasures have been implemented, and selection depends on the organization's appetite for risk. By starting with a basic risk assessment framework, we can begin to understand clearly the interaction between the different elements of the risk process and the importance of appreciating what is happening beyond the organization's boundaries.

Over the coming years rapid changes in technology are likely to have an important impact on how risk assessments are completed. This is why it is important to have a good understanding of the basic principles. As the need for more flexible and dynamic risk assessments increases, it is important that information security risk managers understand the basic principles if they are to define their own assessment processes to meet changing business requirements.

12

Risk Analysis

In this chapter we outline the process and issues that need to be considered when undertaking a risk assessment. We start by examining the overarching risk assessment process as outlined in Chapter 11 before moving on to address each component. We conclude by considering how risk should be mitigated in the light of the results of the risk assessment.

The basic risk assessment process is outlined below. There are variations of this process, but in general the individual elements remain broadly the same:

- Identify and value information assets
- Define the threats
- Define the vulnerabilities
- Combine this information to assess the risk and assign a risk level
- Define countermeasures
- Mitigate risk to an acceptable level

This staged model for risk assessment can be time consuming to carry out, but it is often possible to undertake the threat assessment stage in parallel with the consideration of the vulnerabilities. It largely depends on the time and resources available for carrying out the risk assessment. Later stages may need to include input from other parts of the business. This is particularly true with the final stage where the information security risk manager should mitigate risk to an acceptable level. The definition of an acceptable level of risk should come from the business and, preferably, be endorsed at Board level.

An important point to note about the risk process is that it is iterative. Risk assessment needs to be kept current and to incorporate changes in both the internal and external environment. Furthermore, a cost-to-benefit stage is sometime inserted into the risk process after countermeasures have been defined. This is a very useful activity but one that is very difficult to carry out objectively. It should be included in the risk assessment even if it is not achieved to any depth of granularity.

The basic aims of the risk assessment process are to minimize the amount of risk to which the organization is exposed by recognizing which assets are most important to the business, identifying and anticipating threats, and closing vulnerabilities. The risk assessment process helps to prioritize activities while recognizing that not all risk can be mitigated. There will always be a residual level of risk that has to be accepted if the organization is to function successfully in the current dynamic business environment.

In this chapter we focus on walking through the risk assessment process without software support. This is a perfectly acceptable way of addressing risk assessment and is the best way to understand how a specific organization can implement its own risk assessment process before deciding on spending to roll out an off-the-shelf solution. Indeed, one of the requirements for certification to British Standard 7799(2) is that any process for risk assessment can be used as long as the organization understands the process and can justify its use.

Some organizations carry out risk assessment in two stages. The first stage considers the value of the information assets and the impact on the organization if they were compromised in some way. This first step is often carried out as a business impact assessment (BIA) to baseline those projects and initiatives that have a sufficiently high asset rating to progress to a full risk assessment. Alternatively, the baseline approach will also highlight those projects or initiatives with a relatively low impact on the organization and do not need to be subject to a full risk assessment. The danger with the BIA approach is that some projects have low BIAs when taken in isolation but could have a higher impact when interdependencies are taken into account and yet a full risk assessment will not be carried out.

The first stage of the risk assessment then is to identify the information assets. It is important to consider what type of assets we mean. Information assets obviously include information in the organization, whether it is information that is important because of intellectual property rights, customer information, or internal management information such as accounts or personnel details. Today information assets are not just held in paper form (which necessitates attention to physical security) but are more commonly held and manipulated electronically (which means that the security of the technology supporting the information has to be considered). A further vital part of an information asset is the process that surrounds it, and this could be physical, electronic, or a mixture of both. The business process that determines how an information asset is used sometimes needs to be assessed as an asset in its own right and yet this is something that is often overlooked. It is the business process that brings together all aspects of the information asset; in effect the business process determines the information asset in use.

If asset registers do not exist (and often they don't, or they are incomplete and out of date), then this first step can be addressed through a workshop or through a series of interviews. As assets are identified, they need to be valued according to their worth within the business and the impact that would be caused if they were compromised in some way.

Once the information assets are identified, linkages and dependencies that exist need to be understood. By this we mean the physical and technological infrastructure that supports how the information asset must be linked to the asset itself, the business process that determines how it is used, and the personnel who are involved.

Some organizations have up-to-date asset registers, but these do not usually show the linkages and dependencies we described. If these asset registers are up to date (and many are not), then they can provide a starting point. Other ways of generating an understanding of the information assets can be to convene a workshop to brainstorm ideas or, depending on the time and money available, a risk assessment expert can be used to gather the information. This is usually achieved by talking to individual members of staff about how they carry out their work.

The scope for identifying information assets can be quite daunting unless it is bounded in some way. It is recommended that it is initially restricted to a particular project or implementation. Alternatively, it could focus on a department or a specific product, service, or channel to market. The scope should be defined carefully at the start of the risk assessment and should suit the expectations of those who will be the customer for the final risk report.

After identifying the information assets that need to be protected, the next step is to consider the threat agents. This should be done by carrying out a full threat assessment (as outlined in previous chapters), but as a starting point the information security risk manager should identify a number of generic threat agents, for example

- Insider threat agents
- Pressure groups
- Competitors

- Terrorist groups

- Hackers

- Organized crime

Many organizations are ill-equipped to carry out a threat assessment of this nature, and it does require the use of trained analysts to get the best results. Some large organizations do have this capability, however, but those that don't often rely on official threat assessment information (the availability of this will depend on the type of organization and its role in its country's critical national infrastructure). Software tools for risk assessment often rely on a generic threat table that is broken down into a small number of broad categories. Any organization that is serious about information security risk assessment should aim to be developing and maintaining an understanding of the threat environment if it wants to carry out rigorous risk assessments.

The generic threat categories outlined above can become the focus for a threat assessment workshop or a questionnaire to help identify specific threats to the organization. It is worth spending as much time as possible in identifying these initial threat agents. These are useful for developing a full threat assessment if time allows but can also be used as part of an indicators and warnings system to identify if changes take place in the threat landscape.

The next step is to define the vulnerabilities in the information assets, from the information itself to the physical and technological infrastructure, the people, and the business processes. There are a number of ways of identifying these vulnerabilities and, once again, the choice depends on existing practice in the organization and the resources available.

It does not take long for a group of individuals to identify the main vulnerabilities in the organization's assets. One approach that works particularly well is to use a series of scenarios to structure the thinking in the workshop. These scenarios could just be in outline form, preferably based on incidents that have occurred in the past or that have had an impact on competitors. An example of such as scenario could be based on the recent "phishing"[1] attacks experienced by the finance sector and another could be a distributed denial of service attack. Nontechnical scenarios could include social engineering attacks through the human resources department.

---

1. Phishing attacks use "spoofed" e-mails and fraudulent websites designed to fool recipients into divulging personal financial data such as credit card numbers, account user names and passwords, and social security numbers (Anti-Phishing Working Group, *www.antiphishing.org*).

Penetration testing can be used to assess both physical and technological vulnerabilities. Many organizations now have, at least, six monthly penetration tests carried out by a third party, with interim tests carried out internally. These give detailed reports on the vulnerabilities that are found and should be studied carefully and incorporated into the risk assessment process. Physical penetration testing takes place less frequently but is just as valuable. In this case, individuals aim to move around the organization, gain access to information, and generally breach physical security restrictions in the organization. A further type of testing for personnel vulnerabilities can be carried out using social engineering. Here the aim is to see whether it is possible to persuade members of staff to give away passwords or company confidential information by presenting the request in a semi-legitimate manner. Each of these types of penetration testing can expose vulnerabilities in actual systems. They should be treated with some caution, however, and handled with sensitivity because they can cause staff to feel they are not trusted or are being made to look stupid, and disaffected staff can have the effect of increasing risk in the organization.

Other ways of assessing vulnerabilities include walk-throughs. This can be used to assess an information technology or physical architecture that is being proposed. With a network diagram or an architectural plan, it is possible to step through the alternative ways of compromising information assets to ascertain where the vulnerabilities lie. This is particularly useful for new projects where the technological or physical infrastructure has yet to be implemented or where a migration to a new infrastructure is under consideration.

As with threat assessment, the assessment of vulnerabilities can be done through workshop sessions with members of the business and the project team or through structured interviews and questionnaires. It depends largely on the culture of the organization and the time and money available for doing this part of the risk assessment as to which method is used. Whatever method is selected, it is necessary to make sure that the right people are involved at this stage. There should be a broad selection of roles and responsibilities and good facilitation to ensure that coverage is complete and that no one individual manages to dominate this part of the assessment. It is also important that the vulnerabilities remain at a credible level; very often in a workshop environment it is easy for groups of individuals to become carried away with thinking up new ingenious methods of exploiting their own systems. Although these may pose possible vulnerabilities, it is important to keep these issues in perspective.

So far we have focused on the information gathering part of the risk assessment process. We should now have a detailed understanding of the information assets that are important to the organization within the scope defined. We also have an understanding of the threat environment at a level of granularity that is determined by whether we have undertaken a full threat assessment or have focused solely on identifying generic threat categories. Finally, we should also understand where the vulnerabilities lie in the information assets, the physical and information technology infrastructure, the business processes, and the personnel. The next step is to combine the information to understand the level of risk.

Let us first remind ourselves of the basic definitions of risk assessment. A risk is the probability that a threat agent will exploit a vulnerability, thus causing harm to an information asset. We need both a threat agent and a vulnerability for there to be a risk to the information asset. The basic formula for assessing information security risk is as follows:

$$\text{Risk} = \text{threat} \times \text{vulnerability} \times \text{impact (asset value)}$$

Many risk assessment methods aim to be as objective as possible. This is a worthwhile aim as long as it is kept in mind that it is not possible to apply definitive metrics to the elements of the risk formula; at best, the metrics will be relative. They can provide a good quick indication of where risk is at its highest, but this is all they can offer. It is possible to have a robust transparent process without having hard and fast metrics, and this should be kept in mind so that the risk assessment does not end up claiming to offer an objective answer that it cannot substantiate.

Having said this, however, assigning metrics is a good way of being able to communicate risk across the various stakeholders in the organization. If you can say that out of a maximum score of 12 (to indicate the highest risk), risk A has a value of 10 and risk B a value of 3, then it is easy to appreciate that risk A should have a higher priority for risk mitigation than risk B. When carrying out a risk assessment, it is often necessary to add qualifying statements to judgments that have been made, because this provides a further reason for ensuring that there is no confusion over what the metrics represent. We are merely assigning numbers to the risk formula to show the relative levels of risk present in the organization.

Although many software tools and methods purport to offer a more quantitative approach to measuring risk, they should be approached with some caution, and the information security risk manager needs to question whether the solutions offered are in fact as rigorous and objective as they portray themselves. This is not to say that there are not risk assessment methods in place in other fields that offer a quantitative approach that is well developed; the field of corporate finance has a number of techniques for measuring risk that are well established but perhaps not easily transferable into the information security arena. Different types of risk assessment processes are discussed in more detail in Chapter 16.

Without software support the simplest way to assess which assets are most at risk is to use a two by two matrix, such as the one shown at Figure 12.1. The matrix should have threat and vulnerability as its axes so that the various assets that have been assessed can be plotted on a simple high/low scale. The value of an asset can be depicted by size or color. For example, the matrix in Figure 12.1 shows five information assets (labeled A, B, C, D, and E); these are mapped against threat and vulnerability ratings (from High to Low). We can see that assets C and D have both high vulnerability and high threat ratings. Asset D is shown larger than asset C, however, indicating that asset D is of a higher value to the organization. To flesh out this example, we could imagine asset C being personnel records and asset D being the processes, technology, and information surrounding client payment details. The matrix shows that the risk to asset D is greater than the risk to asset C. As a result, asset D should receive a high priority for risk mitigation activity. If we look at the other assets on this diagram, we can see that asset E has a high level of vulnerability but a low level of threat. Here we need to remember the formula for risk management. If there is not a credible threat to exploit a vulnerability, then there is a relatively low level of risk. Accordingly, risk mitigation for asset E is not a high priority. The final assets are A and B. These are both in the low vulnerability and low threat category; however, asset B not only has a slightly greater vulnerability and threat rating than asset A but it is also larger (meaning that it is of greater value to the organization).

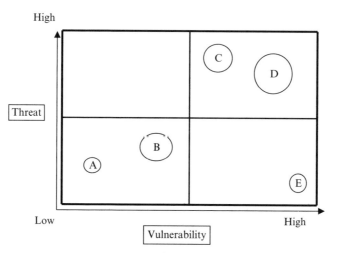

Figure 12.1. *Risk assessment matrix.*

The prioritization of the risks shown in the matrix appears to be in the order of asset D, C, B, A, E. The matrix also shows, however, that this simple assessment may require some more complex judgments to be made. For example, should asset A be a higher priority than asset E? Asset A is slightly smaller (but not much), and although asset E has a low threat rating it is very vulnerable, and the threat rating could change very rapidly. It is at this point that we begin to recognize the subjective nature of risk assessment. The assessment of risk will not be binary but will depend on a range of factors (many of them ill defined) in a rapidly changing environment.

A slightly different way of depicting risk is through a probability/impact grid. This is basically the same as the matrix that was used previously but plots probability of the risk occurring against impact. In our opinion this only serves to hide the subjectivity of the risk assessment process. The probability/impact grid suggests that the probability of the risk occurring is knowable, and this really is not the case. The best estimate of probability that we can make is based on the levels of threat and vulnerability, and in our opinion it is better to be clear about this from the start.

A further way of visualizing risk is through the volume of a risk cube as shown in Figure 12.2. The large cube shows the volume of risk at the time of the assessment. It is measured by combining impact, threat, and vulnerability. The smaller cube depicts the amount of risk exposure that remains after mitigation strategies have been put in place. Although this is a useful way for visualizing the effects of the risk process, understanding how the risk formula works, and conveying the achievements of risk assessment it still suggests that impact, threat, and vulnerability can be measured to produce a risk cube of a certain volume.

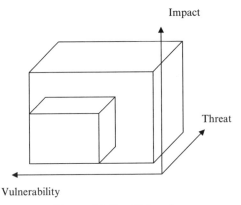

Figure 12.2. *Risk cube.*

The tension between accepting a qualitative measurement for risk and achieving a quantitative result is addressed fully in Chapter 14.

The process of combining asset value (or impact), threat, and vulnerability gives us our level of risk. It is intuitive to prioritize the risks because this process is taking place, but ranking the various risks also gives rise to some unanswered questions and for the need to make explanations and qualifications. As we saw in the example of the matrix, risk assessment is not a binary activity and there needs to be space to capture the questions and the information that explain the prioritization of risks. This is an important aspect of the risk assessment and should not be avoided just because it means that the risk process is not as tidy as we might have hoped. This part of the risk assessment often highlights dependencies in processes, people, and systems not been previously understood.

The best way to capture this information is probably through the inclusion of a table of prioritized risks underneath the matrix, or a probability/impact grid (or whatever other tool has been chosen). It may be that senior managers only wish to see the diagrammatic representation of the risks, but those responsible for making budgetary decisions and for implementing countermeasures need to see the details of the decision-making process.

Risk communication is an important part of the whole process. It may be the case that the diagrammatic representation of risk can also separate out personnel, process, and technical risks so that they can be easily assigned to the relevant departments for mitigation. This could be achieved quite simply through the use of different colors or shapes.

The next step is to assign countermeasures to the risks. These are measures that mitigate the risk to a level that is acceptable within the organization. In some respects the level of acceptable risk is a subjective judgment to be made by the Board (except, perhaps, where it is decided by legal and regulatory requirements). The level of risk that is acceptable to the Board is necessarily defined at a high level. It is the responsibility of the different layers of the risk management hierarchy to understand how this level of risk manifests itself across the organization for each of the risks that are identified.

If possible, a range of countermeasures should be defined for each risk. These can be gathered from a workshop session or by the information security risk manager in isolation. The aim should be to put together a range of alternative countermeasures with some being technical, some procedural, and some physical. The countermeasures should have a range of attributes that ensure they either deter, protect, detect, or react to a security incident. "Deter" is about having a track record and being seen to be acting appropriately and securely (an example of this could be if the organization is certified to a particular information security standard and prominently displays this certification to deter attackers). If this is convincing, then many potential attackers will move on to an organization that looks as if it is easier to attack. "Protect" is about knowing and understanding the information security requirements within the organization and the vulnerabilities and threats that are faced. "Detect" means that if an information security breach occurs, then it is discovered quickly (from a technical perspective this could be through the use of an intrusion detection system). "React" means that in the case of a security breach, the organization has processes in place (both technical and procedural) to ensure that the risk exposure is capped as quickly as possible after an incident.

From the selection of countermeasures defined for each risk, it is then possible to ascertain which will work best in the organization (for example, be most acceptable to staff, have the least impact on working practices) and which will bring about the most benefit for the least cost. This latter determinant for selecting countermeasures is often difficult to achieve in practice, but where more than one countermeasure is put forward this should be considered. In the past it has often been the case that technical countermeasures were considered before all others, primarily because they were easy to understand and implement for the technical staff that often carried out the risk assessments. It is the case now that these so-called point solutions have been recognized as not always offering a good return on investment, and many organizations are now moving to consider countermeasures from a more holistic point of view. An example of this could be that instead of implementing more technical security to counter an internal threat to confidentiality, an organization may find it is easier to implement physical security measures (such as biometric scanners on doors) or to tighten up procedural measures such as implementing thorough background checks for new employees.

When countermeasures have been defined and selected, a project plan should be drawn up to ensure they are implemented within a reasonable time frame. Each countermeasure should be signed off by the person responsible for its implementation. In some organizations it is individual business managers and not the information security risk manager who has the final say on whether a countermeasure is implemented or not. In these cases it is useful for the information security risk manager to get the business manager to sign off the level of risk to which he or she is exposed if he or she refuses to implement a countermeasure. This ensures that the audit trail from the risk assessment process leads back to the accountable business manager to ensure proper responsibility is taken for the risks faced by his or her department or project. Where this measure of risk can be given a monetary value, this too should be included. This ensures visibility and traceability across the risk assessment process.

When the countermeasures have been implemented, this marks the end of this particular iteration of the risk assessment process. The important point to remember is that risk assessment needs to be kept current, and this can be achieved by revisiting the initial risk report and examining issues that have changed (whether they are impacts, threats, or vulnerabilities) or whether any of the supporting information and questions that surrounded the decision-making process are different.

We have seen from this examination of the risk assessment process that many areas cannot be pinned down to a definitive answer or measurement. This is an important facet of the risk assessment process in the current business environment. Risk assessments are only useful where uncertainty and ambiguity are accepted and not ignored. These issues are addressed further in Section V.

13

Who Is Responsible?

In this chapter we introduce the role of risk managers and identify the level within the organization at which they must operate to be effective. It also explores the various stakeholders in the organization who need to be taken into account when developing the risk assessment process. First, we consider what the role of the information security risk manager involves in practice and then suggest areas were it should perhaps evolve before examining the organizational hierarchy and the relationships that need to be built.

The role of the risk manager depends largely on the nature of the organization, the sector in which it operates, and whether there is already an established risk function. The finance sector, for example, traditionally has a well-established risk function. This has primarily been focused on credit risk, but more recently it is starting to take into account operational risk (as a result of regulatory requirements such as Basle II). In organizations such as this, where a risk management function traditionally exists, the role of the information security risk manager can become confused. This is usually because information security risk management is a relatively new area (particular when compared with issues such as credit risk). As the role of the information security risk manager first evolved, it tended to focus on technical risk (as did the risk assessment process itself). The information security risk manager was often a technical expert and for this reason would be based in the IT department reporting through the line management structure already in place. What we often see now is that as IT security risk has evolved to become information security risk, the risk manager is still based in the IT department but may now have a dual reporting line through the IT department and through a broader organizational risk function (in the finance sector this is often the finance director, but now it may also be a risk director). It is often the case that Board responsibility for risk is swept up under the area of finance rather than standing on its own. This is not unusual and is commonly the case with physical security. This may change in the future with the continuing corporate governance pressures; nevertheless, at the current time information security risk managers need to build their own profile so they ensure they can engage with the Board.

In those organizations that are not as mature, the risk manager can sometimes still be located further down the management hierarchy embedded within the audit department or the IT department. In this case the focus of the role usually is still on technical risk in isolation from the broader requirements of the business; in many instances risk is only one aspect of the role. Where risk is only one of many responsibilities it is often given only cursory examination, because the holder of the post may have their efforts diluted on a number of tasks. In this scenario, with limited time available to the practitioner, it often occurs that an established software tool for carrying out risk assessment is imposed with little flexibility. This offers a correspondingly low level of overall benefit within the organization. This is a very narrow vision of the role of the information security risk manager, and although it still exists in too many organizations, it does not normally achieve the required outcome.

Very often the responsibility for risk assessment is divided between the physical security, personnel security, and IT security functions, which can cause confusion and division and does not foster a holistic approach to tackling risk. In these circumstances it is probably most beneficial for one individual to take the role of building relationships between these functions. There is often plenty of scope for this type of initiative because these different areas of security traditionally do not work well together. It is not an easy task to act as a conduit between these areas, but information security is probably the element that most obviously ties them together. When we consider the physical security of information, information in the electronic environment, the security of personnel, and their data, the common theme is the information element. If the information security risk manager wishes to raise his or her profile and to develop a mature business-focused role, then taking on the task of acting as the link between the different elements of security and with the rest of the business is probably worthwhile and may well be the best way to achieve it.

At the most senior level there will usually be a Board member who has responsibility for corporate risk, among other things. Different types of risk managers may then be spread throughout the organization, usually one in audit with a corporate governance role, one for health and safety risk, one for financial risk, and, hopefully, one for information security risk. The information security risk manager should then have access to either a dedicated or virtual team of individuals who can carry out information security risk assessments. The size and structure of this team will be determined by the organization, its size, and the sector in which it operates. These virtual team members usually sit within the security function of the organization. This team should have an outward focus from wherever they sit to foster relationships across the breadth of the organization. This can work well where there are good channels of communication.

On occasion, security is still centralized within an organization and all the staff responsible for information security sit together physically. This has the benefit of ensuring a common approach to information security risk but makes it difficult to devolve this across a large organization (in particular if the organization has an international profile). Often in large international companies this team is distributed globally, with security officers present in various countries reporting into a global security function at the center. This obviously spreads the workload and makes the implementation of security initiatives more efficient, but it is much harder for the information security risk manager to control. It is often the case that local security officers "go native" and implement their own solutions according to the environment in which they operate. This structure makes it much harder to ensure that a common approach is implemented.

Ideally, risk should be represented at the Board level within organizations, and in many cases this does happen, particularly where an organization feels compelled to do so to satisfy corporate governance requirements. It often comes under the remit of the finance director, but more often there is a group risk director. It is important to keep in mind that information security risk is only one element of the finance director's/group risk director's responsibilities. This role usually relies on senior management support to deliver in this area. The senior manager's role is often that of chief information security officer or head of security. It should be at this level that the method and processes for carrying out information security risk assessments are defined. In this way approaches to risk assessment across the organization can be aligned by the group risk director (or the person fulfilling this function within the business). A number of information security roles usually fall below the level of chief information security officer. Many of these are technical roles, and although these are vital, it is also necessary for security to maintain a link to the business and to have a small number of roles that can move quite flexibly between the technical concerns of information security and the broader concerns of business risk. It is only in this way that the important link between information security risk and the business can be maintained.

At each stage in the management chain it is important to have people in these posts who are good communicators and can understand the technical implications but balance these within the broader environment of business requirements. Where risk assessment processes tend to break down is where the outputs cannot easily be appreciated in terms of their impact on the business.

A further danger is where information security risk management is not afforded its proper place at the Board level, usually because it is portrayed as being too technical, or it becomes diluted to the point where the results do not mean anything in an attempt to gather the different types of organizational risk assessment into one single report. These are difficult issues for the risk manager to overcome, because she or he usually operates at the level just below the chief information security officer and so has a limited sphere of influence.

The best way forward is often for the risk manager to look sideways at his or her peers across other functions and to ensure that strong links are built with other stakeholders in the organization. The obvious relationships should be with other security teams that may exist (for example, where physical security sits separately from information security). It is often the case with physical security that this function has a more holistic approach to risk assessment and they are often the ones that successfully tackle the issue of threat assessment in a more rigorous way. This seems to be because many physical security managers have either an armed forces or police background where the concept of threat assessment as described in earlier chapters has a certain level of maturity.

Another obvious group of stakeholders is the IT department itself. Sometimes IT and information security are part of the same overarching group, but in large organizations they often operate separately. Information security is sometimes treated with suspicion by the IT department because it is perceived to be a nuisance factor, an issue that threatens technical developments and hinders the working practices believed to be important in delivering the functionality required. The information security risk manager may have to work hard to build a strong relationship with the IT department and can only do this by demonstrating the value that comes from helping explain technical issues in business terms. The benefit of this is that the IT department becomes more closely integrated with the rest of the business, with the information security risk manager being an effective conduit for this relationship.

As with physical security, the human resources (HR) department is another group with which the information security risk manager could form a profitable relationship. Information security is an important aspect to the functioning of the HR department, particularly with privacy and data protection issues being high profile issues. The information security risk manager can help assess processes and procedures for the protection of personnel records. Many HR departments are still relatively lax in the area of the procedures that they adhere to in following up references and undertaking more detailed background checks on new and potential members of staff. This is often an issue of time and resources but also because communications between HR and the rest of the business are often poor. As is usually the way, it is best to involve HR at an early stage in any project that will involve assessing the security of personnel. These should all be issues that are the legitimate concerns of the information security risk manager. The issue of personnel security extends beyond the policies for deserters and joiners to consideration of the varying requirements (both from a contractual and security perspective) for specific roles in the organization. Furthermore, it is often necessary to address the information security risks surrounding senior management teams in high profile organizations; this extends the information security risk manager's role into the realm of physical security as the two areas overlap with the risk to individual personnel and their families. For example, if the personal information about the senior management team is not adequately protected, there may be a need to use physical security countermeasures so that it may be necessary for the information security risk manager to consider close protection as a risk mitigation strategy.

The risk function within an organization often sits within the scope of the finance director, particularly in the finance sector where risk has traditionally focused on credit risk. In many ways there should be a natural affinity between information security risk and the finance department if only because corporate finance has a range of well-established ways for looking at risk. As yet there has only been limited exploration of using such techniques in the information environment, and it may be that these techniques do not transfer well. Even so, the basic concepts and concerns are very similar. More obvious reasons for a strong relationship between the information security risk manager and the finance department stem from the fact that information security risk assessment should be used as the basis for business cases for security spending, providing evidence to support budgetary requests. Furthermore, the risk assessment process should provide evidence that money is being saved in the organization by using the appropriate security measures and thus having to spend less on incident management. For these reasons the information security risk manager should ensure that the finance director understands and supports the risk assessment process that is used in the organization and that the results of assessments are routinely required for business cases for security spending.

A less likely group of stakeholders could also be found in the marketing or public relations department. Because organizations have started to develop a mature security function, they are increasingly better at understanding the vulnerabilities inside the organizational boundaries but are still poor at looking beyond the organization and examining the threats from the environment in which they are operating. It is often part of the role of the marketing or public relations department to ensure that environmental (or boundary) scanning takes place. This means that they have an awareness of activities, opinions, and issues taking place in the external environment that may affect the organization. In some businesses this is undertaken by the department responsible for developing business strategy. Wherever this activity takes place it means individuals within the organization perform what is basically open source intelligence analysis. The focus is usually on the market and competitors, but some organizations (particularly in the pharmaceutical and oil industries) also monitor pressure groups and political groups that may affect them. Intelligence information of this kind can greatly support the production of threat assessment information either through provision of developed intelligence or through access to data feeds. There are few organizations that use intelligence analysts, but many use business and market analysts who possess the same basic skills and who could be a valuable resource for the information security risk manager.

The benefits of the information security risk manager forming cross-organizational relationships are numerous. The primary benefit has to be that information security is promulgated throughout the organization, and this is the first step in developing an information security culture in an organization. Second, as greater sections of the organization perceive the benefits of information security risk management, the easier it is for the risk manager to get support at higher levels in the organization. If the role is defined and implemented carefully, the information security risk manager can become the champion of security within the organization. This role can be valued for its ability to bring together all elements of security, to set them within the business context, and to communicate information security risk effectively to the business and to the IT department.

Section V

Tools and Types of Risk Assessment

14

Qualitative and Quantitative Risk Assessment

In this chapter we outline the difference between qualitative and quantitative risk assessments and suggest why one approach may be better in some circumstances than another. It should be noted that here we do not examine either quantitative or qualitative data analysis approaches in detail. This is beyond the scope of this book; however, the risk manager should develop sufficient background knowledge from this overview to research this area further if necessary.

It is widely recognized that qualitative data analysis often reveals a new understanding of a situation—if the analysis is undertaken with experience and sensitivity. By qualitative data analysis we mean the relatively unstructured approach taken during the interviews and workshops often used as the start of the risk assessment process. The analysis of the information gathered means that the review can avoid reducing information to numbers before it is really necessary. After all, numbers are no substitute for the risk manager's understanding of the interviewee or workshop participant, the circumstance of the interview, and the many other small pieces of information that do not mean anything when taken separately but aggregate to give a detailed picture of risk within the organization.

This type of qualitative data analysis is similar to, and can benefit from the principles of, discourse analysis. The information given to a risk manager is encapsulated in language, but this language is always "in use." By this we mean language is not used innocently; it depends on where we are and to whom we are talking, among other factors. The language used by an individual can shed light on values, attitudes, and motivations. For example, the interviewee may be wary of talking to the risk manager and restrict his or her comments accordingly or tone down any criticisms depending on their position in the organization.

Alternatively, someone who is perceived to be in a position of authority may create noise to divert attention from something they do not wish to reveal.

This type of data analysis is often criticized for being too subjective. It is highly dependent on the judgment and ability of the risk manager, but these methods of data analysis and discourse analysis are already widely used and accepted in other professions such as medicine and the law. We suggest that an eagerness to place IT and IT security firmly within the family of the "hard" sciences has done a disservice to those of us who work at the "soft" end of technology. Risk assessment now tends to be moving toward the soft end of technology. Remember, at the end of the day it is the people who are both the problem and the solution. In general, this past focus on the hard science aspects of information security has meant that we have tended to see IT security as a "closed" system, one that is knowable and understandable.

Organizations have tended to treat information security in isolation and have lost sight of the fact that unless it is integrated with the physical procedural and personnel security measures that are taken, it cannot be effective. What we have failed to do until quite recently is appreciate the people and process aspect of security. These are just as important, if not more so, than the technology in ensuring that security is maintained. The introduction of people and processes into our considerations of information security risk means that the picture becomes much more complex. We have to recognize that what we are now looking at are complex "open" systems that interact in different often seemingly irrational ways. With qualitative data analysis we aim to keep the picture of risk as rich as possible for as long as possible. After all, what do the numbers generated by risk assessment software actually mean? Few risk managers have carried out a risk assessment that highlighted a risk that had not been made apparent from the early stages of the risk review. We are not suggesting that we should not progress through to the metrics stage of quantitative data analysis, only that it should be recognized for what it is and not built up beyond that which it can legitimately demonstrate.

Qualitative data analysis can be linked, however, with quantitative analysis. Quantitative data analysis should aim to produce reliable statistical evidence, and we have to accept that in general terms this is something that we have not been able to do in the field of information security risk. The strength of quantitative analysis is also its weakness because questions and answers must be tightly controlled. This limits the breadth of response that is possible and, of necessity, limits the complexity of the risk picture. As we shall see in Chapter 17, this may have been an acceptable approach as information security risk assessment came into being, but it is unlikely to be acceptable with the strategic initiatives that we can see on the horizon.

Of course, for many risk managers qualitative data analysis is something they will probably need to learn about, and many may find it a daunting challenge. Qualitative data analysis aims to look at human motivations, thoughts, feelings, and attitudes. This type of analysis should not been seen as a competitor to quantitative analysis. The decision of which to use should depend on what you are attempting to achieve. One point we believe important, however, is that either method should be undertaken with rigor. Many risk assessment processes may look as if they take a quantitative approach but in fact there is often little rigor underpinning the methods. This is an attribute of many off-the-shelf risk assessment tools and is a factor that we touched on in our discussion of risk assessment tools.

Qualitative data analysis is useful for handling complex subject areas, and it seems that risk assessment will become increasingly complicated with the development of new technologies and the introduction of new business models and strategies for achieving competitive advantage. It is often easier to communicate qualitative data analysis to a wider audience because of the ability to describe the picture of risk in some detail with real examples. The downside is that this can also be difficult to reduce to the type of short briefing paper that the Board may want on information security risk. The risk manager may need to find a way to manage this tension, and this is why it is often necessary to introduce a pseudo-quantitative element to the risk assessment process. This is satisfactory if care is taken to highlight the point that the purpose of this part of the risk assessment is primarily to communicate findings quickly and will not give definitive answers. In general, the warning that is usually given is that quantitative measurements are given to provide relative levels of risk. To this end numbers are often used in place of rankings; therefore, the number 15, 10, and 5 could be used in place of high, medium, and low. Although the use of these numbers does not add anything to our knowledge of the rankings of these risks, there is a perception that the risks are more clearly defined.

Qualitative data analysis depends to a large extent on the skill of the interviewer or data gatherer. It is not something to be attempted lightly; training is needed to support the interviewing process and the subsequent data analysis. It may also be difficult to separate the evidence from the interpretation, and this should be undertaken with care.

Quantitative data analysis often uses methods such as Bayesian networks and Monte Carlo simulations. Bayesian networks (sometimes also called causal models) determine the probability of an event happening under circumstances where nothing is known except that the event occurred a certain number of times and failed to occur a certain number of other times. Monte Carlo simulations imitate a real-life situation where values are randomly generated for uncertain variables over and over to simulate a model. There are many other statistical methods that measure risk. These are particularly well used in the finance sector where such techniques are used to assess credit or insurance risk. Unfortunately, they have not always transferred quite as easily to the field of information security risk.

One of the problems in using these mathematical techniques is that they often require specialized software and knowledge of quantitative methods. They can also be relatively difficult to explain to other stakeholders. It is often the case that the necessary skills and resources to use these techniques are not easily found in most organizations, although they do exist in the finance sector. Indeed, some of these quantitative techniques are likely to cross over into the field of operational risk as methods are developed that can address both credit risk and the broader category of operational risk.

Qualitative and quantitative data analysis is definitely an area where the information security risk manager should develop a working knowledge even if only to recognize when a risk assessment method lacks rigor. It is possible to combine elements of quantitative and qualitative data analysis, and this is the way forward for information security risk assessment. In our opinion, however, it should be a balance of the two rather than a reliance on one or the other. Information security is still a dynamic and rapidly emerging field, and by limiting approaches we could easily miss identifying important risks.

Whether qualitative or quantitative data analysis techniques are used in the risk assessment process, they should be implemented with rigor by the information security risk manager and should be recognizable as having this attribute if they are part of an off-the-shelf product. The information security risk manager should have sufficient knowledge to ask the necessary questions to assess the techniques used. It is unlikely that information security risk managers will be an expert, and they should not have to be. However, they should be able to discuss the subject area with experts to make an informed decision about which methods are most suitable for use in the organization. Finally, we caution against the use of quantitative methods over qualitative methods. It may seem like a less subjective option and therefore easier to justify, but unless implemented carefully it is easy to simplify the risk picture to the point where it yields very little value. Qualitative data analysis helps to develop a rich picture of risk in the organization, and, as we see in later chapters, this could be very important with the emergence of new technologies and new business strategies.

15

Policies, Procedures, Plans, and Processes of Risk Management

In this chapter we explain and provide examples of how to identify and describe risk management duties, responsibilities, processes, plans, policies, procedures, and projects. We provide a high level overview of these issues. This overview cannot be either all encompassing or complete, because the requirements of each organization vary and the way in which they address them is decided on the basis of the level of risk tolerance that the organization has and as the understanding of the situation develops.

Before we start to look at the individual elements that come together within an organization to allow us to undertake risk management, it is worth reminding ourselves of the types of action that can be taken to mitigate risk. For convenience these are conventionally described in four areas, where risk can be avoided, reduced, accepted, or transferred. Figure 15.1 shows the relationship between the different aspects of risk treatment and gives an indication of the type of measure that normally is taken against different types of risk.

DUTIES AND RESPONSIBILITIES

At all times, when considering risk management, it is important to bear in mind the respective duties and responsibilities of those who are involved in the process. After all, if you haven't got this fundamental aspect right, what chance do you have of developing an infrastructure that you can have confidence in? In most organizations, the development of the risk management infrastructure is probably organic or as the result of a sudden realization that such an infrastructure is necessary. It is rare that the infrastructure is developed from the ideal position of a planned implementation brought about as the result of a considered decision derived from the business plan. Whatever the starting point, in most organizations it involves a

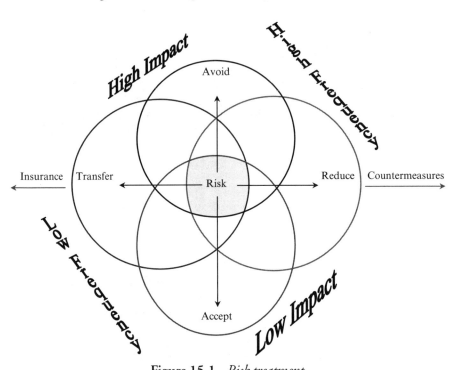

Figure 15.1. *Risk treatment.*

range of individuals from different areas of the business. If their duties and responsibilities are not thought out and clearly defined and documented, the only thing that can result is confusion and conflict. Although the decision as to which individual within an organization will undertake specific duties depends on the size and structure of the organization and also the skills and strengths of the individuals involved, some of the main duties and responsibilities are detailed below. It should always be remembered that for the management of risk to be effectively addressed, it will involve the support of all members of staff from the chairman down to the lowliest laborer.

The Board

The Board is ultimately responsible and accountable for management of all aspects of the business and consequently for ensuring that the risk management and treatment that is in place is adequate. The duties of the Board may, for example, include the following:

- Defining the business objectives and requirements: Risk management is an aspect of the business and must be undertaken within the framework of the overall business.

- Defining the risk tolerance of the business: All organizations have different levels of risk tolerance and it is one of the responsibilities of the Board to determine the acceptable level of risk.

- Identification and allocation of resources: The Board has overall control and responsibility for the organization and has responsibility for determining the appropriate personnel and resources to address risk.

- Acting as the sponsor and champion for risk management: The Board must be seen to be driving and supporting the risk management process. It is helpful, from the point of view of the staff, to have a member of the Board act as the champion for the activity. Also by having a member of the Board directly involved in the process, it ensures that representation and communication of the issues at Board level is improved.

- Developing and communicating the organization's policy for risk management: The Board is responsible for defining all organizational policy, and the risk management policy must be developed and in line with other policies.

- Provide direction: The Board must take the lead if the risk management process is to be successful. It is only with leadership and direction from the Board that the process can be effective.

Risk Manager

This individual has overall responsibility for the success of the whole process and is responsible, ultimately, for the level of recommended risk the business accepts and is mitigated in one way or another. Remember that at the end of the day, you can only treat risk in one of four ways: you can avoid it through business planning to avoid the risk, you can reduce it through the application of countermeasures, you can transfer it through actions such as insurance or by contract, or you can accept it. It is worth repeating that you can never eliminate all risk; all you can do is manage it to a level that is acceptable.

The duties of the risk manager normally include the following:

- Developing a risk management environment: The risk manager needs to ensure all aspects of the approach to risk management are addressed and that the infrastructure is developed to help the organization become risk aware.

- The whole risk management process: This includes all phases from the identification of risks through the assessment of risk to the monitoring and control/mitigation of the risk.

- Communications: Because this activity covers all areas and levels of the organization, a good level of communications is essential. It is necessary to communicate the objectives of the exercise and its importance to the organization. The communication skills are also required to generate an atmosphere of cooperation between the business unit managers, to communicate the results of the risk management process, and to ensure that the controlling/mitigating actions are implemented. The risk manager should communicate regularly with the Board to ensure they are informed with regard to progress, significant issues and developments, and the level of residual risk.

- Coordination: As described above, with the activity affecting all areas and levels of the business and involving a range of activities, the coordination of activities is essential if the investment and the process itself is to be effective.

- Facilitation: The collection of information from a range of resources requires a variety of techniques to ensure that the most suitable information is collected. To achieve this it may be necessary to facilitate a range of meetings, workshops, and surveys. It is also necessary for the risk manager to facilitate the introduction and implementation of the risk control/mitigation measures, because this potentially requires actions to be taken across a number of business units.

Business Unit Managers

These managers ensure that, within their areas of responsibility, the procedures that have been identified in the policy are adhered to. They have responsibility for the operational risks in their areas, including their identification, assessment, and mitigation. They also have a responsibility to keep the Board and their nominees informed of developing risks, because they are closer to the situation and should be well placed to recognize problems at an early point. Within each business unit, the manager is responsible for ensuring that the staff understands their risk management responsibilities and the levels of risk that the members of staff are allowed to take.

Employees in Posts of Core Functions

These employees include human resources, auditors, finance department, and a host of others who hold positions that may cross the business unit boundaries. These are members of staff that can provide a useful insight into the differences between the operation of the individual business units and can identify issues that may not be apparent within an individual business unit. The duties of these employees include the identification of personnel with appropriate skills to undertake key risk management processes and to support and advise management in their specializations.

The Staff

The staff of an organization, if they are aware of the issues and have "bought into" the process, potentially have a huge impact on the detection of incidents and whether the measures being taken to mitigate the risk are being implemented and are actually effective.

PROCESSES

A range of processes need to be developed or adopted to address the requirements of the organization. Some of the processes that are almost certainly required include the following:

- Issue identification and context setting: A preliminary step is to identify the issues that need to be addressed and to provide some type of context to enable people to understand why they are important and the priority they should be addressed in. This process includes activities such as a stakeholder analysis and the definition of the problems and their scope and context.

- Assess current risk management capacity: A preliminary step is an evaluation of the current capability of the organization for risk management. After all, it may be that the Board of the organization decides, in light of the infrastructure already in place, there is no requirement for further action. In a mature environment, this may be a rational, if brave, decision.

- Perform internal and external environmental scans: This is necessary to understand the state of the organization in terms of the type and source of risks. The internal scan provides information on existing policies and awareness of risk within the organization, whereas the external scan provides information on the state of the environment and the position and attitude of key external stakeholders and partners.

- Key risk area identification and assessment: Once the internal and external scans have been completed, it is necessary to analyze the context and results to understand the types or risk identified and any local or organization-wide issues that are relevant. A sample of the type of template that might be used to catalogue identified risks is shown in Figure 15.2. This figure captures, at a high level, all the basic information required.

- Determining probability and impact: Once the risks have been identified and assessed, it is possible to determine the level of exposure, defined in terms of the probability of impact.

- Risk ranking or prioritization: Once risks have been identified, they have to be allocated a ranking on their importance and prioritized for action to be taken to control or mitigate them. The risk tolerance state of the organization should be taken into account during this process.

- Determining required states: Once the risks have been prioritized, it is necessary to determine the expected and required outcomes in both the short and long term. In other words, what is the required end state that must be achieved after the risk has been controlled or mitigated?

- Identifying and investigating options: It is necessary to develop a policy for the identification and investigation of options for the control or mitigation of risks to ensure a consistent and coherent approach is taken. In this process, the tools and approaches for the treatment of the risk are evaluated to ensure that the selected option has the maximum effect.

Risk	Impact Level			
	Date	Low	Medium	High

Figure 15.2. *Risk template.*

- Develop an initial risk response: During the risk identification and assessment processes, some risks are identified that either require urgent attention or can be easily addressed. To address these risks, it is necessary to develop a process for tackling them.

- Strategy definition and implementation: A strategy for the management of risk that is consistent with the organizational ethos, values, and risk tolerance of the organization should be identified and implemented.

- Monitoring and adjusting: When risks have been identified, assessed, ranked, and prioritized, a process is required for the ongoing activity of monitoring the state of exposure and the effect of the measures being taken. This can be used to adjust the measures that are being taken to control or mitigate the risk.

- Document the corporate risk profile: Once the risk management cycle has been completed, it is important to document the corporate risk profile.

PLANS

There is a very old, but true, adage that to fail to plan is to plan to fail. Plans for the management of risk are increasingly being seen as essential to the business in the future. A failure to make plans for the management of risk within an organization means that any actions taken are reactive and unlikely to be coordinated. What this would actually mean is that the organization is not managing the risk but is actually managing the outcome of a failure to manage the risk. This may seem self-evident, but it unfortunately true that in many organizations, it is the reality. The purpose of the risk management plan is to provide a tool for documenting the initial state and for managing the reduction of risks during the process. The plan should provide a documented framework for the organization through which risk status and issues can be communicated, and it can also document the risk mitigation strategies used to reduce identified risks. The plan may also contain financial information to inform decisions on the strategies that are proposed and allow informed decisions to be made.

The types of headings that may be appropriate for a risk management plan are the following:

- Introduction
- Authority

- Scope
- Definitions
- Strategy and approach
- Organizations and responsibilities
- Process and procedures
- Planning
- Risk assessment
- Risk control/mitigation
- Risk monitoring

A range of other related plans is needed, and these must be derived from the business requirements and must be coherent with, and an integral part of, the business plan. These are required to address different aspects of the process, including the following:

- Plans for the collection of the information that allow risk assessments to take place: It is essential that this activity is planned from the outset, because it requires input from all areas of the organization.

- Plans for the risk analysis and assessment process itself and the scope and frequency with which the assessments take place: The analysis and assessment of risk is complex and multifaceted and must be carefully planned and coordinated if it is to be effective and occur in a realistic timeframe.

- Plans for the treatment of the risk and the measures implemented and the way in which the elements are addressed: Because the treatment of risk takes a variety of forms, it is essential that implementation is planned to ensure they are effective and also to ensure that the effects of each of the actions can be measured.

- Plans for tracking and controlling risks: This includes collecting information about a range of factors that affect the risk level the organization is exposed to during any period and the actions taken to treat them. This is the ongoing activity of responding to changes in the business and the risk as they occur and measuring the changing levels of risk that remain.

- Plans for business continuity and the actions to be taken in the event of an incident: These are essential and must be practiced regularly to ensure they work effectively and that the relevant staff understand their roles and responsibilities and are conversant with the procedures that they must follow.

- Plans for awareness and training: There is a need to plan for ongoing staff awareness and training on the risk and the actions that staff need to take to reduce it and to recognize events that increase the level of risk. A failure to develop long-term plans for awareness and training on risk inevitably leads to a fragmented approach and, in time, it being forgotten or the priority it is given being reduced.

POLICIES

The purpose of a risk management policy is to ensure the organization manages risks appropriately. The policy should include the identification of risks related to the business of the organization and the evaluation and control measures for their management. It should address the information infrastructure, the organization's information itself, and the physical, procedural, personnel, and electronic measures used to protect the organization's information assets.

The policy is produced under the authority of the Board of the organization and normally starts with a statement of its purpose, its objectives, an explanation of any definitions, the rationale of the principles that have been applied, a statement of the responsibilities, and a statement that acknowledges that some risks encountered will have to be accepted and that not all risk can be eliminated. The policy also identifies and outlines an implementation strategy. An example of the types of headings that may be appropriate for a risk management policy are as follows:

- Introduction
- Authority
- Scope
- Definitions
- Strategy and approach
- Organizations and responsibilities
- Process and procedures

- Planning
- Risk assessment
- Risk control/mitigation
- Risk monitoring

A range of other policies is required and many of them, such as policies for information security, physical security, health, and safety, should, and hopefully will, already exist. If the list of policies seems similar to the list of plans, this should be of no great surprise!

PROCEDURES

Once you have developed policies to state the organization's position on a topic, it is essential that procedures are defined to interpret the policy into the actions required by those involved in the process and by all members of staff within an organization. The procedures are, effectively, the instructions to the staff on the actions that must be taken in a range of situations. Procedures need to be produced to address each area that requires staff to take actions. The types of procedure that are likely to be required include the following:

- A procedure for risk information collection
- A procedure for risk assessment
- A procedure for risk control/mitigation
- A procedure for business continuity

Note: Procedures are produced to ensure consistency of approach in the way in which an activity is addressed. The policies also act as an organizational repository for knowledge on best practice in each area.

PROJECTS

In the process of developing and implementing risk management within an organization, a range of projects should be initiated to ensure a successful conclusion. It is likely that in most organizations it will be necessary to develop projects for the following:

- Data collection
- Risk assessment
- Risk mitigation
- Monitoring
- Training

The creation of a project allows for the effective management and control of an activity. By undertaking each activity as a project, it can be planned, managed, priced, and monitored to ensure that the outcome meets the objectives defined at the outset.

SUMMARY

In this chapter we covered a wide range of issues that need to be taken into account if the management of risk is to be tackled in a comprehensive and coherent manner that is driven by business requirements. It may seem that the list of processes, procedures, plans, and duties is excessive, but many of the elements may already be in place. The areas addressed have been given to provide some guidance into the range of issues and as an aide-mémoire for when you are in the middle of a number of processes and can no longer see the forest for the trees.

16

Tools and Techniques

In this chapter we describe a number of the more common tools and techniques that can be used when carrying out an information security risk assessment. We describe the features of the tools, the advantages and shortcomings of various techniques, and compare them against each other. We also seek to explain why one approach may be better for some organizations than another.

Several forms of risk assessment are performed in organizations, and although here we focus on techniques for assessing information security risk, it may be the case that techniques and processes can be borrowed from other areas. The main areas to consider include health and safety risk, safety critical risk, and corporate finance and investment risk. Although these are not examined in this chapter, they all have unique features. Health and safety risk assessments are usually well promulgated throughout an organization. Although they are relatively high level, they are often underpinned by a rigorous process examination because they are driven by legal and regulatory requirements. Risk assessments on safety critical systems are usually, from necessity, very thorough. They often focus on software code validation and are resource intensive processes that rely on specialist skill sets. Risk assessments to support corporate finance and investment decisions often focus on market risk. This is the measurement of financial risk that cannot be diversified away by having a portfolio of investments. Market risk measures the sensitivity of an individual investment to the movements of the financial markets. A great deal of research has been carried out in this area, and some of the techniques and principles developed may offer some insight into ways of tackling information security risk. This is particularly the case where a return on investment has to be demonstrated.

The aim of this chapter is to demonstrate the techniques and software support that are available to assist the risk manager to deliver information security risk assessments. This builds on the thorough understanding the risk manager has of the individual elements of the risk process and the way these elements fit together. It is unlikely that any of the tools discussed in this chapter are suitable for an organization to use without tailoring. When tools and techniques are not tailored, it is often the case that the risk assessment process becomes fractured as tension appears between the tool and the established processes that exist in the organization. The tools discussed in this chapter have been chosen as representative of risk assessment tools—there are certainly many more out there. There are also tools emerging that offer support for operational risk, and, of course, information security risk is part of operational risk. This is particularly the case in the finance sector where these tools are being implemented to achieve regulatory compliance. Operational risk tools often bring together a useful understanding of business processes together with mathematical formulae for assessing risk (for example, using Monte Carlo simulations and Bayesian modeling techniques). Many have still to be rigorously tested, but this is an area of development of which the information security risk manager should be aware.

There are a number of tensions inherent in implementing an information security risk process:

- Moving away from a discrete risk assessment to a process that is embedded in the organization and aligned with business strategy.

- Presenting technical solutions in business terms.

- Defining countermeasures that do not restrict the business and are acceptable within the organizational culture.

- Achieving stakeholder and Board level buy-in to the process.

As a guide, the following criteria for evaluating approaches to risk assessment and risk management are a good starting point. These are based on those recommended by National Institute for Standards and Technology[1] for judging hazard analysis techniques and have been amended to meet the requirements of assessing information security risk.

1. The results from the technique shall enhance the understanding of the way risks arise, are prevented, or reduced (for example, they will produce meaningful metrics).

---

1. L. M. Ippolito, D. R. Wallace, *A Study on Hazard Analysis in High Integrity Software Standards and Guidelines.* NIST, NIS-TIR 5589, January 1995. http://hissa.nist.gov/HHRFdata/Artifacts/ITLdoc/5589/hazard.html

2. The technique shall permit the modeling and evaluation of a wide range of failure models.

3. The technique shall enable systematic analysis to be carried out in a manner that is auditable, repeatable, and verifiable.

4. The technique shall be appropriately matched to the expertise of staff (not too labor intensive but sufficiently so to ensure that project managers and resource owners have to think about the issues).

5. The technique shall be appropriate for a system of the given complexity operating in the given domain and containing the given hazards (graphical notation can be used to minimize complexity).

6. The technique shall give valid results using data of the quality and quantity actually available (ideally it should be flexible enough to cope with information that is incomplete).

7. The technique shall be appropriate for the particular life cycle phase at which it is to be applied (where possible, it should be integrated into the project/process life cycle).

8. Tools of adequate integrity or standard templates shall be available commercially to support the technique or shall be able to be supplied.

9. The technique shall be defined by a national or international standard or a published reference book, or a definition and instruction for its application shall be able to be supported.

10. The tools and techniques selected should be aligned with organizational processes and culture.

The tools examined in the remainder of the chapter include the CCTA (Central Computer and Telecommunications Agency) Risk Analysis and Management Method CRAMM, fundamental information risk management (FIRM), simple to apply risk analysis (SARA) and simplified process for risk identification (SPRINT),[2] COBRA, and operationally critical threat, asset, and vulnerability evaluation (OCTAVE).

---

2. It should be noted that FIRM, SARA, and SPRINT are tools, produced by the Information Security Forum and are only available to their members (www.securityforum.org).

CRAMM

CRAMM was first developed in 1985, so it is a well established tool for assessing information security risks. It is still owned by the U.K. Government and is the "government preferred" method for risk assessment. Insight Consulting is now the sole licensee for CRAMM, which is used in many companies around the world. It also offers explicit support for the implementation of ISO 17799.

CRAMM follows the basic risk assessment model already outlined, but it has a strong qualitative element to data gathering and a comprehensive database of countermeasures. Countermeasures can be generated at three different levels ranging from policy statements to technical implementation. CRAMM has a poor reputation in some sectors, probably because it is the oldest and most structured information risk assessment methodology and tool. It also takes a certain amount of expertise to drive the software with any skill, and someone who only undertakes the occasional review will not achieve this.

The qualitative element to data gathering in CRAMM is an important strength. Too many risk assessment tools try to play down the value of qualitative input to a risk assessment and instead push forward the pseudo-science that often underpins the quantitative metrics they produce. After all, as we have pointed in previous chapters, numbers are no substitute for the reviewer's knowledge of the interviewee, the circumstances of the interview, and the many small pieces of information that don't mean anything when taken separately but aggregate to give a rich picture of the information security risks. Methods of qualitative data analysis are already widely used and accepted in other professions such as medicine and law. The downside is that gathering and processing qualitative data analysis is labor intensive.

The first and final stages of the CRAMM review are often the most valuable. These stages encompass the information gathering and final reporting, and if these are carried out sympathetically and with perception, then CRAMM can be an effective means of bringing management and technical staff together. CRAMM reports can present information to management that is high level and supports what-if decision-making scenarios as well as justifying expenditure and strategy. At the technical level, CRAMM can direct staff to the practical implementation of countermeasures, albeit in a platform neutral environment. The fundamental problem with CRAMM is that even if someone was trained in the use of the tool and the methodology, unless the process was undertaken regularly it is highly unlikely they would be able to get the most out of the tool.

The CRAMM process follows three stages:

1. The first stage establishes the review boundary, builds an asset model, and assesses data assets and physical assets.
2. Assets are grouped to show their dependencies and are then related to assets. From this a threat and vulnerability assessment is carried out and measures of risk are calculated.
3. The final stage allows for the generation of countermeasures.

At each of these three stages it is possible to produce a management report. There is also the option of carrying out a rapid risk assessment where, instead of requiring the organization under review to answer the threat and vulnerability questionnaires, the reviewer relies on his or her experience. The obvious downside to a rapid risk assessment is that the information supplied is largely subjective.

FIRM

FIRM is a high level approach for risk assessment and risk management. FIRM comes in the form of two documents and supporting software. The first document is an implementation guide, and the second provides supporting materials for the FIRM process and its use. The FIRM documentation is very thorough, and for organizations new to the concept of risk assessment, it is an excellent starting point.

A 10-stage process is outlined for the implementation of FIRM. The stages move from identifying resources that need to be monitored to an information gathering stage (taking a balanced scorecard approach), analyzing the responses and advising on results before producing a report on the condition of the enterprise with regard to information risk. The whole process is divided into two phases. The first phase is called "Encouragement" and is an opportunity to establish a relationship with the owners of resources and to achieve some quick wins. The second phase is "Reporting," and during this phase balanced scorecards are reissued for completion, but this time the process is taken through to reporting to senior management on the condition of security across the business.

The implementation guide discusses "information risk management" but is, in fact, only considering information stored on IT systems. Therefore, assessing the risks to information under other circumstances (for example, transmitted via phone or fax or taken off the premises in hard copy) would need to be addressed separately. As the guide points out, monitoring the effectiveness of information security must entail consideration of what the information is to be used for, but FIRM only goes part of the way to address the risks. The risk management process should indeed allow risk to be considered in business terms, but risk mitigation strategies need to be defined in practical terms, and there seems to be little support for this in the FIRM structure. Although the guide suggests that results should be produced for different levels of decision making, it is acknowledged that FIRM only offers support down to the level of resource owners. In many cases these owners then need assistance to turn the results of the FIRM process into technical countermeasures. The process for achieving this and assessing success is not defined or supported by FIRM.

FIRM also requires that the information gathered is quantitative. It would be more helpful if both qualitative and quantitative information is gathered to assess risk systematically across an organization. Quantitative data are necessary but hide the point of view and assumptions made by the individual who supplies it. FIRM recognizes that "dubious" data and inaccurate data may be input onto the balanced scorecard. Without qualitative data to support the balanced scorecard, this can happen relatively easily. The gathering of qualitative data at an early stage provides useful supporting information against which the quantitative data can be fully understood.

FIRM claims that the balanced scorecard approach leads to a "balanced view of risk" between threat, vulnerability, and assets. The primary advantage of FIRM over other risk management tools is that it does not rely on one individual to carry out the whole risk management process but devolves the process to resource owners via local coordinators. The individual who takes the role of what FIRM calls the "driving force" supports the process, analyzes the responses, and reports on the findings. In this way FIRM would be better suited than other risk assessment tools for use in a large organization.

FIRM also appreciates the need for buy-in across the organization—from high level management to resource owners. The two-phase monitoring process ("encouragement" before "for real") is a good idea, because it is often possible to identify quick wins at the "Encouragement" stage. Feedback is certainly essential to maintain momentum in the process.

SARA AND SPRINT

SARA and SPRINT are complementary tools for carrying out and managing security risk. SPRINT is a fast-track risk assessment method that is split into three phases: assessing the business risk, assessing the threats, assessing the vulnerabilities, and controls before producing an action plan. Once the first phase of SPRINT is completed, it should be possible to assess the criticality of the system and to decide whether an in-depth risk assessment should be undertaken (using SARA) or whether it is sufficient to take SPRINT to completion.

A SPRINT review is undertaken via mediated interviews with the business owner for the system. The documentation suggests that a SPRINT review can be completed in a few working days over a 2- to 3-week period. There is an accompanying document for SPRINT that details the controls that can be implemented to mitigate risk.

The benefits of SPRINT, as outlined in the documentation, are that it can be used on existing systems and those still in development, it is business oriented, it is structured but easy to apply and simple to understand, and it can be conducted by individuals with limited experience of risk analysis.

SARA is intended to be used for analyzing the risks associated with business critical systems. There are four main phases identified for SARA and these mirror those used by CRAMM quite closely:

1. Defining the scope and objectives, identifying participants, and planning the review.

2. Identifying business requirements for security, understanding the environment, the business impact, and fact gathering via interviews and workshops.

3. Assessing the threats, vulnerabilities, and control requirements via one or more of the workshops.

4. Production of a report, drawing together the key findings and recommendations and outlining an action plan.

This is a strong methodology for risk assessment but, like CRAMM, could prove to be rather labor intensive. Again, it should be noted that these tools are also only available to those organizations who are members of the Information Security Forum.

COBRA

Cobra was originally designed within one of the United Kingdom's major banks but is now owned by C&A System Security Ltd. Cobra has a similar underlying methodology to CRAMM but does not have the same extensive range of countermeasures. One of the benefits of Cobra lies in its use of questionnaires. This can speed up the risk assessment process quite considerably. Cobra is made up of a number of modules that fit in the overall risk engine. This gives the tool a broad range of flexible options; for example, it can be used to undertake a compliance check against ISO 17799 or a full risk assessment. Alternatively, specialist modules can be designed for incorporation into the tool. The full risk assessment starts with a business impact questionnaire. Once this has been answered, Cobra then selects further questionnaires for the risk assessment based on the answers given. The disadvantages of using Cobra are that some organizational priorities are difficult to measure in financial terms and the initial business impact questionnaire tends to rely on this information. Furthermore, the countermeasures generated by Cobra are at a very high level and need significant interpretation before implementation.

OCTAVE

OCTAVE is a risk assessment method developed by the Carnegie Mellon Software Engineering Institute. A second version of the method, called OCTAVE-S, is designed for use in small organizations. OCTAVE considers the same elements as other risk assessment methods but does not focus exclusively on information technology. The method aims to balance operational risk considerations with security and technology requirements. This is a more forward looking aim than some of the other risk assessment tools that we examined. OCTAVE's value comes from the fact that it is self-directed (and should therefore be easier to align with an organization's business practices) and encourages the use of interdisciplinary teams bringing together personnel from both Information Technology and business units. Explicit recognition of the benefits of a pan-organizational approach demonstrates the maturity of thinking behind the method.

An OCTAVE assessment may take at least 12 workshop sessions.[3] This seems to be a heavy load and one that most busy organizations would find difficult to accommodate. It could also be difficult to keep the momentum going in the process if the workshops are spread out over too long a period of time. The method does recognize, however, that the number of workshops held depends on a range of factors, including the scope of the assessment and the resources and time available for its completion.

---

3. OCTAVE Frequently Asked Questions, http://www.cert.org./octave.faq.html

The OCTAVE approach covers three phases:

Phase 1: This is an information gathering phase. During this phase information assets in the organization are examined. Their importance to the organization is used to prioritize them, and current protection strategies are examined. For critical assets security requirements are defined and threat profiles are identified.

Phase 2: This is an assessment phase. During this phase infrastructure vulnerabilities are identified and flows of information across the organization are examined for weaknesses.

Phase 3: This is the countermeasures phase. During this phase risks are identified and strategies for risk mitigation are developed.

Essentially, the first phase focuses on the organization, the second on technology, and the third on strategy and planning. This seems to present a well-balanced approach to the risk assessment process and one that could fit in well with other risk assessment initiatives in an organization (particularly those with an operational risk focus).

Most usefully, OCTAVE is basically a set of principles and attributes that are combined into the OCTAVE and OCTAVE-S method. This gives scope for flexibility within a framework. An OCTAVE analysis gives a baseline understanding of risks within an organization that is then kept current through the implementation of a plan-do-check-act cycle. The incorporation of the plan-do-check-act cycle is another indication of the maturity of this approach because it is both recognition of the quality assurance role in risk management and embraces the spirit of ISO 17799.

One of the most interesting areas of the OCTAVE method is an attempt to develop threat profiles for critical assets. Although the OCTAVE method defines threat as "an indication of an undesirable event,"[4] a different definition than we use in this book, it does go on to expand the definition and refer to "a situation in which a person could do something undesirable."[5] The method goes on suggest that threats consist of a number of properties and these include actors (or, in our terms, threat agents), motives, and access. These last two properties are considered optional. OCTAVE also includes assets and outcome as properties of the threat. The threat profiles are mapped onto the technical infrastructure that exists to explore attack paths and define areas of vulnerability.

---

4. C. Alberts, A. Dorofee, *OCTAVE Threat Profiles*. Software Engineering Institute, Carnegie Mellon University.
5. Ibid.

One element that does seem to be explicitly lacking from the OCTAVE method is the recommendation that organizations should look beyond their own boundaries, at the external environment. The information for developing the threat profiles all comes from the workshops that are held during the first phase—the information gathering part of the assessment.

OCTAVE seems to offer a mature and flexible approach to risk assessment. It is broad in its approach, aiming to place information security within the wider concerns of operational risk. It offers a structured framework within which organizations can align their own processes while ensuring they follow the principles of OCTAVE. It offers a way of assessing threat that goes beyond what we have seen in other risk assessment methods and tools.

In this chapter we have examined a number of tools for carrying out information security risk assessments. This was not intended to be a comprehensive review of the techniques and software support available to the information security risk manager but was meant to give a flavor of the variety of approaches currently being used. It is hoped that we have shown both strengths and weaknesses of these methods. The information security risk manager needs to decide whether or not to use one of these tools and, if so, which one will best meet the requirements of his or her organization. This is why we have spent some time explaining the basic principles of risk management to ensure the information security risk manager is equipped to evaluate these tools in the context of his or her organization's practices, processes, and culture. It may be the case that the risk manager decides not to use an off-the-shelf method or product but to develop one specifically for the organization. This is a legitimate approach, and this book should help to start the process off. Alternatively, if the risk manager decides to use one of these tools, or even a different tool, he or she should be in a position to understand how to customize it for his or her organization without distorting the basic risk assessment principles.

For many organizations, most value is gained from using the principles of one of these methods but swapping the method of delivery to suit the circumstances. For example, sometimes it is more suitable to do the information gathering part of the assessment through workshops rather than questionnaires. OCTAVE gives a flexible framework for managing the overall process and has closer links to operational risk than some of the other tools examined. This is particularly useful in the current climate in the finance industry. For organizations that need to introduce the concept of information security risk management to the whole organization, FIRM is a useful way of achieving this. The balanced scorecard approach is one with which most managers in an organization feel most comfortable. For those in the public sector, those who require a more structured approach, or those who are going to use external consultants for delivery, CRAMM might be suitable. For information security risk assessments that have a well-defined and relatively narrow scope, COBRA, SARA, or SPRINT could be used.

On a final note, organizations might well find that they start off with one approach to risk assessment that then needs to mature over time. For example, many organizations start off at the level of assessing information security risk within discrete projects. This is a safe place to start, but in time the information security risk manager is likely either to devise an enterprise-wide approach or to contribute to such an approach. At this point a broader framework is necessary, and this is probably where OCTAVE (or something similar) will be useful. OCTAVE's appreciation of the role of threat assessment within the information security risk assessment gives a strong indication of its suitability for an organization with a mature approach to risk assessment. The information security risk manager should now be in a position to act as an informed user of risk assessment tools, techniques, and software.

17

Integrated Risk Management

In this chapter we address the management aspects of the risk assessment process and suggest ways that information security risk management should be integrated into organizational business processes. In particular, we focus on business strategies, specifically with regard to compliance, regulation, and corporate governance. We consider the impact this will have on the structures for delivering a successful risk assessment process across the organization.

The world of risk management is changing rapidly, with greater emphasis on governance and transparency and a seemingly relentless push toward tighter regulation. This picture is complicated further with the emergence of new technologies such as pervasive computing which can lead to the creation of virtual and dynamic business environments.

In the light of these changes, it is perhaps now time to reflect on those organizational structures that support the process of information security risk management and to consider the business strategies that will shape risk management practice in the future. If this opportunity is ignored, then we may well end up with a fragmented approach to risk. This could easily cause a vicious circle where we add greater complexity to our systems and processes with diminishing returns to the business in terms of both security and compliance.

We consider the various elements that sit around the concept of information security risk management and explore how they interrelate, how they change over time, and why it is important for organizations to be able to influence these relationships. We move on to examine the relationship between risk, compliance, and regulation and then look at how changing business models and new technologies are having an effect on the world of risk management. We look at examples of changing strategies and structures that highlight how risk management practices need to change to maintain a balance between the elements of the risk environment and provide an integrated approach across the business. Finally, we suggest changes that should be considered if information security risk management is going to successfully continue to deliver value over time.

Figure 17.1 depicts the environment in which risk management is situated. At the bottom of the diagram is the concept of trustworthiness. In turn, this has a direct relationship to governance processes in an organization, and this influences an organization's ability to demonstrate compliance. Compliance is a complex area that sits between risk and regulation. In this figure we can see risk assessment depicted as being an attribute that is part of the internal and external organizational environment. This is still a factor that is often forgotten. Risk is not just determined by the vulnerabilities within an organization, but also by the activities that take place beyond the organization's boundaries—whether this is through regulatory requirements, stakeholder expectations, or the threat environment.

It is important to keep in mind why we carry out risk management. Of course, we do it to secure our systems and processes, but the aim underpinning this is primarily to build trust. The trust we build from our position as information security risk practitioners increasingly has to extend across a broad community so that it encompasses not only the organization itself but goes beyond its boundaries to customers, partners, shareholders, and regulators.

So what do we mean by trust and trustworthiness? Trust in the context of information security has been described as "a predisposition to expose oneself to

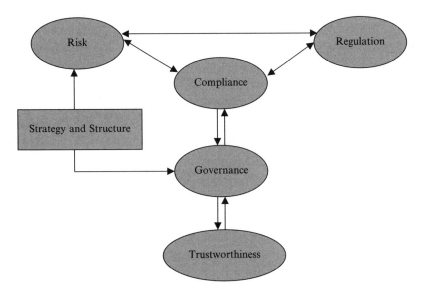

Figure 17.1. *Risk environment.*

a security risk."[1] In this definition we can see a direct link between the concepts of risk and trust, but under what circumstances could we expect someone to expose themselves to a security risk, thereby exhibiting trust? Perhaps trust is given because an organization displays certain attributes. We would suggest that these attributes could include, but are not limited to, good governance and compliance.

An example of this can be seen in the recent flotation of the Internet search engine, Google. The company was recently criticized by Institutional Shareholder Services, America's most powerful shareholder group. Google was criticized for having poor standards of corporate governance and was warned they would not be "taken seriously within the investment community"[2] if they didn't rectify the situation. This clearly illustrates the link between good governance and trustworthiness.

Governance and compliance are a two-way relationship. They are instrumental in defining each other, and they change over time both in terms of their individual states and in the balance of the relationship between themselves. To be successful, an organization needs to find ways of strengthening its trustworthiness. This can be achieved by improving the governance processes, because, in turn, this puts the organization in a strong position to convince external auditors that they are compliant with current regulations. This linkage between trust, governance, and compliance is an important factor in an organization's ability to demonstrate value for its stakeholders. As we can see, this is not a straightforward relationship but relies on negotiation and the ability to balance a number of attributes with risk as a key factor.

Compliance itself is the interface between risk and regulation and the boundaries between these areas is becoming increasingly blurred. Bridget Hutter and Michael Power, both academics researching the area of risk regulation, point out that, "Compliance is fundamentally a creative process of negotiation and interaction between regulatory agencies and those they regulate."[3] This suggests that we should not expect compliance to consist of getting the right ticks in the correct boxes but rather we should be looking to understand and internalize the spirit underlying the requirement for compliance. This means that "compliance is emergent,"[4] and, as such, it will fluctuate as our understanding and perception of risk changes and the regulatory environment expands or contracts according to events, incidents, changes in processes, and technology.

---

1. S. Zaba, HP Labs, Bristol, UK.
2. *Sunday Times*, 22 August 2004, UK.
3. Ibid.
4. Ibid.

If we accept that what constitutes compliance changes over time, then we should try to understand how to take this into account when we assess the risks that an organization faces. At the moment we do not easily accept the subjective nature of risk. The temptation is to drive toward an objective process for assessing risk. In the main this comes from the background that many information security practitioners have as scientists or engineers. For decisional certainty risk, "closure" is necessary. But no systems are really closed even though we find it simpler to treat them this way. Systems are open and they evolve. This means that we have to accept uncertainty, and this uncertainty requires judgment.

We have to expand our understanding and accept other aspects to risk (other than impact, assets value, and threat) that distort our understanding of risk. Mark Fenton-O'Creevy and Emma Soane refer to the need to take into account "the fear factor—how much we dread the potential outcome—and the control factor—the extent to which we are in control of events."[5] A combination of both can increase our perception of risk. This is the reason why a terrorist attack is perceived to be a high risk at the current time—it is something that we fear and something that we also believe we have little control over. We use heuristics to gauge risk; that is, we gauge risk by locating it within our own experience. However, much as we would like to believe we assess risk rationally, we have to accept that we do not. We need to acknowledge this and engage with the "individualistic and variable nature of risk perception."[6] In particular, we need to do this if we are going to ensure that changes in risk assessment mirror the changing concept of compliance.

Regulation is determined by external events and driven by the overriding perception of risk. Regulations are usually broadly defined to allow flexibility for any changes that may take place in the future. For example, regulations have to be sufficiently flexible to accommodate the emergence of new technologies. We can see risk and regulation as the two ends of a see-saw, with compliance as the balance point between them. When risk assessments can be demonstrated to be fit for purpose, then regulatory activity should be less prominent. Conversely, when risk assessment activities are not believable, then regulatory activity is likely to increase. In the past we have seen the swings between the two states as something that is relatively gentle. It seems likely that the movement between the two will become increasingly turbulent in the near future.

5. M. Fenton-O'Creevy, E. Soane, "The Subjective Perception of Risk," UK FT. *Mastering Risk, Part One.* Tuesday, April 25, 2000.
6. Ibid.

We now need to move on to uncover why this should be the case and what organizations can do to influence where the balance point is between risk and regulations while building trustworthiness for its stakeholders. The emergence of pervasive, or ubiquitous, computing has a significant impact on the requirements demanded of risk assessments. There are many unresolved difficulties in assessing risks across intertwined systems (particularly with regard to critical infrastructure protection). These difficulties have still to be fully addressed and yet the world of risk will become even more complex as we see more wearable devices, networks that are configured on the fly, and grid computing, allowing us to share processing power. The Cyber Trust and Crime Prevention Project recently completed by the U.K. Department for Trade and Industry highlighted some of the issues. The European Commission IST Advisory Group suggested that security requirements will change over time and that the "new paradigm will be characterized by 'conformable security'."[7] This means that security requirements change with circumstances and context, just as perceptions, motivations, and actions alter. We need to take account of these changes in an equally dynamic way. Crucially, the report highlights the need to "understand the relationships between human factors and risk and trust if a relatively secure cyberspace is to develop in the future."[8] This highlights the need to examine the links between these concepts and to broaden our understanding of risk. It is no longer merely a good idea but will soon become a necessity if we are to continue to produce meaningful risk assessments.

The new business models supported by these technological advances will move toward greater specialization. Organizations will use outsourcing to enable them to concentrate on their core business. In turn this will spawn businesses that focus on specific niche areas of competency. With time, organizations will need to accept they have to rely on their business partners to deliver a complete solution. In particular, business models that focus on cooperation will distinguish successful businesses. This strategy of specialization and cooperation will require "far more than connectivity and interoperability" as it will "rely on management, control, security, privacy and governance."[9] We need to find a way of ensuring the delivery of these attributes if these new business models are going to succeed, because in many respects it seems as if these will be the dominant strategies whether we can manage the risks or not.

It has already been pointed out that the United Kingdom will be at the forefront of offshore outsourcing in Europe over the next decade.[10] It has also been

---

7. Cyber Trust and Crime Prevention, CTCP Technology Forward Look, p. 5.
8. Ibid., p. 6.
9. "A Perfect World? A Model for Transformation." IBM Business Consulting Services, April 2003.
10. B. Goodwin, "UK IT Staff to Bear Brunt of Offshore Job Losses." IT Management, *Computer Weekly*, August 19, 2004.

suggested that this is almost inevitable as "To outsource offshore is not a political decision ... It's an economic decision with political ramifications."[11] From this we can conclude that offshoring will take place, and the political fallout from this must be managed. It is apparent that some of the political consequences that we witness will stem from security and from our ability to manage risk. For example, we are already seeing data protection issues raised surrounding a U.K. bank's transfer of personal customer information outside the European Economic Area. Action is being taken by a trade union to attempt to prevent this activity. The grounds for this action are that under U.K. data protection legislation this activity cannot take place unless customers have given their express consent. The political ramifications are exemplified in the involvement of a trade union attempting to protect the rights of U.K. workers whose jobs are threatened by offshoring. The likely outcome is that this action will play on the perception of risk shared by the bank's customers. In turn they will look for reassurance that the risk is being managed through proof of compliance and good governance. However, offshoring does highlight the difficulties of replicating processes and procedures in different countries and different cultures. As part of the assessment of information security risk, it is important to recognize that procedures are not internalized in the same way across the globe but are mediated by the different cultures in which they are implemented.

A further example is the recent case of a Pakistani worker who was part of an outsourcing offshore contract and who threatened to post U.S. patients' medical data on the Internet if she did not receive back pay.[12] Even more worrying, the U.S. General Accounting Office has noted the possibility of "malicious changes to code since significant US air traffic control system Y2K work had been sub-contracted outside the US without mandated background checks."[13] This high-lights the desperate need to bring together physical and information security and to assess risk holistically.

From these examples we can begin to see how there could easily be a backlash from employees, partners, and consumers against the strategy of outsourcing off-shore. The Union Bank of California recognized that this could be a problem and set up a dedicated sourcing office to manage the risks. The office handles con-tracts and staff, strategy, and communications. This initiative by the Union Bank of California highlights the need of organizations to look beyond their own boundaries and to understand the security risks in their business environment.

---

11. J. King, "Damage Control: How to Combat Offshore Outsourcing Backlash." *Computerworld* July 12, 2004.
12. L. Weinstein, "Outsourced and Out of Control." *Communications of the ACM*, February 2004, vol. 47, no. 2, p. 120.
13. Ibid.

Finally, there is the example of Pilot Network Services, an outsourcing organization that went bankrupt, leaving customers of its managed network services severely exposed. This case highlights the need for organizations to develop processes for cooperation and brings home sharply the realization that if you implement outsourcing strategies you have to recognize that someone else's business becomes part of your business and vice versa.

Current regulatory requirements also demonstrate how the demands on risk assessment need to change. The Sarbanes Oxley Act raises issues of governance, specifically monitoring and reporting aspects. If we examine recent surveys that focus on organizational preparedness for demonstrating compliance with Sarbanes Oxley, we can see very conflicting messages. For example, Silicon.com reported that "Two thirds of firms claim they've nailed it,"[14] yet only a few weeks later they reported that many banks use instant messaging but have not thought through the risks or understand the requirements for compliance. Similarly, many seem to believe that they can transfer their regulatory responsibilities through an outsourcing strategy. Noncompliance with Sarbanes Oxley could have huge repercussions for organizations in terms of fines, damage to reputation, and the impact on share prices. Such conflicting messages are not surprising when we consider what compliance entails and the fact that regulations do not deal with specific technologies; this is where the need to negotiate comes into play, and it is difficult to negotiate from a strong position if you cannot demonstrate that you understand the risks.

One of the ways of handling the risks inherent in the changing environment is by changing our strategies for security. We have to find a way of dealing with complexity, balancing paradoxes and contradictions. Information security risk has to confront issues of relationship management, merger and acquisition activities, alignment between parent companies and their subsidiaries, and knowledge management.

The CIO of British Airways recently said, "We don't want to entrust our future to one external supplier" because "Nobody can forecast where technology will be in five to ten years time, it's much better to retain strategic control, but still work with suppliers."[15] With the changes that we expect to see in the business environment, this could be a short-sighted approach. This demonstrates a customer/supplier approach that leads to an all or nothing solution—they will either win by selecting the "right" technology provider or lose because they haven't. The risks are high in this instance. A partnership approach would mean

14. A. McCure, "Compliance: Two-Thirds of Firms Claim They've Nailed It." Silicon.com, July 2, 2004.
15. J. Milne, "Holy Grail or Poisoned Chalice." Managing Information Strategies, *www.misweb.com*

they would minimize the risks by establishing a strong relationship with a partner and helping them to develop the technical solutions that they need. There is a subtle but important difference in this relationship because it treats customer and supplier as peers. The technology risks may be more controlled in this instance, but the risks have now been transferred to the ability of individuals to manage this new type of relationship. In this case it seems that the CIO of British Airways believes that his organization can retain the ability to use IT for competitive advantage. This may not be the case if computing power becomes a utility; then they will have to rely on other specializations to deliver an advantage.

With mergers and acquisitions it is often the case that too much attention is paid to the financial details of the organizations without considering the integration of technology at an early enough stage. This raises a number of security risks for the organizations involved. Information security professionals need to be able to articulate these risks in a rigorous business focused manner if they are to be managed effectively.

There are perhaps lessons to be learned from a group called the Jericho Forum[16] and from what they are trying to achieve. They believe "they need both to prepare for this new 'deperimeterised' world and get the software vendors to support them."[17] They are focusing on defining the requirements for technology to minimize the security risks that they see. This is fairly typical of the development of security initiatives. The technology requirements of necessity have to be addressed first, but we would suggest that somebody also needs to think about the business processes that need to be put in place to manage these challenges. As always, we need to address information security risks across people and processes as well as technology. The risks from the emerging world of new technologies and business models need to be understood to develop the requirements, but there also needs to be risk management processes in place that can evaluate the changing environment on an ongoing basis.

We need a structure for information security risk management that reflects these changes in business strategy. As information security becomes more of an organizational and social concern, we should give more thought to the way that information security risk managers portray themselves. It is perhaps time for information security risk managers to think about the type of identity they wish to construct for themselves within the organization. It seems unlikely that their current roles (which often consist of either being the policemen of the

16. http://www.opengroup.org/projects/jericho/
17. *Secure Computing* magazine.

organization or the technologists) will help develop a role for the individual who wishes to be taken seriously at a strategic level.

This is an important point. With the growth of outsourcing activities, the information security risk manager needs to demonstrate that he or she can rise to the challenge of being a strategic player. The new infrastructure put in place by the Union Bank of California and required for successful outsourcing needs "contract management experts, procurement specialists and relationship."[18] In this environment there is a need for risk management professionals who can think strategically to manage the risks across these different strands of activity. Crucially, the successful risk manager will need to be able to develop relationship management skills as he or she deals with more stakeholders who are external to the organization and knowledge management skills to avoid repeating mistakes and to ensure that lessons are learned. Without these skills the information security risk manager will not be able to move his or her role closer to the strategic center of the organization.

It seems then that to develop an integrated approach to information security risk management in the twenty-first century, there is a need to understand the role that information security risk assessment will play with the advent of new technologies and new business strategies. The risk manager needs to explore broader attributes of risk and to look beyond organizational boundaries. Only in this way will information security risk management become integrated with the day-to-day processes of running the business. To achieve this, and to be taken seriously, the information security risk manager needs to consciously construct an identity that moves away from that of the policeman or the technologist and moves closer to that of the businessperson. The management of information security risk is key to developing trustworthiness, and for the organization to appreciate this, risk needs to be integrated across the boundaries of business strategy and technology.

Holy Grail or Poisoned Chalice', Jaine Milne, Managing Information Stratetgies, www.misweb.com"

Section VI
Future Directions

18

The Future of Risk Management

As the global marketplace continues to change and become more dependent on technology, the need for corporate risk management will become greater and the problem more complex. Risk aware organizations will increasingly need to be staffed with professionals who are technologically aware. The stereotypical view of the type of an individual tasked with risk management as being an ex-policeman or an auditor is totally unrealistic both now and in the future. In this chapter we address some of the current trends in both business and technology and how they relate to the need to provide protection to a company and how these changes affect the risk management professional.

In the global marketplace, organizations, to continue to develop and expand, are increasingly dependent on the new technologies and the adaptation of existing technology. As the communications and computer technologies have converged, it has allowed a huge range of possibilities to be realized that were previously not achievable and organizations to structure themselves and operate in ways that were not previously possible. These developments, particularly in communications and computing, have allowed the marketplace to expand and the organizations to become more flexible, responsive, and efficient. This, together with the legislation that has been introduced to control this new environment, has exposed organizations to a range or risks they had not previously experienced and to a level of complexity that had not previously existed.

As a result of this evolving environment, organizations that are to survive and to prosper must become more risk aware. The staff who carry out the risk management function need to be increasingly skilled and professional and have an awareness of technology that was not necessary in the past. Historically, the people who were made responsible for security and, if it was carried out at all, risk management were typically either from an audit background or were retired police officers or ex-military. The auditor filled this type of post largely because the role grew from the audit and security areas, and, after all, auditors are good at communicating and operating at all levels of the organization and are used to finding out what is actually happening. Because they have to have access to all areas of the operation in their audit role, they also tend to be trusted members of staff. The retired police and military individuals were selected because of their knowledge of crime and physical security and their honesty. The selection of these types of individual was, in the past, both sensible and logical, because few other career backgrounds would provide access to the type of knowledge and experience required to carry out these roles. Unfortunately, in the new environment, these credentials are no longer even remotely adequate to meet the organizational needs. If the management of risk is to be addressed effectively, the practitioner must now have a far wider range of knowledge and experience. They must not only know of the implications of the security issues and the countermeasures used, they must also understand the technologies and, most importantly, the business itself.

As discussed in the earlier chapters, getting the staffing of the risk management function correct is essential. Who is the super person that will fit the bill? They will need to operate at the appropriate level within the organization, because they will require the authority to interface with the decision makers and will need to operate at a level above the functional stovepipes that are created at an operational level. They will, of course, have to be good communicators, because they will have to interface with all the elements of the business and persuade not only the management that, where appropriate, change and investment is required, but also with the functional managers to persuade them to give their effort and their precious information to someone that they cannot control. They will also have to have experience in the business of the organization and experience and training in risk assessment, the underpinning technologies, information security, current and developing legislation, and a host of other areas. It is true that the size and the complexity of operation of the organization will vary greatly and so, as a result, will the difficulty of the task of the risk manager, but even in a relatively small and straightforward organization, you can see that it will be difficult to capture all of these skills in one person.

What is the answer? As with a number of other areas that involve the technologies we are relying on, the solution may well be not to try to create a super person (who would be very expensive to create and very difficult to retain once they had gained the skills and experience) but to manage the assets that already exist in the functional areas; we are talking about using management techniques in a business environment. It would be totally unrealistic to expect one individual to keep up to date with developments in all the disparate areas involved, so the sensible solution is to use the best and most effective resources available.

This potentially reduces the breadth of the required skill set for the risk manager to knowledge and experience of how to carry out risk assessments, communication skills, and management skills to enable the risk assessment to be enacted and presented to the relevant authorities for the development and implementation of a plan of how to manage the risks identified.

The global marketplace and the business environment continue to change as organizations adapt to survive and to remain competitive. This situation is likely to continue for the foreseeable future, and, as a result, the issues that must be addressed in understanding and managing risk will continue to become more complex. To meet this ongoing situation, the infrastructures that organizations implement to address the problem of risk management must also be forward thinking and flexible. On the positive side, as more organizations become risk aware, there will be an increase in the level of knowledge, awareness, and experience on the subject. Also, with this improved awareness and as demand increases, there will be legislation, guidance, procedures, tools, and techniques developed to aid the practitioner and to address the issues.

A number of significant technologies have continued to develop and have also continued to converge, with computing and telecommunications becoming increasingly reliant on each other. Telecommunications systems are now all digitally controlled, which means they are controlled by computers, and computer systems are, in turn, totally reliant on the communication systems to achieve the networking requirements that are demanded of them. A number of the more advanced telecommunications providers are now moving from analogue to voice over IP technology for voice communications and are using the protocols that were developed for computing to make more efficient use of the available bandwidth.

This integration of technologies has provided business with the capability to achieve its aspirations and its aims but has in itself been the root of many of the risks that the organizations are now exposed to. As with many developments, the need for additional functionality and flexibility has been the driver of their development, and it is only when the technologies have been deployed and experience gained with them that the risks of their use starts to be understood. A classic example of this is the introduction and deployment of wireless networks. They can provide a cheap and flexible method for creating network infrastructures within a building or a geographical area. From the introduction of the technology, it has always been possible to encrypt wireless networks and to make them relatively secure and ensure that unauthorized terminals did not connect to the system and that attempts to do so could be identified. Unfortunately, partially through lack of experience with this new technology, systems were, and still are, being deployed in an unprotected manner. This leaves the system open to interception and to intruders and the business exposed to potentially cata-strophic risks. If risk management had been applied from the design and devel-opment stage, before it was taken into operational use within an organization, this could have been preventable.

For businesses to be competitive and to continue to grow, they have had to adapt their practices and become more flexible and responsive in the way they operate. One example of this is that, as a result of the improved information flows, the days of large warehouses full of costly inventory are, for the most part, a thing of the past. The structure of supply chains has been refined and business now relies on "just in time" supply with minimal stock holdings and reduced warehousing costs. With the use of technology, organizations have become more mobile and staff now only visit the office when required. Their staff expect to have access to all the resources and information they need while they are on the road or in a hotel room with the result that they are more efficient and productive than in the past. Working practices have also changed, and we now have the concept of "home working" where staff will operate from their homes and save traveling time and expense. The old concept of staff that had "jobs for life" and as a result gathered a high level of corporate knowledge and gave loyalty has also largely been replaced by a short-term workforce that is also more mobile.

Finally, with the globalization of business, organizations have had to become more mobile. As businesses have become increasingly international and multina-tional, to increase efficiency, reduce cost, and to meet market needs, the risks that are encountered are continuing to change and grow.

Another issue that must be considered is that of the corporate boundary. In the past, corporate boundaries were mostly well defined and relatively stable. In the current and developing environment, the boundaries are increasingly flex-ible and poorly defined. In addition to mergers and divestitures, organizations increasingly form into partnerships and other relationships to achieve their busi-ness goals. This is made even more complicated, as an organization that is a part-ner, perhaps as part of a consortium, for one set of business may be a competitor for business in another set of business.

The current trends in both business and technology are having a profound effect on the way in which we need to approach the whole subject of risk. The main business trends are for a more dynamic environment in which the operat-ing basis is less stable. The globalization of business has increased competition and created the demand for ever more efficiency and cost reduction. We have also seen many more acquisitions, mergers, and divestitures as organizations have maneuvered to maintain and improve their market share and to capitalize on any opportunities. Globalization itself has meant that organizations that previously operated inside national boundaries are now operating in multinational environments that draw on and expose them to a range of cultural, legal, and business issues they have not previously had to consider. Look at the example of an American company moving into China as a market. What additional risks is your organization going to face in this environment? How will you deal with this foreign government to gain the necessary agreements and permits? What do you know about the way in which business is carried out in this new arena and the cultural issues that exist there? What risks are the new venture going to face and which of these risks may affect the U.S. based organization? If the loss of the Intellectual Property Rights (IPR) on which your U.S. operation is based is a risk in the new area of operations, would it cost market share in the home market and could the company survive?

As technologies have developed, converged, and become ubiquitous, they have been widely adopted in a drive for reduced costs and greater flexibility and efficiency. A result of this is that we have become so dependent on these technologies that we can no longer operate without them. In most cases the failure of these technologies means that organizations can no longer operate. The option of reverting to a system run on pen and paper is no longer viable.

These changes affect the risk management professional in a number of ways. As with many other areas related to information technology, the rate of change has been increasing for more than two decades. In the past, when organizations had little technology and, where it did exist, it was isolated, it was normally fully under their control. In this environment the use of physical, procedural, and personnel security measures could be used to create an environment where organizations were comfortable that the risk was controllable. With globalization, because of the convergence of technologies that has resulted in the arrival and adoption of the Internet and World Wide Web, along with the pressure and potential for increased efficiency, organizations have been forced to use the technologies to compete and survive.

We hope this book has given you, the practitioner, an insight into a range of the issues that you will have to deal with in the course of understanding, measuring, and managing risk in your organization. The concepts discussed here cover a wide range of ideas to consider and provide some ways to address them. Although not a universal panacea, this book should provide a basis for constructing the organization and procedures needed to reduce the level of risk to which your organization is exposed.

Index

419 scams, 177, 178–179

A

Academia, Internet benefits to, 170
Acceptable risk levels, 195, 203
Accidental disasters, 14–15, 43
Accidental threats, 43–45
Accounting fraud, 16
Actuarial data, 45
  lack of, 8
Adobe Acrobat 4.0, Easter egg in, 146–147
ADSL, 151
Adware, 144
Agent-based technology, risk associated with,
  191
Allied nations capability, in threat assessment
  for nation states, 58
Amazon.com, 171
Amplifiers, 45
  for malicious threat agents, 47, 50–51,
    193
  threat assessment method for, 79–81
AN PHOBLACT website, 177
Anti-Terrorism Crime and Security Act
  (U.K.), 21
Application vulnerabilities, xvi, 143–147
  in COTS software, 153–155
ARPANET, 165
Arthur Anderson accounting firm collapse, 16
Ascend Routing Hardware Vulnerabilities,
  138
Ashenden, Debi, xxi
Asian countries, software piracy in, 146,
  154–155
Asian monetary crisis, 19
Assessment phase, in OCTAVE software,
  239
Asset identification, 192
  Board responsibility for, 221

Asset registers, 189, 197
Assets
  defined, 38
  value of, 187
Asynchronous broadband connections, 12
Asynchronous digital subscriber line (ADSL),
  12
Attacks
  on Cisco IP telephones, 138
  preempting, 8
  probability of successful, 40
  via FrontPage Personal web server
    vulnerability, 144
Audit requirements, 29
Auditability, of risk assessment process, 192
Auditing failures, 16
Availability of information, 192
  defined, 38
  in risk assessment, 185

B

Back doors, 137
  system recovery via, 135
Background checks
  importance in outsourcing ventures, 248
  for new employees, 204, 210
Balance, maintaining, 31, 32
Balanced scorecard approach, 235–236,
  240
Bank of International Settlements, 4, 28
Banking systems
  pillars of Basel Accord, 20
  strengthening confidence in, 19
Barings Bank collapse, 19
Basel Capital Accord, 19–21
Basel II Accord, 4, 5, 7, 28, 207
Bayesian modeling, 217–218, 232
Beta testers, users as, 150
Biometric scanners, 204

Blackmail, 177
of on-line gambling establishments, 179
Board
achieving buy-in by, 232
as champion of risk management, 221
duties and responsibilities of, 220–221
endorsement of acceptable risk levels by,
195
engaging the, 6–7
lack of support by, 210
policy responsibility of, 227
presenting risk issues to, 6
risk representation at level of, 209
Breadth of thinking, 30
Break-ins, sites monitoring frequency of, 135
Brick and mortar companies, 166
Bridging skills, 26, 32
British Standard BS 7799, 5, 39
Broadband connections, 12
Budget process, xvii
Bulletin boards, 12
Business, increased reliance on electronic
infrastructure, 168–169
Business continuity planning, 13, 190, 227
procedure for, 228
Business impact assessment (BIA), 196
Business impact questionnaire, 238
Business knowledge, required of risk
managers, 26
Business management professionals, xi
Business objectives
Board responsibilities for, 221
identifying with SARA and SPRINT, 237
Business processes, as information assets,
196–197
Business risk, 3, 22–24
assessing in SARA and SPRINT, 236–237
qualitative vs. quantitative, 189
Business Software Alliance, 145
Business strategy, 243
aligning with risk assessment, 185, 232
need to align with IT, 9
Business unit managers, roles and
responsibilities of, 222

C
Cable service providers, 12
Capability
components of, 49
of malicious threat agents, 46, 49, 193
Capital adequacy process, 28
Capital expenditures, 17
Carnegie Mellon Software Engineering
Institute, 238

Catalysts, 45
for Chinese nation state sponsored threat
agents, 105–106
for commercial organization threat agents,
118–119, 122–123
components of, 52
for French nation state sponsored threat
agents, 98–99
for hacker threat agents, 128–129
for malicious threat agents, 46, 51–52
for terrorist threat agents, 111–112
threat assessment method for, 84–86
Central Computer and Telecommunications
Agency Risk Analysis and Management
Method (CRAMM), 233–235
CERT Coordination Center, 139–140
Chester, Pam, xix
Chinese nation state sponsored threat
agents
catalysts for, 105–106
factors influencing, 99–101
threat amplifiers for, 104
threat inhibitors for, 104–105
value weighting for, 102–103
CIAC advisory notices
Advisory I-038, 138
Oracle 9iAS Default Configuration
Vulnerability, 139
Cisco Security Advisory on Multiple
Vulnerabilities, CISCO IP telephone
vulnerability, 138
Classified information, involvement in laptop
theft, 175
Closed systems, 246
Cloverdale Kids, 42
COBRA software, 190, 233, 237–238
Commercial imperative
as catalyst factor, 52
for malicious threat agents, 51
Commercial off-the-shelf (COTS) software,
149–152, 162
Commercial organizations, 89
as malicious threat agents, 48
threat assessment method for, 68–71
threats posed by, 43
Commercial prudence, effect on security
features, 153
Commercial sector disasters, 15–17
Commercial threat agents
Aerospaciale France, 119
catalysts for, 122–123
motivational factors for, 123
threat amplifiers for, 121–122
value weighting for, 120

Boring Aerospace and Defense, 113–115
  catalysts for, 118–119
  factors influencing, 113
  motivational factors for, 119
  threat amplifiers for, 115–116
  threat inhibitors for, 117–118
  value weighting for, 114
Communications skills, 33
  required of risk managers, 26, 209, 222,
    256
Communications technologies, convergence
  with computer systems, 11
Competitiveness
  as catalyst for malicious attacks, 51
  as factor in risk management, 24
Competitor threats, xiv, 197
Compliance strategies, 243, 244, 245
  changes over time, 246
  relationship to risk and regulation, 243
Comprehensive asset registers, 189, 197
Computer Emergency Response Team
  (CERT), 133
  CERT Coordination Center, 139–140
Computer hygiene, of international system
  builders, 154
Computer Incident Advisory Capability
  (CIAC), 133
Computer-related crime, improved detection
  of, 180
Computer theft, 174, 175
Computers
  convergence with communications
    technologies, 11
  risks to, ix
Confidentiality issues, 8, 9, 192
  in risk assessment, 185
Confidentiality of information, defined, 38
Conflicts of interest, 16
Connectivity and dependence issues, xvi
Consequential effect, 27
Consumers
  as beta testers, 155–156
  as greatest security problem, 139
  lack of concern for security, 153
Context
  importance to risk managers, 25
  setting, 223
  understanding, 32
Control factor, 246
Copyright violations, 174
Core functions, duties of employees in, 223
Corporate excesses, high profile, 18
Corporate finance risk assessment techniques,
  6, 231

Corporate governance, xv, 22, 27–28, 29,
  207–208, 243, 245
  relationship of trustworthiness to, 244
  tightening of, 7
  in wake of Enron bankruptcy, 28
Corporate power abuse, 16
Corporate scandals, 7
Cost-benefit ratios, for risk countermeasures,
  204
Cost-effective security, xiii
Cost-effective software, COTS applications,
  150
Cost of development, for custom software,
  159–160
Cost of participation, as inhibitor, 50
Cost reduction, driving globalization of
  business, 258
Cost-to-benefit stage, of risk analysis, 196
Costs vs. risks, x, xiii
COTS software. See Commercial off-the-shelf
  (COTS) software; Off-the-shelf software
Council of Europe, resolution on lawful
  interception of telecommunications, 180
Counterfeit software, 154–155, 174–175
Countermeasures, 26, 31, 40
  acceptability to business culture, 232
  assigning to risks, 203
  comprehensive database in CRAMM, 234,
    235
  cost-benefit analysis of, 204
  defining, 193–194, 195
  implementation plans for, 194, 205
  understanding implications of, 29
Countermeasures phase, in OCTAVE
  software, 239
Crackers, 133
  responsible, 134
CRAMM software, 6, 190, 233–235
Creativity, 32
  required of risk managers, 29
Credibility, link to technical understanding,
  30
Credit card numbers, identity theft of, 179
Credit risk assessment, 4, 28, 211
Crime detection improvements, 180
Criminals, 89, xiv
  Internet crime, 172–176
  as malicious threat agents, 48
  threat assessment method for, 71–74
Critical National Infrastructure, 43,
  169–170
Cult of the Dead Cow website, 145
Cultural factors, in threat assessment for
  nation states, 58

Custom software
advantages and disadvantages of, 158–160
historical trends of, 149
Customer information, as information asset, 196
Cyber stalking, 173
Cyber Trust and Crime Prevention Project, 247
Cyberterrorism, 15

D
3D Pipes screen saver, Easter egg in, 136
Data analysis skills, 32
Data collection projects, 229
Data-gathering skills, 30, 33
Data Protection Act, 7
Data protection issues, related to outsourcing, 248–250
Databases, of operating system vulnerabilities, 133
Default configurations, as sources of vulnerability, 139–140
Default passwords, 140
Denial of service attacks, 172, 173
attack on Cisco IP phones using, 138
in blackmail of on-line gambling establishments, 179
exploiting router vulnerabilities, 139
in NetMeeting application, 153–154
as second most expensive computer crime, 176
using user systems as launch platforms, 140
Department of Homeland Security, 169
Depreciation, 17
Detection, 203
of security incidents, 204
Deterrence, 203
Development cycle
of COTS software, 150, 151–152, 160
of custom software, 158–159
Development team Easter eggs, 147
Digital subscriber line (DSL), 12
Directory protection, inappropriate, 140
DirectX, in Easter egg software, 146
Disaffected employees, 56, 90
as malicious threat agents, 48
threat assessment method for, 75–79
Disasters
commercial sector, 15–17
malicious, 15
natural and accidental, 14–15
Discourse analysis, 215
Distributed denial of service (DDoS) attacks, 173, 198

Distributed systems, 190
Divestitures, 258–259
Documentation
of corporate risk profile, 225
in risk management process, 225–227
Dot com revolution, 166
Doubledot bug, 144
Downstream speeds, 12
Drenth, Arnold, xix
Drink or Die counterfeiting group, 154–155
Duties and responsibilities, 219–220
Board level, 220–221
business unit managers, 222
employees in core function posts, 223
risk manager, 221–222
staff, 223

E
E-business, 166
E-buyer, 171
E-commerce, 166
E-mail systems, historical introduction of, 165
Earthquake threat, 44
Easter Egg Archive website, 136
Easter eggs, 135–137, 146–147
in pirated software, 146
Electronic infrastructure, increased business reliance on, 168–169
Electronic shopping malls, 166
Employee backlash, in outsourced businesses, 248
Employee loyalty, disappearance of, 258
Empowered small agents, 186
Encouragement phase, in FIRM software, 235–236
Enron scandal, 15–16, 28
Enterprise lending, 20
Enterprise-wide risk, 4, 6
Ethical issues, 7
European Commission IST Advisory Group, 247
European Union, 20
Events, as catalyst factors, 52
Exchange of information, ease with COTS software, 150
Executables, activation of Internet Explorer vulnerabilities via, 144
Exploitation, of operating system vulnerabilities, 134
External environmental scans, 223–224
emphasis lacking in OCTAVE software, 240

F

Facilitation, by risk managers, 222
Factor value weighting
    for catalysts, 85
        Chinese nation state sponsored threat
            agents, 106
        commercial organization threat agents,
            119, 123
        French nation state sponsored threat
            agents, 98–99
        hacker threat agents, 129
        terrorist threat agents, 112
    for Chinese nation state sponsored threat
        agents, 101–103
    for commercial organization threat agents,
        69–70, 114, 120
    for criminal group threat agents, 72–73
    for disaffected employee threat agents,
        77–78
    for French nation state sponsored threat
        agents, 92–94
    for hacker group threat agents, 75–76,
        124–125
    for motivational factors, 87
        Chinese nation state sponsored threat
            agents, 112
        commercial organization threat agents,
            119
        French nation state sponsored threat
            agents, 100
        hacker threat agents, 129
        terrorist threat agents, 112
    for nation state threat agents, 59–61
    for pressure group threat agents, 66–67
    for terrorist threat agents, 63–64, 107–108
    for threat amplifiers, 80
        Chinese nation state sponsored threat
            agents, 104
        commercial organization threat agents,
            116, 121
        French nation state sponsored threat
            agents, 96
        hacker threat agents, 126
        terrorist groups, 109
    for threat inhibitors, 83
        Chinese nation state sponsored threat
            agents, 105
        commercial organization threat agents,
            117, 122
        French nation state sponsored threat
            agents, 97
        hacker threat agents, 127–128
        terrorist threat agents, 111
Fear, as inhibitor, 50

Fear factor, 246
Feature-rich software
    as COTS disadvantage, 150
    operating systems, 151
Federal Aviation Authority Air Traffic
    Control, 15
Federal Bureau of Investigation, laptop theft
    at, 175
File protection, inappropriate, 140
File Transfer Protocol (FTP), introduction of,
    165
Finance sector, 5, 223
    risk weighted assets in, 28–29
    role in risk management, 211
Financial Accounting Standards Board, 15
Fire threat, 44
FIRM software, 6, 190, 233, 235–236
Firmware, vulnerabilities in, 137–139, 161–162
First European Conference on Combating
    Violence and Pornography on the
    Internet, 180
Flaming wars, 181
Flexible adaptation, 191
Flight delays, due to security disruptions, 15
Fraud, 173
Fraudulent websites, 177
Freeware
    advantages of, 154
    insertion of spyware into, 144
    Linux-based, 157
    low level of security for, 163
    reputable sources of, 158
French nation state sponsored threat agents
    catalysts for, 98–99
    factors influencing, 91–92
    motivational factors for, 99
    threat amplifiers for, 95–97
    threat inhibitors for, 97–98
    value weighting for, 93–94
FrontPage Personal web server, vulnerability
    in, 144
Fundamental Information Risk Management
    (FIRM), 233, 235–236

G

G8 countries, 20
Global business environment, xiv, xv, xvii, 11,
    257
    dependence on new technologies, 255
    insurance industry lack of experience in, 23
    risk assessment problems in, xiii
    vs. local accountability, 17
Global information infrastructure (GII),
    166–168

GNU General Public License, 146, 162
GNU project, 156–158
Google search engine, 245
Governance requirements
  increase in, 191
  relationship to compliance, 245
Government type, role in threat assessment
  for nation states, 58
Gross domestic product, in threat assessment
  for nation states, 57
Group of Eight (G8), 180
Group risk director, 209
Gulf War hardware modifications, 160

H
Hacker websites, 144, 145, 154
  Hacker Index, 145
Hackers, xiv, 56, 90, 123–124, 172, 198
  applications produced by, 144, 154
  catalysts for, 128–129
  factors influencing, 124
  as malicious threat agents, 48
  motivational factors for, 129
  theft of Windows source code, 152
  threat amplifiers for, 124–127
  threat assessment method for, 74–75
  threat inhibitors for, 127–128
Hardware modifications, 160
Hardware vulnerabilities, 160–161
  related to operating systems, 137–139
Hazard analysis techniques, NIST
  recommendations for judging, 232–233
Health and safety risks, 231
Heuristics, gauging risk with, 246
Hideaway.net website, 145
Hobbes' Internet timeline, 13
Home working, 12, 258
Hong Kong piracy, 154–155
Hostile nations, xiv
Hot standby, 144
HTASPLOIT, 144
Human failings, 186
Human resources department, 223
  role in risk management, 210
Hurricane damage, 44
Hypercompetitive environments, 10
Hypertext application interpreter,
  vulnerabilities in, 144

I
Identity theft, 177
Impact
  determining, 224
  levels of, 220
  in risk definition, 8

Implementation
  of countermeasures, 204
  documentation of, 226
Indicators of active capability, for nation
  states, 59–60
Industrial espionage, 172, 173
Industry sectors, risk by, 8
Information assets
  destruction vs. degradation, 187
  determining value of, 187
  identifying and valuing, 195, 196–197
  inappropriate use of, 18
  leakage of, 188
  risks to, x
  scope for identifying, 197
Information Assurance Advisory Council, 6
Information gathering
  with CRAMM software, 234
  in OCTAVE software, 239
Information leakages, 3
Information Security Forum, 190, 237
Information security metrics, 189
Information security risk, 3, 185
  and corporate governance, 22
  evolution from IT security risk to, 207
  lack of actuarial data on, 8
  people and processes in, 3
  in public sector, 6
Information systems
  cost-effective defenses for, xiii
  and individual privacy issues, 18
  risks to, ix
Information systems security, x
Information Technology (IT) systems, 3
Information warfare, 160–161
Infrared microcomputers, 160
Infrastructure
  lack of control over, 165
  as tool to launch attack on other nations,
    172
Inhibitors, 45
  components of, 50
  of malicious threat agents, 46–47, 49–50,
    193
  threat assessment method for, 81–84
Innovation, role of encouraging, 10
Insider threat agents, 197
Instant messaging
  compliance issues related to, 249
  social engineering attacks via, 140
Insurance industry, risk management
  experience of, 23, 44
Integrated risk management, xvii, 243–251
Integrity issues, 7, 192
  in risk assessment, 185

Integrity of information, defined, 38
Intellectual property rights, 196
  loss through outsourcing, 259
Intellectual property theft, 172, 173
  potential in international development
      practices, 150
Interdependence issues, xvi, 4, 18
  Internet related, 172
Interdisciplinary teams, 238
Internal environmental scans, 223–224
International law, 20
  and Internet crime enforcement problems,
      176
International software development, 150
International standards, 5. *See also* Standards
  International Standard 17799:2000–Code
      of Practice for Information Security
      Management, 38
Internet
  downside of, 172
  effects of increasing use of, 165
  expanded use of, 13
  history of, 165–166
  interest of commercial sector in, 171
  lack of control over, 165
  move to home usage, 166
  number of users, 165–166
  real and potential benefits of, 170–171
Internet access, in threat assessment for
      nation states, 57
Internet blackmail, 177
Internet crime, 172
  attention by United Nations, 180
  computer theft, 174, 175
  copyright violations, 174
  counterfeit software, 174
  cyber stalking, 173
  denial of service attacks, 172
  effects of new technologies on, 177–180
  fraud, 173
  hackers, 172
  industrial espionage, 172, 173
  intellectual property theft, 172, 173
  phishing, 173
  pornography and pedophilia, 173
  prosecution problems, 176
  software piracy, 174
  spying, 172, 173
  terrorism communications, 173
Internet Explorer, vulnerabilities in, 144
Internet language population, 14
Internet relay chat, social engineering attacks
      via, 140
Internet Request For Comments (RFC)
  Glossary of terms, 37

Internet search engines, 245
Internet time, 166
INTERPOL initiative, 180
Intrusion detection sensors, 8
Investment risk, 231
Iraq
  alleged printer modifications in, 160–161
  weapons of mass destruction, 41, 56
Irish Republican Army, 177
ISO 17799, 39
Issue identification, 223
IT department, risk managers based in, 207

J
Jericho Forum, 250
Jobs for life, disappearance of, 258
Joined up government, 171
Jones, Andy, xxi
Just in time principle, 258
  and business disruption risks, 24

K
Kazaa, 143
Knock-on effect, 27
Knowledge, and capability, 49
Kobi earthquake, global shortages arising
      from, 161
Kovacich, Dr. Gerald L., xi, xix

L
Laptop theft, 175
Last-minute.com, 171
Law enforcement problems, 176
Leakage of information, 188
Legal accountability, 15
Legal regulations, 7
Life cycle
  of COTS software, 150
  of custom software, 158–160
Lightning damage, 45
Linux, 156–158
  Easter egg in, 136
  secure version collaboration with National
      Security Agency, 162–163
Listewnik, Mark, xix
Literacy levels, modifying threat levels, 57
Local accountability, 17
Loss write-off, by multinational corporations,
      20

M
M-commerce, 166
Macintosh operating system, 151
Malicious code, 145
  due to outsourcing, 248

Malicious disasters, 15, 43, 153–154
Malicious threat agents, 45–47
  capability factors, 49
  groupings of, 48
    components of, 47–48
  inhibitors of, 49–50
Market discipline, 20
Market shortages, vulnerability to, 161
Mathematical techniques
  limitations in risk analysis, 218
  for risk assessment, 232
MAX router, vulnerabilities in, 138–139
MCI Group, 17
Measurement, of threats, 55–56
Media manipulation, 188
Mergers, 258–259
Metrics management system, xvii, 200, 216, 232
Mexican Zapatista group, 177
Microsoft Excel 2000, Easter egg in, 146
Microsoft MSHTA.EXE program vulnerability, 144
Microsoft Windows development, 151
Military IT systems, 5
Minimum capital requirements, 20
Mitigation strategies, 27, 40. See also Countermeasures
Modernizing Government program, 171
Money laundering requirements, 7
Monitoring projects, 229
Monte Carlo simulations, 217–218, 232
Morrison, George, xix
Motivational factors, 193
  for Chinese nation state sponsored threat agents, 106
  for commercial organization threat agents, 119, 123
  difficulty in quantifying, 86
  for French nation state sponsored threat agents, 99–100
  for hacker threat agents, 129
  for malicious threat agents, 45–46, 52–53
  for terrorist threat agents, 112
  threat assessment method for, 86–87
MSHTA.EXE, vulnerability in, 144
Multinational corporations, 19
  control of infrastructure by, 18
  regulatory problems with, 20
  security complications introduced by, 11

N

Nation state sponsored threat agents, 89
  threat assessment method for, 57–62
National information infrastructure, 168

National Infrastructure Security Co-ordination Centre (NISCC), 169–170
National Institute for Standards and Technology, 232
National security breaches, 23–24
Natural disasters, 14–15, 43
Natural threats, 43–45
Need-to-know culture, 31
Negotiating skills, 33
NetMeeting application, denial of service vulnerability in, 153–154
Network configuration file entries, 140
Network criminals, difficulty in identification and prosecution, 181
Network scanning tools, 193
Network self-configuration, 191
New technologies
  dependence of global marketplace on, 255
  effects on crime, 177–180
  emergence of, 243
New York Mercantile Exchange, 15
Nokia Communicator mobile phone, 160
Nonrepudiation issues, 8, 192
  in risk assessment, 185–186
Nonvolatile memory, 161
Norton System Doctor, development team Easter egg, 147
Novell, 151

O

Obsolescence, with custom software, 159
OCTAVE software, 190, 233, 238–241
Off-the-shelf software, xvi
  lack of rigor underlying methods of, 217
  for risk analysis, 196
Office scruples survey, 141
Offshoring, 248–250. See also Outsourcing
On-line fraud, 177–180
On-line gambling establishments, blackmail of, 179
On-line stores, 171
Open source intelligence analysis, 212
Open Source software, 156–158, 162
Open systems, 246
  inadequacy of quantitative analysis in, 216
Operating costs, reducing through risk management, 24
Operating system software, market shares, 151–152
Operating system vulnerabilities, xvi, 133–135, 152–153
  back doors, 137
  comprehensive databases of, 133
  Easter eggs, 135–137

hardware/firmware related, 137–139
social engineering attacks, 140–141
system configuration related, 139–140
Operational risks, xv, 22–24, 232
balancing with credit risk, 28
balancing with security and technology
requirements, 238
Operationally critical threat, asset, and
vulnerability evaluation (OCTAVE),
238–241
Opportunity, for malicious threat agents, 46
Oracle 9iAS Default Configuration
Vulnerability, 139
Order fulfillment, impact of system failures
on, 169
Organisation for Economic Co-operation and
Development, 21
Organizational boundaries, risk beyond, 10
Organizational culture, 7, 27, 32
risk manager's understanding of, 31
Organizational loyalty, decline of, xiv
Organizational politics, 30
Organizational priorities, 238
Organized crime, 198
Outlook Express, Easter egg in, 147
Outsourcing, 247
implications for risk, 248–251

P
Packet switched networks, 165
Participative environment, 30
Password crackers, 144
Password security, 140
most common passwords, 141
UNIX system issues in, 139–140
Patch solutions, 133, 134, 155–156
vs. problem solving in Linux, 157
Peer perception, as inhibitor, 50
Peer review, of scientific manuscripts via
Internet, 171
Peer-to-peer file sharing applications, 143
Penetration testing, 188, 193, 199
People and processes
assessing vulnerability, 192–193
defining countermeasures in context of, 193
difficulty in addressing issues of, 7
in security risk, 3, 5, 216
Personal circumstances, as catalyst factors, 52
Personnel security, 190, 210
responsibliity for risk assessment, 208
Pervasive computing, 243
impact on requirements of risk
assessments, 247
risk associated with, 190–191

Phishing, 173, 177, 198
Physical assets, 41
assessing vulnerability of, 192–193
Physical penetration testing, 199
Physical recovery, 9
Physical security weaknesses, 186
responsibliity for risk assessment, 208
in risk assessment, 190
Pilot Network Services, 249
Pirated software, 145, 154
Point solutions, 204
Policies, xvii, 219, 227–228
Political considerations, 9
Population, in threat assessment for nation
states, 58
Pornography, 173
on-line, 180
Power consumption, in threat assessment for
nation states, 57
Power losses, 14
Pressure groups, 90, 197
as malicious threat agents, 48
threat assessment method for, 65–68
Prioritization of risk, 202, 203
Privacy issues, 15, 18
Probability/impact grids, 202, 224
Procedural countermeasures, 204
Procedures, 219, xvii
adherence by business unit managers,
222
difficulty of replicating in different
countries, 248
types required, 228
vulnerabilities in, 189
Processes
developed in risk management process,
223–224
difficulty of replicating in different
countries, 248
as information assets, 196
of risk management, 219
vulnerabilities in, 189
Processing speeds, 12
Profitability, as disadvantage of COTS
software, 150
Programmable read-only memory (PROM),
161–162
Project-level information security risks, 3, 5,
27
Project risk assessments, 29
Protection, 203
from security incidents, 203–204
Proxy servers, use in terrorism, 177
Psychological recovery, 9

Public domain software, xvi, 149, 162
  case for, 154
Public perception, sensitivity to, 50
Public sector IT systems, 5
  suitability of CRAMM for, 240–241
  information security risk in, 6

Q

Qualitative risk assessment, xvii, 189
  labor intensive nature of, 234, 237
  vs. quantitative risk assessment, 215–218
Quality control, with custom software,
  160
Quantitative risk assessment, xvii, 189
  in FIRM software, 236
  inadequacies of, 215–218
  measuring relative levels of risk, 217
  oversimplification of risk picture through,
    218
Questionnaires
  ability to design, 32
  use in COBRA software, 238
Quotes file, Easter egg in, 136

R

Radio school concept, 171
Reaction, to security incidents, 203
Read-only memory (ROM), 161
Recognition and respect, as amplifiers,
  50–51
Recovery, varying definitions of, 9
Regulation
  driven by overriding perception of risk,
    246
  push toward tighter, 243
  relationship to risk and compliance, 243
Regulation of Investigatory Powers Act
  (U.K.), 21
Regulation strategies, 243
Regulatory requirements, xv
  increasing levels of, 18–21
Remote Desktop Sharing, 154
Reordering systems, automation of, 168
Report writing skills, 32, 33
Reporting phase, in FIRM software,
  235–236
Required states, 224
Residual risk, 40, 196
Resources
  Board responsibility for identification of,
    221
  and capability, 49
Return on investment, for security
  countermeasures, 204

Reusable passwords, 140
Risk
  aligning with business strategy, 185, 188
  assigning monetary values to, 204
  definitions of, 8, 9, 186
  formula for measuring, 186
  impossibility of elimination, 221
  management *vs.* elimination, 23
  relationship to compliance and regulation,
    243
  residual, 40, 196
  subjective nature of, 246
  types of, 22–24
Risk acceptance, 188, 219
Risk analysis, xiv, xvi, 195
  documentation of, 226
Risk appetites, 187
Risk assessment, 29, 185, 193, 224
  aligning with business strategy, 232
  balanced scorecard approaches, 6
  as business process, 39
  critical nature of, x
  defined, xvi, 194, 200
  documentation of, 226
  evolution of, 4
  government preferred methods for,
    234–235
  holistic approach to, xiv
  iterative nature of, 193–194
  maintaining momentum of, 194
  mathematical tools for, 232
  non-binary nature of, 202
  procedure for, 228
  qualitative *vs.* quantitative, 215–218
  software tools for, 190, 198
  steps in, 192–194
  subjective nature of, 202
  threat assessment as input to, 37, 38–40
  tools and types of, xvii, 5
  two stages of, 196–197
  value of documented methods for,
    191–192
Risk assessment matrix, 201–202
Risk assessment process, 185
Risk avoidance, 24, 188, 219, 221
Risk awareness, required for organizational
  survival, 255
Risk communication, 190, 203
Risk cubes, 202
Risk definition, complexity of, 187
Risk dependencies, 4, 25, 29
Risk environment diagram, 24
Risk exposure, capping after security
  incidents, 204

Risk information collection, procedure for, 228
Risk levels
    acceptable, 23
    assigning, 195
Risk management, 188
    administrative and management aspects of,
        xvii
    approaches to, 23–24
    balanced scorecards approach to, 235–236
    documentation plans in, 225–227
    duties and responsibilities of, 219–223
    future of, 255–259
    history of, xv, 3–10
    imposing downstream *vs.* upstream, 188
    iterative nature of, 195–196
    policies in, 227–228
    procedures for, 228
    processes in, 223–224
    projects, 228–229
    rationale for, 244
    theories of, xiv, 3–10
    tools and techniques of, xvii
Risk management capacity, assessment of,
    223
Risk management infrastructure, organic
    development of, 219
Risk managers
    analytical capabilities, 33
    business experience required by, 256
    creativity required of, 29
    duties and responsibilities of, 221–222
    ex-policemen and auditors as, 255–256
    as facilitators, 222
    formation of cross-organizational
        relationships by, 212
    identity construction by, 250–251
    maintenance of balance, 31
    negotiating skills in, 33
    report writing skills, 32
    roles of, xvi, xvii, 207–212
    skills required of, 25, 256–257
    supervisory skills in, 33
    verbal communication skills, 32
Risk metrics, 200
Risk mitigation strategies, 31, 195, 236
    four types of, 219
    procedure for, 228
Risk monitoring, 225
Risk prioritization, 202, 203, 224
Risk process, xiv–xv, xvi
Risk reduction, 219, 221
Risk templates, 224
Risk tolerance, Board responsibility for
    defining, 221

Risk weighted assets, 28–29
Routers, vulnerabilities in, 138–139
Russian monetary crisis, 19

S
Safety critical risks, 231
SAINT initiative, 21
SARA software, 190, 233, 236–237
Sarbanes Oxley Act, 5, 192
    governance issues in, 240
Satellite broadcast technology, 12
Scarcity of resources, 188
Scenario modeling, xv
Scott Morton model, 26–27
Secret files, Easter eggs hidden in, 136
Securities and Exchange Commission
    Enron investigation by, 15
    U.S. Sarbanes-Oxley Act of 2002, 21
Security accreditation, 5
Security features
    built into COTS software, 150
    turned off in COTS operating systems,
        152–153
    undermined by hacker applications, 144
Security spending, business case for, 9, 190
Security.nl website, 135
Self-healing networks, 191
Sensitive information, risk of dissemination
    to internationals, 170
September 11, 2001, 13
Shared passwords, 140
Shareware
    advantages of, 154
    insertion of spyware into, 144
    Linux-based, 157
    reputable sources of, 158
Shareware.com website, 158
SimCity 2000, Easter egg in, 147
Simple to Apply Risk Analysis (SARA), 233,
    236–237
Simplified Process for Risk Identification
    (SPRINT), 233, 236–237
Small pressure groups, 186
Social engineering attacks, 140–141, 198
Software, and capability, 49
Software development process
    anonymous nature of, 155
    for COTS software, 151–152
    for open source software, 156–158
Software flaws
    cracker group publicizing of, 134
    fixes unavailable for, 134
    patch solutions for, 134–135
Software patches, 133, 155–156

Software piracy, 145, 174
    by country, 146
Software reuse approach, 159–160
Software solutions, public domain or off-the-shelf, xvi
Software tools, 231–233
    COBRA, 237–238
    CRAMM, 234–235
    FIRM, 235–236
    OCTAVE, 238–241
    quantitative vs. qualitative approaches of, 200–201
    for risk assessment, 190, 198, 208
    SARA and SPRINT, 236–237
Solar Sunrise case, 135
Soviet information warfare, 161
Specialization, and cooperation via outsourcing, 247
Spoofed e-mails, 177
Spreadsheets, custom templates for, 159
SPRINT software, 190, 233, 236–237
SpyHunter9 Easter egg, 146
Spying, 172, 173
Spyware, 144
Spywareinfo.com team, 143–144
Stakeholder groups, xvi, 4, 25, 207
    achieving buy-in by, 232
    analysis of, 223
    Board, 208–209
    external to the organization, 251
    financial director, 211
    IT department, 210
    marketing/public relations department, 211–212
Stand-alone systems, risk in, 3
Standards
    British Standard BS 7799, 5, 38, 39
    ISO 17799, 7, 39
    risk assessment technique defined by, 233
State sponsored malicious threat agents, 48
Stock taking system, automation of, 168
Storage capacity, 12
Strategic alliances, 10
Strategic risk, 22
Strategy definition and implementation, 225
Subjectivity
    of acceptable risk levels, 203
    of qualitative analysis, 216
    in risk assessment, 202
Successful attack, determining impact of, 40
Sumitomo Capital, 19
Supervisory skills, 33
Supply chains, global changes in, 258
Swinburne, Phil, xix

System configuration, vulnerabilities in, 139–140
System failures, impact on commerce, 169
System recovery, via back doors, 135, 137
System related factors, for malicious threat agents, 47
System software, old versions in use, 140

T
Tactical risk, 23
Target system, 47
Targets, relationship of threat agent type to potential, 56–57
Taxes, and multinational corporations, 20
Technical difficulty, as inhibitor, 50
Technical risk, 3
    historical focus on, 27
Technical solutions, presenting in business terms, 232
Technology, and capability, 49
Technology changes, as catalyst factor, 52
Telecommunications, convergence with computing technologies, 167
Telecommunications access, in threat assessment for nation states, 57
Templates, as custom software solution, 159
Terrorism communications, 173
Terrorist attacks, xiv, 13, 246
    effect of new technologies on, 177
Terrorist groups, 42, 48, 89, 106, 198
    catalysts for, 111–112
    factors influencing, 107
    motivational factors for, 112
    threat amplifiers for, 106–110
    threat assessment method for, 62–65
    threat inhibitors for, 110–111
Thinking skills, required of risk managers, 25, 29
Third party connectivity, 9
Threat, 186
    defined, 37–38
    defining, 195
    identifying and anticipating, 196
    measuring level of, 55–56
    sequence of factors involved in, 47–53
Threat agents, xiv, 8, 193
    catalysts influence on, 84–86
    Chinese nation state sponsored, 99–106
    commercial, 68–71, 89, 113
        Aerospaciale France, 119–123
        Boring Aerospace and Defense, 113–119
    comparison of examples, 130
    criminal groups, 71–74, 89

defined, 37
disaffected employees, 75–79, 90
excluding potential, 90
French nation state sponsored, 91–100
hacker groups, 74–75, 90, 123–129
identifying, 197–198
motivational factors influence on, 86–87
nation state sponsored, 57–62, 89
pressure groups, 65–68, 90
relationship to potential targets, 56
sequence of relationships, 48
terrorists, 62–65, 89, 106–112
threat amplifiers influence on, 79–81
threat assessment method for, 55–57
threat inhibitors influence on, 81–84
types of, 43
Threat amplifiers
    for Chinese nation state sponsored threat
        agents, 104
    for commercial organization threat agents,
        115–116, 121–122
    for French nation state sponsored threat
        agents, 95–97
    for hacker threat agents, 124–127
    for terrorist threat agents, 106–110
    threat assessment method for, 79–81
Threat analysts, 41
Threat assessment, xiv, xv, 193
    defined, 38–40
    examples, xv, 89–91
        Chinese nation state sponsored threat
            agents, 99–106
        commercial organization threat agents,
            113–123
        French nation state sponsored threat
            agents, 91–100
        hacker threat agents, 123–129
        terrorist threat agents, 106–112
    as input to risk assessment, 37, 38–40
    methods of, xv
    OCTAVE appreciation of, 241
    in SARA and SPRINT, 236–237
Threat assessment method, 55–56
    for catalysts, 84–86
    for commercial threat agents, 68–71
    for criminal group threat agents, 71–74
    for disaffected staff threat agents, 75–79
    for hacker group threat agents, 74–75
    for motivational factors, 86–87
    for nation state sponsored threat agents,
        57–62
    for pressure group threat agents, 66–68
    for terrorism, 62–65
    and threat agents, 56–57

    for threat amplifiers, 79–81
    for threat inhibitors, 81–84
Threat environment, 190
Threat inhibitors
    for Chinese nation state sponsored threat
        agents, 105
    for commercial organization threat agents,
        117–118, 122
    for French nation state sponsored threat
        agents, 97–98
    for hacker threat agents, 127–128
    for terrorist threat agents, 110–111
    threat assessment method for, 81–84
Threat levels
    assessment of, 189
    vs. levels of vulnerability, 201
Threat profiles, for critical assets in
    OCTAVE, 239
Threat tables, 198
Time scales, for physical action, 41
Tools and techniques, xvii, 231–233
    alignment with organizational culture, 233
    COBRA, 237–238
    CRAMM, 234–235
    FIRM, 235–236
    OCTAVE, 238–241
    SARA and SPRING, 236–237
Tornado damage, 44
Torvalds, Linus, 156
Traceability, of risk assessment process, 192,
    204
Tracking plans, 226
Training plans, 227, 229
Transferral of risk, 188, 219, 221
    harmonizing with outsourcing strategies,
        249, 250
Trust relationships, 151
    unknowability with software agents,
        191
Trustworthiness, 244–245
Tucows website, 158
Turnbull, Nigel, 22
Turnbull Report (U.K.), 5, 22, 192

U
Ubiquitous computing. See Pervasive
    computing
Unacceptable risk, x, xiii
Uncertainty principle, 246
Underground News website, 145
Undocumented features, 135, 147
Unexpected system access, 3
Union Bank of California, dedicated
    outsourcing office, 248, 251

UNIX systems, guidelines for configuration of, 139–140
Upstream speeds, 12
U.S. Central Intelligence Agency, alleged hardware modifications by, 161
U.S. Department of Defense
  computer systems penetration, 42
  medical Web page penetration, 15
  Solar Sunrise case, 135
U.S. Department of Justice, Enron investigation by, 15
U.S. National Information Protection Center, 169
U.S. National Institute of Standards and Technology, definition of global information infrastructure, 167
U.S. National Security Agency, and secure version of LINUX, 162–163
U.S. Sarbanes-Oxley Act of 2002, 21
U.S. State Department, laptop theft at, 175

V
Value weighting. *See* Factor value weighting
Verbal communication skills, 32
Victimless crimes, 176
Vigilantism, 181
Virtual workforce, xiii
Visibility, of risk assessment process, 204
Volcano screen saver, Easter egg in, 136
Vulnerability, xvi, 8, 40
  application related, 143–147
  assessing with SARA and SPRINT, 236–237
  assessment of, 198–199
  in context of risk assessment, 186
  in COTS applications software, 153–155
  defining, 195, 198–199
  in event of global conflicts or natural disasters, 161
  in firmware, 137–138
  hardware based, 137–139, 160–161
  human failings, 186
  identifying with SARA and SPRINT, 237
  importance of exploitable, 47
  operating system, 133–141, 152–153
  in physical security, 186
  in processes and procedures, 189
  responsibility for, 207–212
  in routers, 138–139
  social engineering attacks, 140–141
  in system configurations, 139–140
  in telephones, 138
  types of, xiv
  vs. threat level, 201
Vulnerability assessment, 192–193

W
Warez sites, 144
Water damage, 45
Weapons of mass destruction, 41
Wearable computing devices, risk associated with, 190
Web presence, business need for, 166
Websites
  Cult of the Dead Cow, 145
  Easter Egg Archive, 136–137
  fraudulent, 177
  hacker sites, 144
  Hideaway.net, 145
  Security.nl, 135
  Shareware.com, 158
  Tucows, 158
  Underground News, 145
  warez sites, 144
  WWW.HACKER.AG, 145
  Ziff Davis, 158
  Zone-H, 135
Whale Sounds Easter egg, 146–147
Widget Aerospace Company, 89–91
  threat assessment examples, 91–129
Wind threat, 44
Windows 95, Norton System Doctor development team Easter egg, 147
Windows 2000, Easter eggs in, 136
Windows NT, security features in, 150, 152
Windows source code, theft of, 152
Windows XP Professinal, Easter eggs in, 136
WINMAIN.EXE exploit, 143–144
Wireless connectivity
  and changing definitions of hardware, 160
  introduction of new risks through, 257–258
  operating system upgrades for, 151
Wordplay.com, 179
Workforce mobility, 258
  security consequences of, 12
Working from home, 12
World Wide Web, 12
  historical introduction of, 165
Worldcom scandal, 16–17

Z
Ziff Davis website, 158
Zone-H website, 135